Turning O

Studies in Medieval and
Renaissance Book Culture

Erik Kwakkel,

Rosamond McKitterick

& Rodney Thomson

Turning Over a New Leaf

Change and Development

in the Medieval Manuscript

Leiden University Press

Cover illustration: Leiden, Universiteitsbibliotheek, MS Vulcanius 46, f. 130r (detail)

Cover design and layout: Mulder van Meurs, Amsterdam

ISBN   978 90 8964 155 7
E-ISBN   978 94 0060 074 4 (PDF)
E-ISBN   978 94 0060 075 1 (EPUB)
NUR   613 / 615

Contents

Preface

The three studies in this book are devoted to changes and developments in the physical appearance of medieval manuscripts between the ninth and thirteenth centuries, and to the circumstances in which these books were produced. They were originally presented as the inaugural Lieftinck Lectures on the theme of 'change and development in the medieval book', but are here greatly expanded. The lectures formed part of the programme organized in Leiden University Library in 2010-11 in relation to the research project 'Turning Over a New Leaf: Manuscript Innovation in the Twelfth-Century Renaissance', directed by Erik Kwakkel, Institute for Cultural Disciplines, Leiden University, and in collaboration with Leiden University Library's Special Collections and the Scaliger Institute. The Lieftinck Lectures are delivered four times a year to commemorate Gerard Isaac Lieftinck († 1994), who held the Chair of Palaeography at Leiden University until 1972 and who made a significant impact on the study of the medieval book, especially the development and nomenclature of script in the Middle Ages.

In Peter Gumbert's tribute to Gerard Lieftinck, delivered at the first Lieftinck Lecture and included in this volume, Lieftinck's career as a manuscript scholar in Leiden is described. He worked in various capacities, from September 1939 as keeper of the *Bibliotheca Neerlandica Manuscripta*, an archive containing descriptions of some 20,000 Middle Dutch manuscripts; from 1942 as keeper of manuscripts; from 1948 as lecturer in medieval palaeography and codicology; and from 1963 to 1972 as Professor of Palaeography. Gumbert, who was Lieftinck's pupil as well as his successor in the Chair, discusses the scope of

Lieftinck's interests and accomplishments, as well as the impact he had on the study of the medieval book, not least in his cataloguing, his pioneering comparative approach to the study of medieval manuscripts in the Low Countries and his contributions to the great enterprise of the *Catalogues des manuscrits datés*.

Rosamond McKitterick's paper addresses the degree of innovation as well as emulation in the production of books and transmission of knowledge in the Carolingian period, and the problem of interpretation these can present for modern scholars. She explores the relationship between Carolingian copies of ancient texts and their exemplars and the ways in which the presentations of the text may form a bridge to the classical past. Her discussion encompasses new kinds of books being produced in the Carolingian period, as well as new genres of texts and is based on close consultation of the surviving manuscripts. For some books, when the earliest extant manuscripts are Carolingian but are certainly or arguably based on older exemplars no longer extant, there is the question of their relationship to these older (or possible) exemplars. How should one think about readers of these manuscripts? What kinds of aids were devised for the reader? How may we eliminate, or at least allow for, our inevitably subjective assessments of manuscript page layout as modern scholars? Such questions are addressed by focusing on history books and world Chronicles from late Antiquity and the early Middle Ages, as well as encyclopaedias and glossaries. Both categories are well represented in the extraordinarily rich and important Leiden collections. The compilation of glossaries with their long lists of words presented particular challenges to the scribes, to which they responded in a number of ways. As McKitterick demonstrates, the manuscripts offer interesting puzzles in themselves about the transmission, not only of knowledge but also of the presentation of this specific kind of information, how scribes coped with the difficulties, how the books functioned and the way the texts were copied and organized.

Erik Kwakkel's study of the transformation of script during the long twelfth century explores the theme of change and development by tracing how one physical dynamic of the medieval book, script, evolved over the course of the period c. 1075 to c.1225. During this century and a half the physical book received a number of new features. This chapter focuses on script exclusively and shows how the handwriting of scribes slowly changed as the book evolved from one prolific book format to another – from Caroline minuscule to Gothic. Based on a source that has not hitherto been used to this end, the *Catalogues des manuscrits datés*, the development of eight palaeographical traits is mapped in order to determine when the characteristic features of Gothic writing replaced those of Caroline minuscule. He is able, for the first time, to place 'time stamps' on each of these developments.

Rodney Thomson focuses on a further aspect of this relationship between book production and intellectual culture during the same crucial period of change and development as that examined by Erik Kwakkel. He does so from the perspective of the contributions to book production made in Germany during the long twelfth century. In seeking to describe and account for the 'Twelfth-Century Renaissance', historians have generally concentrated upon northern France and Paris in particular, on the rise of scholasticism and on brilliant individual figures such as Peter Abelard. The German-speaking areas of Western Europe have been comparatively neglected, with the implication that they were conservative and backward-looking. Thomson reconsiders the work of German scribes using as evidence the twelfth-century library catalogues as well as the surviving manuscripts themselves. He draws attention to the remarkable expansion of existing libraries and the creation of new ones, the prodigious quantity of new books produced to a very high standard and the ways in which the impact of the reform and intellectual innovation of this transformative period can be charted in the libraries of the German empire. The libraries reflect a burst of book copying activity, not only of the staple patristic works and books related to the seven liberal arts, but also of the texts of the new learning emanating from Paris and elsewhere.

The authors wish to thank Steven Vanderputten (Ghent) and Marco Mostert (Utrecht) for their very useful and constructive comments on an earlier draft of this book, Peter Gumbert for his introduction to Gerard Lieftinck, the University Library for their generosity of waiving much of the cost for the images in this book as well as their reproduction rights, Jenny Weston (Leiden) for her meticulous copyediting and the staff of Leiden University Press for their help in seeing this book through the press.

EK, RMK, RT
Leiden, November 2011

List of Figures and Plates

Black and white images presenting details of these manuscripts, referred to as 'Figures', are placed within the text. Colour images depicting the full pages, referred to as 'Plates', are to be found at the back of this book.

Abbreviations

BAV	Biblioteca Apostolica Vaticana
BL	London, British Library
BM	Bibliothèque municipale
BNC	Biblioteca nazionale centrale
BnF	Paris, Bibliothèque nationale de France
Bodl.	Oxford, Bodleian Library
BPL	Leiden, Universiteitsbibliotheek, Bibliotheca Publica Latina
CUL	Cambridge, University Library
KB	Koninklijke Bibliotheek
ÖNB	Vienna, Österreichische Nationalbibliothek
Scaliger	Leiden, Universiteitsbibliotheek, Scaliger
SB	Stiftsbibliothek
UB	Universiteitsbibliotheek
UBi	Universitätsbibliothek
VGQ	Leiden, Universiteitsbibliotheek, Vossianus Graecus Quarto
VLF	Leiden, Universiteitsbibliotheek, Vossianus Latinus Folio
VLQ	Leiden, Universiteitsbibliotheek, Vossianus Latinus Quarto
VLO	Leiden, Universiteitsbibliotheek, Vossianus Latinus Octavo
WLB	Württembergische Landesbibliothek

Gerard Isaac Lieftinck

(† 1994)

Introduction:

Gerard Isaac Lieftinck

J.P. Gumbert

Palaeography, in various forms, has long been known in the Netherlands. One might mention the excellent engravings after charters given by Adriaan Kluit (1735-1807) in his *Historia critica comitatus Hollandiae et Zeelandiae*, 1777-82; the useful description of the Egmond Gospels, also with fine engraved (and partly coloured) plates, in H. van Wijn (1740-1831), *Huiszittend Leeven II*, 1812; the 17 lithographed plates of script specimens and text booklet, published (as a school-book!) by Jacobus Koning (1770-1832), *Algemeene ophelderende verklaring van het oud letterschrift*, 1818; or, in a different field, the famous Leiden Hellenist Carel Gabriel Cobet (1813-89), who used his knowledge of Greek letterforms as a crowbar for emending Greek texts. From a later period one should certainly not forget to mention Bonaventura Kruitwagen OFM (1874-1954), if only for his studies about the scripts used by the Modern Devotion (reprinted in his *Laat-Middeleeuwsche Paleografica* [...], 1942). But all of this is not what we would call modern. Modern palaeography and codicology begin, in our country, with Lieftinck.

Gerard Lieftinck lived a long life: his dates are 1902-94. But during the last fifteen years or so he lived a life of retirement, so that already at his death there was a whole generation who had never seen him.

1. Lieftinck, De Middelnederlandsche Tauler-handschriften.

2. Lieftinck, Codicum in finibus Belgarum ante annum
1550 conscriptorum qui in
Bibliotheca Universitatis asservantur, Pars I.

He started his career studying medicine, but after some time his interest in medieval mysticism led him to switch to Dutch studies, and he decided to study the Middle Dutch translations of the fourteenth-century German mystic Johannes Tauler – and found he could not, because they had not been well published; one had to study the manuscripts first. So he went to Willem de Vreese, at that time the foremost scholar for Dutch manuscripts, a Fleming but in exile in Rotterdam; in 1936 his doctoral thesis on the Tauler manuscripts appeared.[1] He also got involved with the Bibliotheca Neerlandica Manuscripta (BNM), the huge card file on all Dutch manuscripts that De Vreese spent his life compiling. When, after De Vreese's death in 1939, the BNM went to the Leiden library, Lieftinck went there too, and eventually became Keeper of Manuscripts. He also started to teach, combining this with the Keeper's job, until the teaching became full-time and his rank that of professor until 1972 – the retirement age for professors then still was 70.

His training with De Vreese, combined with the work in the stacks of the Leiden manuscripts, gave him a deep knowledge of Dutch manuscripts. I think that one of his colleagues also played an important role: K.A. de Meyïer, a Greek scholar. Being handicapped (he was virtually deaf, and his speech was very difficult to understand), he could not work with the public. Following the habits of the time he was permitted to work in the hidden parts of the library, at first for nothing, later for a pittance, and did excellent work there. He prepared himself for cataloguing the Vossius manuscripts, and by way of exercise did a smaller catalogue, the Perizoniani, in 1947. In the same time Lieftinck prepared a catalogue of an important section of Dutch manuscripts, which appeared in 1947 (dated 1948).[2] The two catalogues follow the same model, which the two scholars probably elaborated together. Lieftinck explicitly names De Vreese's description of the Ruusbroec manuscripts as his model; but his is clearer and better – and, in fact, modern. They not only give a listing of the texts, but also a material description, including a good collation, identification of watermarks, description of decoration and binding; and they show an awareness, at least in the more evident cases, of the problems of composite manuscripts. Such catalogues had not earlier appeared in our country.

During the work on the catalogue he also came, following the lead given by Kruitwagen, to a clearer understanding of Dutch palaeography, recognizing the script he called 'bastarda' (later rebaptized 'hybrida') as a historical entity.

In his later life he made several valuable contributions to the study of Medieval Dutch literature and its manuscripts, which I shall not discuss here.[3]

But his interest widened. Already in 1948 he studied the Martinellus that an eleventh-century bishop of Utrecht gave to his church: he identified it as a work of a South-German scriptorium, and drew historical conclusions from this fact.[4] I think he was wrong: it was made in Utrecht, not in Augsburg. But if Lieftinck's result was wrong, his approach was right: he looked at the book with the eyes of a palaeographer and a codicologist, which no one had done before; and he saw the likeness to German script – at that time nobody had realized that Utrecht was, in that period, very much a province of the German empire. The same with his study of the Egmond Gospels (1949): the solution was not quite the right one, but the approach was perfectly right and perfectly novel.[5] He travelled in Belgium and Northern France; these travels resulted in 1953 in a study of the twelfth- and thirteenth-century manuscripts of the Flemish Cistercian abbeys Ter Duinen and Ter Doest.[6] Again he tackled them with what is obviously the right approach: distinguishing the house products from the books that had been produced else-

3. These include Lieftinck's 'Het Ridderboec als bron voor de kennis van de feodale maatschappij in Brabant omstreeks 1400'; 'Drie handschriften uit de librije van de abdij van Sint Bernards opt Schelt'; '"Methodologische" en paleographische opmerkingen naar aanleiding van een hert met een wit voetje'; 'Middelnederlandse handschriften uit beide Limburgen: Vondsten en ontdekkingen – Het Lutgarthandschrift'; Problemen met betrekking tot het Zutphens-Groningse Maerlant-handschrift; 'Pleidooi voor de philologie in de oude en eerbiedwaardige ruime betekenis van het woord'.

4. Lieftinck, Bisschop Bernold (1027-1054) en zijn geschenken aan de Utrechtse kerken. This publication was Lieftinck's inaugural lecture as Lector.

5. Lieftinck, 'Het evangeliarium van Egmond' and 'Het oudste schrift uit de abdij van Egmond'.

6. Lieftinck, De librijen en

scriptoria der Westvlaamse
Cisterciënser-abdijen Ter
Duinen en Ter Doest.

7. Lieftinck, 'Pour une
nomenclature de l'écriture
livresque de la période dite
gothique'.

8. Lieftinck, Manuscrits datés
conservés dans les Pays-Bas I.

where. Again, not all his results are final. But again, this had never been done for any of the Belgian abbeys – and, what is worse, it has, as far as I know, not ever been done, for this or any other Belgian abbey, in the almost sixty years since then. It is evident that, from studying manuscripts because they contained interesting texts, he had gone on to study manuscripts as archaeological objects: what we now call a codicological view.

On these travels he gained many friends, the most important ones in England, among them Roger Mynors, Neil Ker and Ian Doyle. He also was among the founders of the Comité de paléographie latine. In that context he presented his views on Dutch palaeography.[7] He was not understood by the audience, because they were all accustomed to the manuscripts of their own countries, and at that time no one realized that Lieftinck's distinction of hybrida from cursiva, according hybrida the status of a separate script type, was a perfectly real, but regionally limited phenomenon. In Germany and France it simply is not so; but in our country it is. Lieftinck's way of seeing things therefore met with scepticism and aversion, instead of the comprehension and moderate acceptance which it deserved.

This 'blindness' of knowing only the manuscripts one has at home should, in the course of time, have been remedied by the great undertaking of the Comité: the Catalogues des manuscrits datés. Lieftinck immediately and energetically (and virtually single-handed) started on the Dutch part of this series; volume I, concerning the manuscripts of non-Dutch origin kept in our country, appeared in 1964.[8] (Volume II, on the Dutch manuscripts, was not finished until 1988, by his successor). Again he had an original approach: for each manuscript he indicated how it fitted into his system of script types; and he ordered the plates not simply by date, as all the other countries did, but by country of origin and script type – for was not palaeographical clarity the aim of the whole project? Neither his distinction of hybrida as a separate script type (which was actually much less clear in volume I than it was to be in the Dutch volume II), nor his use of the term cursiva for a formally defined script type (and not as an equivalent of 'speedy and/or sloppy script'), nor his ordering of the plates were appreciated by his international colleagues. Rare were those who realized that Lieftinck had made an important contribution to the knowledge of late-medieval script, and to the form in which clear knowledge is always expressed: terminology (which for this subject is called 'nomenclature'). But Julian Brown once wrote to me: 'I bless his name every time the subject comes round.'

Of other work, I mention: his discovery of the Fulda Gellius manuscript in Leeuwarden (1955), his facsimile edition of the Corbie Servius (1960), and his contribution to the discussions about 'imposed' manuscripts (1961).[9]

In his later years his interest shifted to art history, the culmination of which is his study of the Master of Mary of Burgundy (1970).[10] Art historians do not judge this work very favourably; this, together with the not particularly clear presentation, regrettably obscures the many excellent observations of details that are hidden in it.

Lieftinck was not a man of systematic clearness, neither in teaching nor in writing. But he was a man of taste and a feeling for quality; and he was often modern in his way of tackling matters – more modern than his contemporaries, and perhaps he himself, realized. And he was also a gentleman and a very nice man. Although he is perhaps not to be counted among the really 'great' palaeographers, he certainly was the man who put the Netherlands 'on the map' as far as manuscripts are concerned. He will do very nicely as a 'patron saint' for palaeography and codicology in the Netherlands.[11]

9. Lieftinck's 'Le ms. d'Aulu-Gelle à Leeuwarden executé à Fulda en 836 (Leeuwarden, Bibl. Prov. de Frise, ms. B.A.Fr. 55)'; 'The "Psalterium Hebraycum" from St Augustine's Canterbury rediscovered in the Scaliger bequest at Leyden'; Servii Grammatici in Vergilii carmina commentarii; and 'Medieval Manuscripts with "Imposed" Sheets'.

10. Lieftinck, Boekverluchters uit de omgeving van Maria van Bourgondië.

11. A full bibliography of Lieftinck's publications is found (in installments) in Gumbert and De Haan, Essays Presented to G.I. Lieftinck.

æopacto

...conpetat dicimus. Conpetere. reicaui...

o/ei/uierg   q:meminisse aut constant ualere fallitur

& cognos   tur historiarum lib t sicuero quasi formi

respicere   dine attonitus neq: animo neq: auribus

otu cognio   aut lingua conpetere

quoquia   INCIPIT PER D LITTER

tulliusin

canaliu   Damnare e damno adficere un

is reipubl   de et condempnare dictu; etcom

nectute   rio nullo damno adfectu undempnem pl

etiadequi   mus Damnare est exheredare lucilius

cognoscere   satirarum lib xr cassius gaius hicoper

partepuer   rius quam cefalonem dicimus sectoren

derepubl   furium q; hunctullius quam index he

onsuetudi   dem facit et damnari alii omnes. Dam

rrosesq;ul   nare necessitate constringere etuis

Glossaries and Other Innovations in Carolingian Book Production

Rosamond McKitterick

Carolingian book production needs to be understood within the context of the communication of knowledge, the transmission of ideas across time and space and the consequent formation of what can be described as a cultural map in Europe.[1]

One of the things this entails is the practical means by which ideas could be exchanged, that is, modes of communication and consequently the role of books, the evidence for the exchange of ideas, connections between individuals and institutions and examples of texts and types of knowledge. The importance of the theme of the migration of ideas in relation to books and texts is reflected in the attention increasingly being paid to it, not least in the Leiden-Palermo-Groningen project on the 'Storehouses of wholesome learning and transfer of encyclopaedic knowledge in the early middle ages' directed by Rolf Bremmer, Kees Dekker and Patrizia Lendinara,[2] the Martianus Capella project under the direction of Mariken Teeuwen at the Huygens/ING Institute in Den Haag,[3] and, more generally, the 'Francemed' project based at the German Historical Institute in Paris on 'Processes of cultural transfer in

1. This is the general theme of the book on which I am currently engaged, provisionally entitled *The Migration of Ideas in the Early Middle Ages*, to be published by Cambridge University Press.

2. Bremmer and Dekker, eds., *Foundations of Learning* and Bremmer and Dekker, eds., *Practice in Learning*.

3. Teeuwen et al., eds., *Carolingian Scholarship and Martianus Capella*, 1st edn. November 2008, http://martianus.huygens.knaw.nl/, accessed 23 May 2011.

4. See the online report, http://hsozkult.geschichte. hu-berlin.de/tagungs- berichte/id=3032, accessed 8 June 2011.

5. For an excellent survey, see Martin et Vezin, eds., *Mise en page et mise en texte du livre manuscrit*.

the medieval Mediterranean' led by Daniel König, Rania Abdellatif, Yassir Benhima and Elisabeth Ruchaud.[4]

Concerns with how knowledge was transferred are particularly germane to Erik Kwakkel's enquiries about the relationship between the physical features of medieval manuscripts and the texts they contain, and the extent to which any group of scribes at a particular moment may have made radical innovations in the presentation of their texts. Is it possible for modern scholars to extrapolate, from the layouts of the texts themselves, how books might have been used and what the needs of readers were at any period in the middle ages? In what ways do medieval manuscripts provide the evidence for how such needs may have changed and been accommodated?

Such questions will obviously prompt a host of different responses according to the type of text and context in which that text might have been produced. That the responses would be different cannot be stressed enough. Liturgical, pedagogic, judicial, administrative and scholarly needs may all have had to be accommodated, in that these required different physical presentations. It may make generalization inconveniently difficult, if not impossible. Each and every particular example, whether of a succession of copies of a particular text across a wide chronological and geographical range, or of one single representative of a text written in a particular time, context and place, will contribute nevertheless to a wider understanding of book production in the middle ages, and enable us to identify innovation in the presentation of texts to readers.[5] It may also help to trace any continuities, or a revival of older features that may have died out between the Carolingian period and the twelfth century. I shall concentrate for the most part in this chapter, therefore, on two categories of text: early medieval history books, and dictionaries and glossaries compiled in the eighth and ninth centuries. History books written for one audience may have a different impact in new contexts and can be redeployed for different educational and ideological purposes. Collections of Latin word definitions or glossaries, given that words in themselves are the most basic form for the conveyance and migration of ideas, potentially offer a guide to the intellectual as well as practical preoccupations of the time. They may also represent new formats designed to present information, especially words, needed in new contexts. I shall discuss both these categories of book – history books, and glossaries – in the second and third sections of this paper, for both are highly significant as demonstrations of different ways Carolingian scribes treated the physical page. But first of all there are some general points about physical form in relation to texts in the early Middle Ages that need to be made.

Physical Form, Scribal Practice and Aids to Readers
If we are to determine whether or not Carolingian book production introduced many innovations to the appearance of the books, a principal question has to be not only how much Carolingian scribes may have inherited by way of scribal practice but also how many of the physical characteristics of the categories of text they copied were taken over from their exemplars.[6] There are Carolingian examples of many features of the presentation of texts that we now take for granted, such as quire marks at the end of a gathering, the marking out of sections, paragraphs or verses with enlarged capital letters, the practice of setting out a text *per cola et commata* (in relation to reading it aloud) and marginal key words summarizing the principal contents of a section. Various systems for citations and differentiation of quotations from the main text were deployed. One was quotation marks in the form of commas all

6. See the useful observations of Caillet, 'Caractères et statut du livre d'apparat carolingien'.

Fig. 1. Leiden, Universiteitsbibliotheek, MS BPL 67 E, fol. 7r (detail, enlarged). Latin glossary chrestomathy, France, s. ix³⁄⁴, showing notes of authorities cited in the margin.

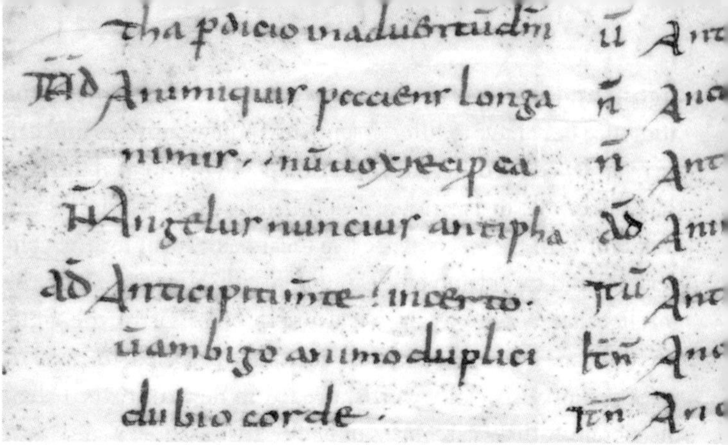

Fig. 2. Leiden, Universiteitsbibliotheek, MS VLQ 9, fol. 24v (detail, enlarged). *Liber Herbarius*, Italy, s. vi², showing a quire mark.

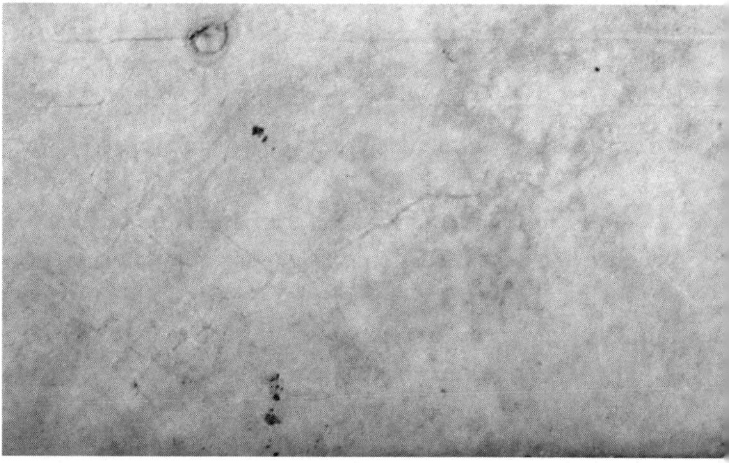

Fig. 3. Leiden, Universiteitsbibliotheek, MS BPL 114, fol. 38v (detail, enlarged). *Epitome Aegidiana* Bourges, s. viii/ix, showing the running titles.

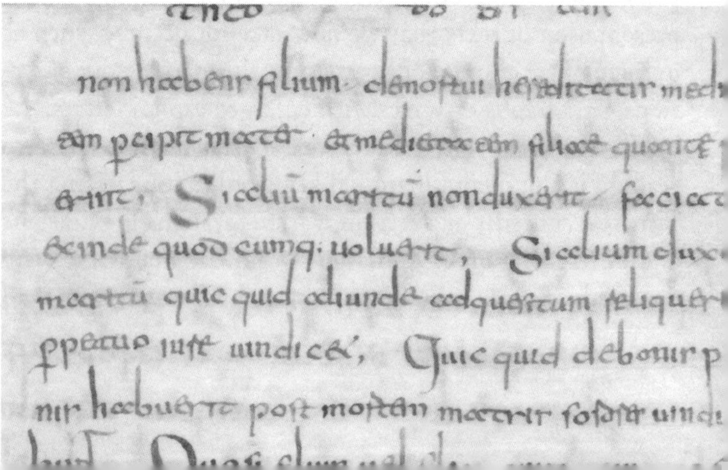

down the paragraph, such as the ninth-century Reichenau copy of Augustine's *Retractationes* in BnF lat. 17394. Another was the use of abbreviated names of authorities as marginal reference tools, such as 'AUG' for Augustine, 'AM' for Ambrose, 'GG' for Gregory the Great. Both these devices were established by the late eighth century at least, and can be especially observed in manuscripts containing biblical exegesis. An example is St Gallen, SB, MS 283, p. 46, citing Augustine.[7] In BPL 67 E, fol. 7r (Fig. 1/Plate 1), sources of words in the A-section of the glossary are offered. Most if not all of these reading aids can be found in late-antique codices as well. Many of these aspects, furthermore, can be illustrated from early medieval manuscripts in the Leiden University Library collections.

Quire marks, as a system, for example, were a standard feature of the organisation of a late-antique codex such as VLQ 9, fol. 24v (Fig. 2/Plate 2), a Herbal written in Italy in the second half of the sixth century, even if the position in the bottom margin changes from the left corner to the middle over time.[8] Running titles in the top margin of a page, most usually in a different type of script from that employed for the main text, are present in the oldest Latin manuscripts extant from the fourth and fifth centuries, and would appear to be a consequence of the development of the codex form of the book.[9] One example in Leiden is BPL 52, fol. 100r, *Servius in Lib. V–XI Aeneidos*, probably written at Corbie at the turn of the eighth century, with running titles in uncial or minuscule, and illustrated here is BPL 114, fol. 38 (Fig. 3/Plate 3), *Epitome Aegidiana*, of the sixth-century *Lex Romana Visigothorum*, copied s. viii/ix, in which the running titles are in capitals or in minuscule. In both cases the main text is written in minuscule.

The elaborate cross reference system for comparing the Gospel narratives of Christ's birth, teaching, miracles and pas-

7. Illustrations of the St Gallen examples cited can be found on the *Codices Electronici Sangallenses* website, www.cesg.unifr.ch/en/, accessed 16 November 2011. Manuscripts in St Gallen, Stiftsbibliothek are paginated.

8. See Lowe's 'Some Facts About Our Oldest Latin Manuscripts' and 'More Facts About Our Oldest Latin Manuscripts', reprinted in his *Palaeographical Papers*, ed. Bieler, Vol. 1, 187-202 and 250-74, respectively, from which subsequent references to these two articles are cited.

9. Lowe, 'Some Facts' and 'More Facts'. On the codex, see Roberts and Skeat, *The Birth of the Codex*.

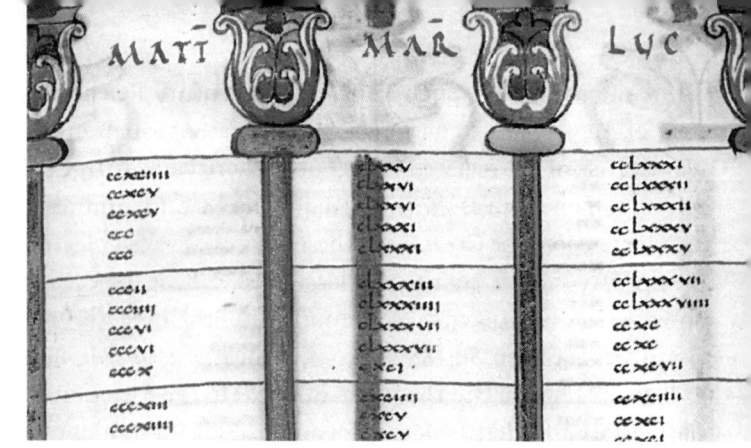

Fig. 4. Leiden, Universiteits-bibliotheek, MS BPL 48, fol. 8v (detail, enlarged). The so-called 'Ghent Livinus Gospels', St Amand, s. ix³ᐟ⁴.

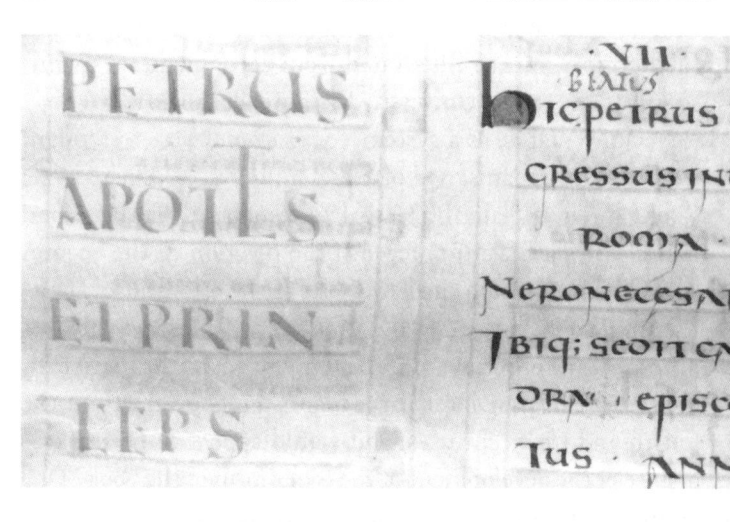

Fig. 5. Leiden, Universiteits-bibliotheek, MS VLQ 60, fol. 8v (detail, enlarged). *Liber pontificalis*, St Amand, s. viii/ix, showing different script types and ornament-ed coloured initials.

Fig. 6. Leiden, Universiteits-bibliotheek, MS VLF 82, fol. 120v (detail, enlarged). Isidore of Seville, *Etymologiae* and glossaries, Paris, St Germain-des-Prés, s. ixⁱⁿ, showing a hierarchy of scripts and the T-O diagram to represent the world.

sion was devised by Eusebius in the fourth century and is to be seen in the synoptic canon tables in Gospel books such as the Ghent Livinus Gospels now BPL 48, fols 8v-9r (Fig. 4/Plate 4), written at St Amand in the third quarter of the ninth century.[10]

Many late-antique and early medieval scribes created interplay between various text colors, rubrication and different coloured headings. An early example is again the sixth-century Italian codex, *Liber herbarius*, VLQ 9, fols 24v-25r (Fig. 2/Plate 2) with alternating red and black uncial, the same script as the text, or VLQ 60, fols 8v-9r (Fig. 5/Plate 5), a copy of the *Liber pontificalis* from St Amand, dated to the late eighth or early ninth century which deploys different script types as well as ornamented initials and colours.[11] In many instances the interplay between different grades of script was formalized as a hierarchy of scripts, particularly practised at Tours in the ninth century, but familiar in many early medieval books, such as VLF 82, fol. 120v (Fig. 6/Plate 6), from the Paris region or the Canon Law collection in The Hague, Museum Meermanno-Westreenianum, MS 10.B.4, fol. 53v, both dated s. viii/ix.[12]

A variable use of two-column or long-line layout on each page is to be observed in the oldest extant Latin manuscripts.[13] It is a commonplace, moreover, that the essentially square format of many late-antique codices appears to have been reproduced by many Carolingian scribes when copying classical and late antique texts. Surviving manuscripts of Horace, on the other hand, are more often than not presented with more regular proportions rather than square.[14] A layout that visually distinguished between main text and 'add-ons' such as glosses or fuller commentary is familiar in ninth-century copies of older texts and may have been taken over from earlier exemplars. So might the deployment of different sizes of script for

10. On the arrangement of Gospel books see McGurk, *Latin Gospel Books from A.D. 400 to A.D. 800*. Cf. the review by Wright, 'Latin Gospel Books from A.D. 400 to A.D. 800 by Patrick McGurk'.

11. Lowe, *Codices Latini Antiquiores* (henceforward CLA), X, Nos 1582 and 1583.

12. CLA, X, No. 1581.

13. Lowe, 'Some Facts', ed. Bieler, 201.

14. Lowe, 'More Facts', ed. Bieler, 270-1. See also McKitterick, *History and Memory in the Carolingian World*, 201-4. I am grateful to Erik Kwakkel for his summary of the appearance of Horace codices.

15. Duchesne, *Le Liber pontificalis*, XLIX-XLVII; Geertman, 'La genesi del *Liber Pontificalis romano*'; and McKitterick, 'Roman Texts and Roman History in the Early Middle Ages'.

16. Butzman, ed., *Corpus Agrimensorum Romanorum* and *CLA*, IX, No. 1374. See also the comments by Michael Reeve in Reynolds, ed., *Texts and Transmission*, 1-6 and Dilke, *The Roman Land Surveyors*, 126-32.

the main text and the annotations, such as the Leiden copies of Servius (BPL 52) and Martianus Capella, VLF 48.

Tables of contents are also familiar from both chapter headings preceding biblical books and contents of law books, as well as the Vossius copy of the *Liber pontificalis* mentioned above, VLQ 60, where on fols 5v-7r the list of the popes whose biographies are included in the book is placed at the beginning in numbered sequence, or BPL 114, fols 8v-9r, listing the contents of a law book. A remarkable instance of the provision of contents' details is the eighth-century miscellany from St Gallen, St Gallen, SB, MS 225, pp. 3-4, which has itemized all its contents. These would appear to be elements of the presentation of the text developed when the texts themselves were being compiled. In the case of the *Liber pontificalis*, the list of popes acting as an indicator of the contents appears to have been part of the original conception of the text in the sixth century.[15] The detailed lists at St Gallen, however, are more likely to be the product of a particular enterprise at St Gallen in the eighth century that I explore more fully below.

Similarly, diagrams were probably derived from late-antique exemplars, and familiar from such texts as the famous *Agrimensores* corpus in the Codex Arcerianus A (Wolfenbüttel, Herzog August Bibliothek, MS Aug. 2° 36.23), later owned by Erasmus.[16] They are found in a number of texts relating to astronomy, cosmology, mathematics, geometry, music and the like. Thus they mostly occur in such texts as Pliny the Elder's *Natural History*, Macrobius's *Commentary on Cicero's Somnium Scipionis*, Martianus Capella's *Marriage of Philology and Mercury* and the translation of and commentary on Plato's *Timaeus* by Chalcidius, as well as encyclopaedic compilations composed in the early Middle Ages such as the *De natura rerum* and *Etymologiae* of Isidore of Seville. These diagrams function as illustrations, interpretations, further information, clarification and even interrogation of the texts they serve. Examples among many possible are the planetary configurations in the Leiden *Aratea*,[17] VLQ 79, fol. 93v, the representation of the equinox in a Leiden copy of Martianus Capella, *De nuptiis Philologiae et Mercurii*, written at Auxerre in the second quarter of the ninth century, VLF 48, fol. 92v, and the T-O diagram to represent the world, common in copies of Isidore of Seville's *Etymologiae*, here illustrated from VLF 82, fol. 120v (Fig. 6/Plate 6) written at St Germain-des-Prés at the turn of the eighth century.[18]

Knowledge of the study of Carolingian science has increased enormously in the past two decades, not least as a result of the meticulous examination of the Carolingian copies of many of the relevant classical texts, which as Eastwood has stressed, were revived, copied, disseminated and studied from the time of Charlemagne onwards.[19] The idea of diagrams as visual elucidations of a text is clearly as old as some of the disciplines concerned, not least Euclid's geometry, but it is also the case that Bruce Eastwood and Gerd Grasshoff have been able to identify and classify innovative astronomical and planetary diagrams introduced into manuscripts to assist readers from the Carolingian period.[20] Anna Somfai has also traced how the process of trying to understand the cosmology in Plato's *Timaeus* precipitated further explanatory diagrams in the ninth and tenth centuries.[21]

The ways in which particular texts and functions of texts can determine format is of course in evidence for liturgical texts designed to be read aloud, but it is no less pertinent for particular layouts of text appropriate to their format, such as verse. An example is the poetry of Lucretius, *De rerum natura*, lib. VI in VLF 30, fol. 22v (the *Codex Oblongus*) (Fig. 7/Plate 7). Annals and Easter tables such as those assembled in Scaliger 28, fols 17v-18r

17. See the facsimile edition, Bischoff, *Aratea: Kommentar zum Aratus des Germanicus MS. Voss lat Q. 79*, Chapter 4.

18. See the useful discussion of early diagrammatic maps by Teresi, 'Anglo-Saxon and Early Anglo-Norman Mappaemundi', and her references.

19. Eastwood, *Ordering the Heavens*. See also Butzer and Lohrmann, ed., *Science in Western and Eastern Civilization in Carolingian Times*.

20. See Eastwood and Grasshoff, *Planetary Diagrams for Roman Astronomy in Medieval Europe*.

21. Somfai, 'The Transmission and Reception of Plato's *Timaeus* and Calcidius's Commentary During the Carolingian Renaissance'.

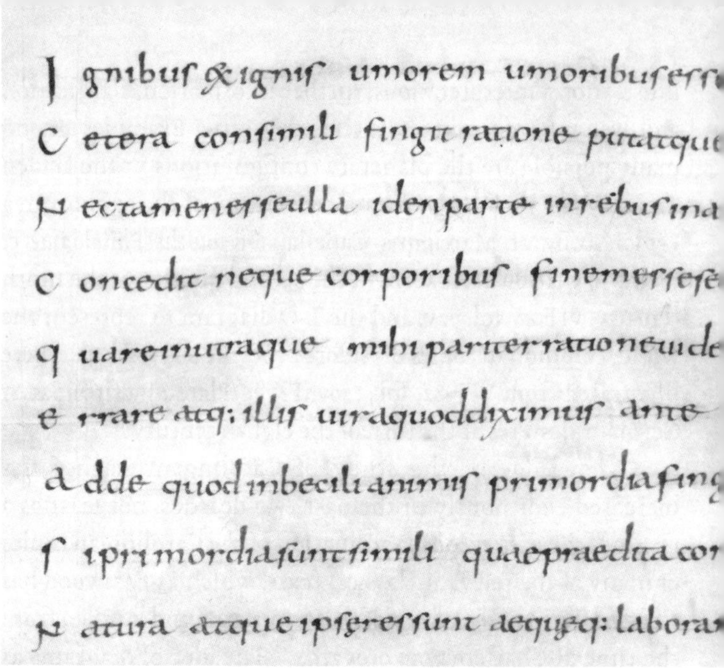

Fig. 7. Leiden, Universiteitsbibliotheek, MS VLF 30, fol. 22v (detail, enlarged). Lucretius, De rerum natura, lib. VI (*Codex Oblongus*), Northwest Germany, s. ix^(1/4)- ²/⁴ showing layout for verse.

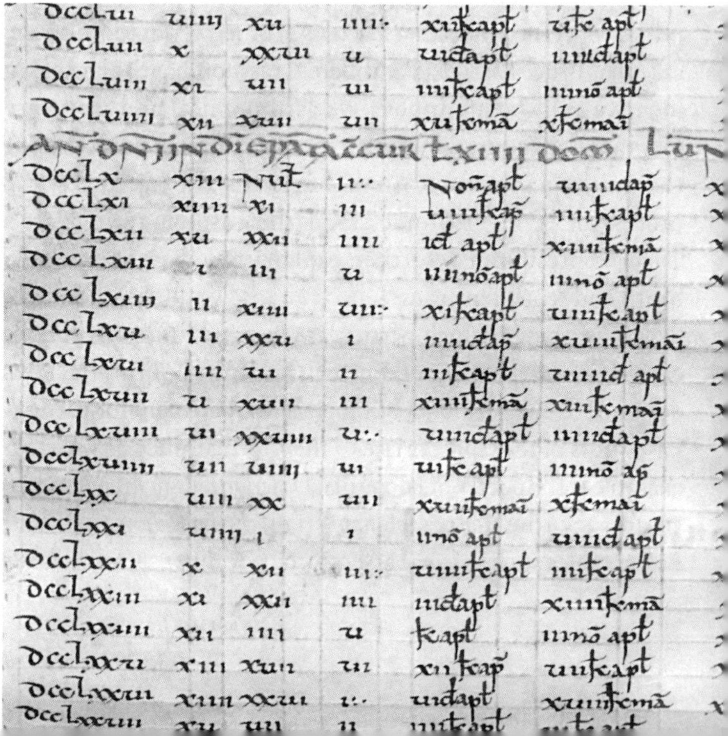

Fig. 8. Leiden, Universiteitsbibliotheek, MS Scaliger 28, fols 17v-18r (detail, enlarged). Flavigny, c. 816, showing layout for Annals and Easter tables.

also required new layouts (Fig. 8/Plate 8). Within a text the requirements of reading and understanding in different periods manifests itself, moreover, in changes in punctuation.[22]

New Genres of Text and New Types of Book

When used in new genres of text we might be inclined to see these as innovations. When the texts are older, the obvious question is: how many of these features are taken over from the exemplar? In particular, how many were demonstrably taken over from late-antique exemplars? We need to distinguish old texts from new, with classical, late antique secular and patristic works on the one hand, and all the array of Carolingian writings and new authors on the other, just as those working on twelfth-century manuscripts need to differentiate between new twelfth-century works and copies of older scholarly, literary, scientific and ecclesiastical texts.

The layout of music in the form of the newly invented neumes in relation to text that is encountered for the first time in the ninth century is an entirely new development, manifest in a number of remarkable manuscripts of the late ninth and tenth centuries.[23] A further example of a completely new kind of text in the Carolingian period is the *Liber vitae* or Book of Life, a book simply filled with names of both the living and dead of a particular community and many other groups of people, lay and monastic with which it had links, and for whom prayers were offered. Nine of these are extant from the Carolingian period, the earliest produced at Salzburg in July 784.[24] The Pfäfers *Liber vitae*, now in St Gallen, Stiftsarchiv, Cod. Fab. 1, for example, was actually part of a Gospel book.[25] Others in this new genre, such as the Reichenau confraternity book, with its 40,000 names arranged in columns according to the institutions to which they belonged, are completely free-standing new designs.[26]

22. Parkes, *Pause and Effect*.

23. See the introduction by Rankin, 'Carolingian Music'; Rankin, 'On the Treatment of Pitch in Early Music Writing'; the examples offered in Demollière, ed., *L'art du chantre carolingien*; and as an example of early music layout, the facsimile of the St Gallen Troper and Sequences, Arlt and Rankin, eds., *Stiftsbibliothek Sankt Gallen Codices 484 & 381*.

24. Geuenich, 'A Survey of the Early Medieval Confraternity Books from the Continent'.

25. Erhart and Kuratli-Hüeblin, eds., *Bücher des Lebens – Lebendige Bücher*, 88. See also the facsimile in Von Euw, ed., *Liber viventium Fabariensis*.

26. Zürich, Zentralbibliothek, MS Rh. Hist. 27, ed. with facsimile Autenrieth, Geuenich and Schmid, *Das Verbrüderungsbuch der Abtei Reichenau*.

27. Bischoff, *Paläographie des römischen Altertums und des abendländischen Mittelalters*, 143-51 and Bischoff, *Latin Palaeography*, 112-8. See also Ganz, 'The Preconditions for Caroline Minuscule'.

The Pfäfers *Liber vitae* example suggests that some of the layout of Gospel texts and canon tables had clearly influenced the scribe's approach to the problem, for liturgical purposes, of listing names of the dead and living. There are other categories and genres of text, such as poetry, letters, history, law, theological treatises, encyclopaedias, dictionaries, liturgy, lives of saints and martyrologies, to which the Carolingians made distinctive new contributions. But the Carolingian scribes may nevertheless have set out their texts in a similar way to the scribes of their ancient Roman and early Christian models rather than devising completely new formats. After all this, is there really very much in Carolingian copies of older texts that was actually introduced into the laying out and presentation of the text for the first time by Carolingian scribes, as distinct from being developed from ideas already offered in exemplars? The elaboration of Caroline minuscule undoubtedly effected a major change.[27] Its role as a book hand appears to have consolidated an attitude to the Roman system of script already in existence - notably the capitals, uncial and half uncial of the book hands - as a hierarchy of scripts on which scribes could draw in their efforts to bring greater clarity and structure to a text. It would be natural to consider whether Caroline minuscule was so vigorously promoted precisely because, once it was accepted as a principal book hand, it opened up an even greater range of scripts and ranks of script for scribes to deploy in laying out a text. That is, in addition to the Roman script system of capitals, uncials and half uncials the minuscule script itself as a text hand offered new possibilities for the ways the older script types could be used in relation to texts written in minuscule. At the same time, the space occupied by the minuscule script, and the different way it filled lines on the page offered new challenges to scribes when laying out their texts, not least if copying from older exemplars written in different script types. How much did Carolingian scribes change when copying a text? How can we establish what they may have changed if we lack extant earlier exemplars? If they changed particular aspects, why did they do so? Do such changes reflect new needs on the part of the users of the book? Were new categories of reader to be accommodated? Did new scribes approach their copying tasks in a different manner? Furthermore, how can we eliminate, or at least allow for, our inevitably subjective assessments of manuscript page layout as modern scholars?

History Books: The Chronicon of Eusebius-Jerome

The books in the BPL, Scaliger and Vossius collections in Leiden Universiteitsbibliotheek make it possible to address these questions, only some of which can be considered in the scope of this paper. Let us look at an example of a late antique history book, copied in the Carolingian period and throughout the middle ages, namely the Chronicon of Eusebius in the Latin translation and continuation of Jerome made soon after 378. There are two fifth-century copies of this text extant, the fragments of one of which is in Leiden, now VLQ 110 A, fols 1v-2r (Fig. 9/Plate 9), written in Italy in the fifth century, though other leaves from this same manuscript are also to be found in Paris and in the Vatican Library.[28] This remnant of the fifth century can be compared with the copy made of it when it was still intact in the ninth century at St Mesmin, Micy in the Loire valley, now VLQ 110, fols 48v-49r (Fig. 10/Plate 10). But there is also an even more sumptuous version of the Chronicon, in four colours, Scaliger 14 from the very late eighth or early ninth century, and very probably made for Charlemagne himself.[29]

The Chronicon does not take the form of continuous narrative about the succession of empires, but is presented in

28. BnF MS lat. 6400 B (fols 1-8 and 285-90) and Rome, BAV, MS Reg. lat. 1709A (fols 34-35): CLA, V, No. 563, CLA, I, p. 34 (illustration and description of Reg. lat. 1709A, no number, between Nos 112 and 113), CLA, X, No. **563.

29. See Fotheringham, ed., The Bodl. Manuscript of Jerome's Version of the Chronicle of Eusebius, 1-7.

Fig. 9. Leiden, Universiteitsbibliotheek, MS VLQ 110 A,
fol. 1v (detail, enlarged).
Chronicon of Eusebius-
Jerome, Italy, s. v.

Fig. 10. Leiden, Universiteitsbibliotheek, MS VLQ
110, fol. 48v (detail,
enlarged). *Chronicon* of
Eusebius-Jerome,
St Mesmin, Micy s. ix^med
copied from VLQ 110 A.

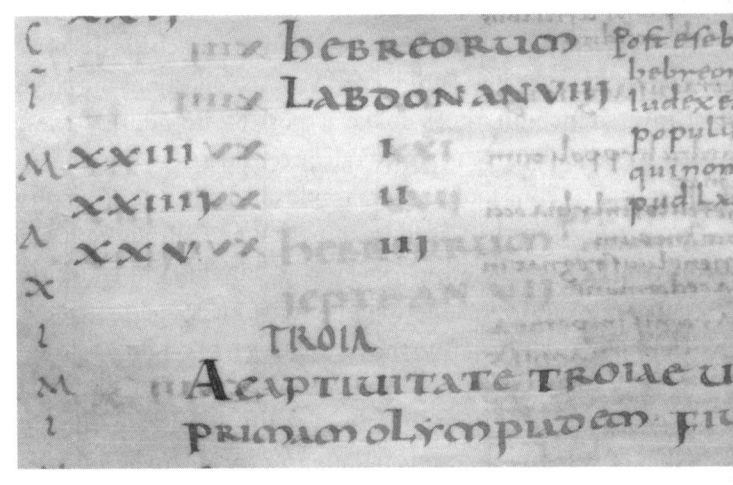

Fig. 11. Leiden, Universiteitsbibliotheek, MS
Scaliger 14, fol. 23v (detail,
enlarged). *Chronicon* of
Eusebius-Jerome, court
circle of Charlemagne,
s. viii/ix, showing column
layout.

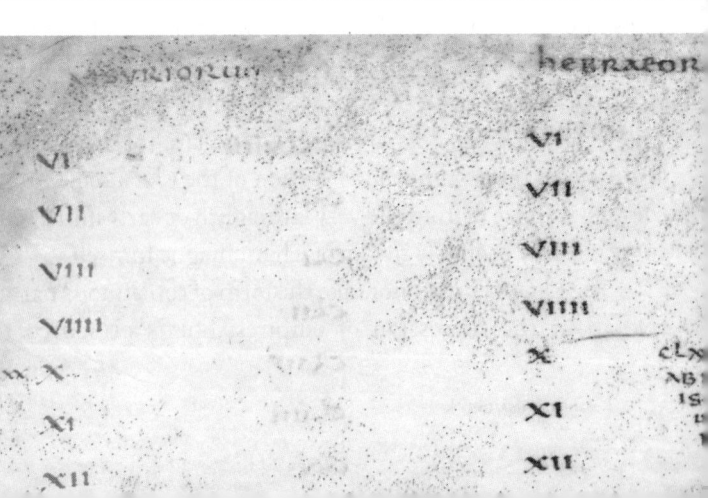

columns, recording different chronological sequences, such as years since the birth of Abraham, Olympiads and the regnal years of kings, judges, archons and emperors. The Chronicle is then constructed in relation to these columns of dates in columns spread at first over two pages or an opening, and later on one page. Sometimes the columns are colour coded, as in Scaliger 14, fols 23v-24r (Fig. 11/Plate 11). They are devoted to the rise and fall of the empires of the Medes, Persians, Athenians, Romans, Macedonians, Hebrews, Egyptians and others, nineteen in all.[30] One or two columns, the section known to modern scholars as the 'historical notes' but adapted from the label *spatium historicum* given it by the *Chronicon's* first editor, Joseph Scaliger, in 1606,[31] then records events, quite briefly, such as the career of Moses and Alexander the Great, the founding of Rome, the victories of Cyrus, the fall of Troy, the birth of Christ, the destruction of Jerusalem and so on. History is visually synchronised and it creates interesting juxtapositions, such as the careers of the poet Homer and King Solomon, or the coincidence in time of the Judge Deborah and King Midas.[32] As Christopher Kelly has noted, however, Eusebius appears to have had serious reservations about the historical notices relating to Greek mythology. Eusebius plotted the mythical events as historical within the framework of the Chronological tables, discussed some of the uncertainties and problems of rationalization, but also retained some of the repeated and irreconcilable chronologies in the classical past while presenting the Hebrew notes as if they were a clear, logical and unproblematic sequence. Thus, in Kelly's words, 'biblical history flows smoothly and securely ... and the shape of the past is indisputably determined by the Old Testament'.[33] As the Roman Empire expands, so the columns contract, and after the destruction of Jerusalem by Titus in 70AD even the sepa-

30. See Burgess, *Studies in Eusebian and Post-Eusebian Chronography*; Burgess, 'Jerome Explained: An Introduction to his Chronicle and a Guide to its Use'; and Inglebert, *Les romains chrétiens face à l'histoire de Rome*, 217-80.

31. Grafton, *Joseph Scaliger: A Study in the History of Classical Scholarship*.

32. Kelly, 'Past Imperfect: The Formation of Christian Identity in Late Antiquity'.

33. Kelly, 'The Shape of the Past: Eusebius of Caesarea and Old Testament History', 27.

34. For further illustrations see Leiden University Library Special Collections, Snapshot 67, https://disc.leidenuniv.nl/view/snapshots.jsp, accessed 8 November 2011.

35. Grafton and Williams, *Christianity and the Transformation of the Book*.

rate column for Jews disappears. The scribes of Scaliger 14 clearly modelled the layout of the text on fifth-century exemplars, such as VLQ 110 A (regarded as the best representative of the original form of the text) with respect to the parallel column arrangement, the colour coding of the different peoples assigned to each column and the distinctions made between various categories of entry in the type of script deployed. In the number of lines on the page and precise elements of the layout of particular entries as distinct from the text as a whole, however, Scaliger 14 does not conform with any other known early manuscript of the Chronicle. This means that the scribe appears to have devised his own version of the layout for each page in reacting to the content of the text, rather than slavishly following any model.[34]

Certainly most of the Carolingian copies of the *Chronicon* maintain the format in general that Anthony Grafton has demonstrated was devised by Eusebius and adapted by Jerome in the fourth century.[35] While the scribe of Scaliger 14 is more creative in relation to his model than some of the other Carolingian copyists of the *Chronicon*, even the colour coding in Scaliger 14 appears to have been part of Jerome's original intention in presenting the text, for it carries out the description in the preface he supplied. Jerome there had explained that the use of different colored inks should be preserved exactly as they had been written

'lest someone suppose that so great an effort has been attempted for the meaningless pleasure of the eyes, and when he flees from the tedium of writing inserts a labyrinth of error. For this has been devised so that the strips of the kingdoms, which had almost been mixed together because of their excessive proximity on the page, might be separated by the distinct indication of bright red, and so that the same hue of colour which earlier parchment pages had used for a kingdom, would also be kept on later ones.'[36]

Accordingly, the beginning of the Chronicon text in Scaliger 14 sets out the Assyrians in red, the Hebrews are in green, black is used for the Scythians, and brown for the Egyptians. When the Argives need to be inserted, another colour – dark red – is used. Apart from the differentiation between the different peoples and empires by colour, there is also an elaborate hierarchy of references orchestrated by changes in script type and size, with entries and headings in differently sized and spaced uncial, historical notes inserted in uncial, but minuscule used for the prefatory matter and for the more substantial sections on Roman history towards the end of the book. Similarly, the ninth-century copy of the Chronicon in Oxford, Merton College, MS 315 also preserves the colour coding, but uses elaborate square capitals and rustic capitals for many of the headings and minuscule for the historical notes.[37]

The Italian scribe of the late eighth- or early ninth-century copy in Lucca, Biblioteca capitolare, MS 490, on the other hand, squeezed as many as seven pages of his late antique exemplar onto one page. Although the chronological sequence was preserved there is a marked loss of clarity and it is very difficult to follow the sequence of events.[38]

Even worse, from the point of view at least of continuity in layout, however, is the version produced at Corbie in 1154, now BPL 30, fols 14v-15r (Fig. 12/Plate 12), whose scribe made a complete jumble of the text. This scribe apparently preserved the chronological divisions as simply spurious text dividers, all kinds of extraneous bits of information are added, and a lot else

36. Eusebius-Jerome, Chronicon, ed. R. Helm, Eusebius-Werke, Vol. 7, 5. English translation: http://www.tertullian.org/fathers/jerome—chronicle—01 prefaces.htm, accessed 23 May 2011.

37. See the online facsimile, image.ox.ac.uk/show?collection=merton&manuscript=ms315, accessed 9 November 2011.

38. Schiaparelli's Il codice 490 della Biblioteca capitolare di Lucca e la scuola lucchese (sec. VIII-IX): contributi allo studio della minuscola precarolina in Italia and Il codice 490 della Biblioteca capitolare di Lucca: ottantatre pagine per servire a studi paleografici.

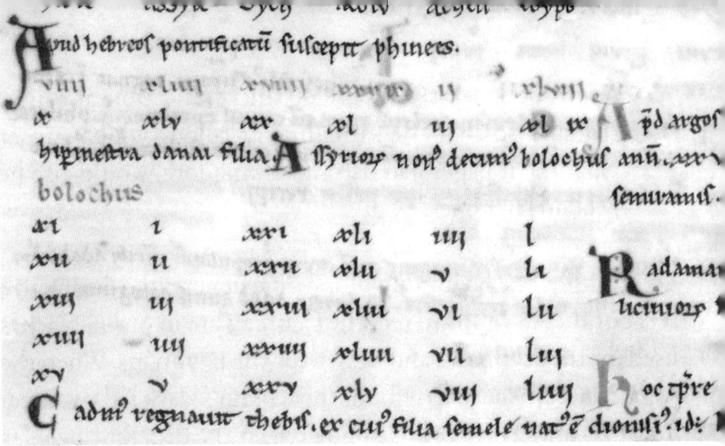

Fig. 12. Leiden, Universiteitsbibliotheek, MS BPL 30, fol. 14v (detail, enlarged). *Chronicon* of Eusebius-Jerome, Corbie 1154, showing how most of the material about Athens from the exemplar has been omitted.

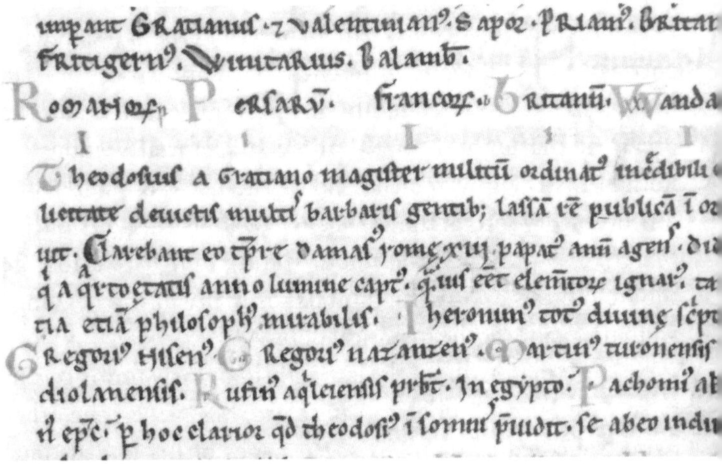

Fig. 13. Leiden, Universiteitsbibliotheek, MS BPL 30, fol. 66v (detail, enlarged). *Chronicon* of Eusebius-Jerome and *Chronicle* of Sigebert of Gembloux, Corbie 1154, showing elements introduced into the layout that appear to echo some of the principles of the Eusebius-Jerome section.

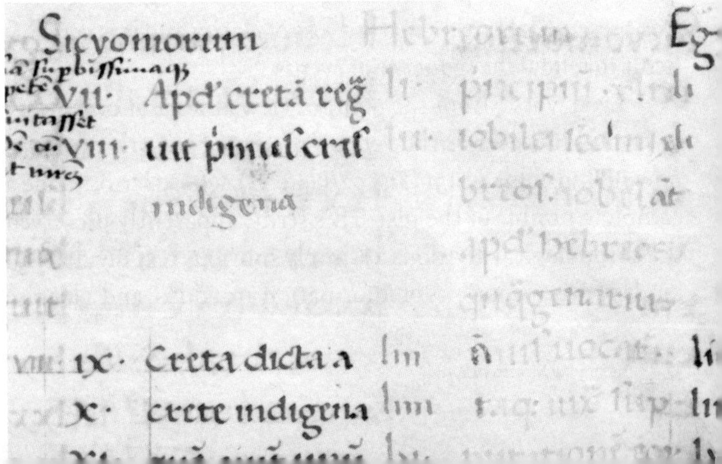

Fig. 14. Leiden, Universiteitsbibliotheek, MS BPL 97 B, fol. 9r (detail, enlarged). *Chronicon* of Eusebius-Jerome, Florence s. xv, showing the reversion to the late-antique layout.

is lost. On the opening illustrated for example, most of the material about Athens is omitted, but elsewhere, such as fols 25v-26r, material on the Hebrews is omitted. But, the scribe treated the *Chronicon* as the preliminary part of the Chronicle of Sigebert of Gembloux. That later text, as can be seen in BPL 30, fols 66v-67r (Fig. 13/Plate 13), has elements introduced into its layout that appear to echo some of the principles of the Eusebius-Jerome section. It would merit further study as an apparent instance of a fourth-century text whose original format, as well as its content, was completely reinterpreted to suit expectations and needs on the part of at least one scribe and his supposed readers of history in twelfth-century Picardy.

The fifteenth-century humanistic scribe copying the text in Florence, whose work survives in BPL 97 B, fol. 9r (Fig. 14/Plate 14), however, reverted to the late-antique layout and reproduced it, though without much recourse to the colour-coding system. Again, the scribe's reasons for doing so need to be considered. He could have been simply faithfully reproducing the late-antique layout of his exemplar out of respect, or because in the light of Jerome's preface it made sense to him. Emulation of this format over a millennium of universal Chronicle compilation may conceivably have given added rationale to the layout in parallel columns, but it is necessary to bear in mind that many universal chronicles, from Bede's *De temporum ratione*, Chapter 66, and the ninth-century universal chronicles of Freculph and Ado onwards, were set out in continuous prose.[39]

These five examples of copies of Eusebius-Jerome's *Chronicon* in Leiden nevertheless offer an opportunity to compare treatment of the same text across a thousand years, from late antiquity to the Renaissance, in which the format for the presentation of the text devised by Jerome largely retained its supremacy, whether as model or inspiration.

39. Bede, *De temporum ratione*, ed. Jones; Freculph, *Chronicon*, ed. Allen; Ado of Vienne, *Chronicon*, ed. Migne. For the context of production see McKitterick, *Perceptions of the Past in the Early Middle Ages*.

40. CLA, VII, Nos 967a and 968-975. For comments on the material palimpsested in the early Middle Ages see Declercq, ed., *Early Medieval Palimpsests*.

Glossaries

I turn now to consider a very different and new kind of book, namely, early medieval glossaries. Here the existence of late antique exemplars of some of the texts contributing content to the glossaries might be surmised, but the early medieval scribes appear to have dealt with a presentation of text comprising words, pairs of words, phrases and only occasionally complete sentences in a creative manner. It is striking that the format of these glossaries varies so considerably, from very small handbooks such as VLO 74, to very lavish folios such as VLF 26. The relationship between the physical features of these manuscripts and the texts they contain is clearly different for each manuscript witness and may therefore suggest a number of different kinds of use. The palaeographical and codicological range of these books and the huge spectrum of physical structures they offer is crucial evidence in its own right of the possible range of intended uses for these books. Even the parchment could vary from small scraps, even recycled scraps, of ill-favoured parchment to large well-prepared sheets. The glossary in St Gallen, SB, MS 912, for example, was written on recycled folios of fifth- and sixth-century grammatical, literary, medical and biblical codices.[40]

With such a diversity of material on which compilers could draw, glossaries need to be regarded as simultaneously old and new texts, incorporating not only samples from eight hundred years of use of the Latin language and transmitting precise (if not always accurate) knowledge in a fundamental way, but also representing a succession of choices and selections of words that were thought to be necessary, appropriate, useful, or interesting for particular contexts and, apparently, a new method of organising the material. It is necessary therefore to determine how relevant to particular contexts of the Carolingian world any of these glossaries might be judged to be. They cannot simply be regarded as products of a schoolroom.

I do not pretend as yet to have made much progress with all the questions these glossaries raise, nor with the work agenda they have precipitated, but in the rest of this chapter I should like to discuss three questions: firstly, that of the initial formation or origins of the early medieval glossaries; secondly, how they might have been used; and thirdly what that use might tell us about reading processes and the reception of knowledge in the early middle ages. All these are germane to the themes of Erik Kwakkel's project on 'Turning over a New Leaf', namely, how knowledge is presented in books, the possibility of changes in the use of texts and the production of new kinds of books.

Early medieval glossaries are predominantly Latin glossaries, with Latin words glossed in Latin, and compiled primarily in the areas ruled by the Franks and to a lesser extent in Anglo-Saxon England. Some Latin:Latin glossaries, such as the Épinal, Erfurt and Werden glossaries, also contain glosses in Old English, Old High German and Old Saxon, either as integral parts of the definitions or as interlinear insertions.[41] There are also Greek:Latin and Latin:Greek glossaries. Leiden has a ninth-century copy of the *Hermeneumata* of pseudo-Dositheus designed for beginners, with the Greek *lemmata* preceding the Latin words arranged in both semantic and thematic sections. The colloquy between pupil and teacher is set out as if it were a glossary, following the logic of the content which functions as a contextualized word list. This is how the scribe in VGQ 7, for example, fol. 6r, appears to have laid out the words.[42] There is also a Latin:Arabic glossary from northern Spain that can be dated palaeographically to the tenth century (Scaliger Or. 31), compiled by a Christian, with the Latin *lemmata* in AB order

41. Bischoff et al., *The Épinal, Erfurt, Werden, and Corpus Glossaries*. Cf. Sweet, *The Épinal Glossary, Latin and Old English of the Eighth Century* (who printed each page of the glossary with a facing transcription).

42. Cf. St Gallen, SB, MS 902 of the early tenth century. It contains the pseudo-Dositheus, written out in continuous text rather than arranged in columns. See also Dionisotti, 'Greek Grammars and Dictionaries in Carolingian Europe' and some comments about use of pseudo-Dositheus included in Derolez, 'Anglo-Saxon Glossography'. On Brussels, KB, MS 1828-30 (185), see Bremmer and Dekker, *Anglo-Saxon Manuscripts in Microfiche Facsimile*, 23-32. See also Kramer, *Glossaria bilingua in papyris et membranis reperta*.

43. My dating differs from that of Van Koningsveld, 'The Latin-Arabic glossary of the Leiden University Library'. I am grateful to Jésus de Prado Plumed for his comments on the Arabic and Arabic script in this manuscript.

44. Goetz, ed., *Corpus glossariorum latinorum*; Lindsay, ed., *Glossaria Latina*; Hessels, ed., *An Eighth-Century Latin-Anglo Saxon Glossary Preserved in the Library of Corpus Christi College Cambridge*; and Hessels, *A Late Eighth-Century Latin-Anglo-Saxon Glossary*. New editions of glossaries in particular manuscripts are being produced by Gatti, for example *Un glossario bernense* (Bern, Burgerbibliothek, A. 91 [18]).

and with both the Andalusian Arabic and the Visigothic minuscule in a very accomplished script.[43] The alphabetical ordering of these glossaries was sometimes very basic, that is, into sections of A-words, B- words and so on. Others organized them into AB order, and some were even more sophisticated.

The glossaries with non-Latin glosses appear to originate in a bilingual context, mostly one in which Latin was being learnt as a second language, whether in England or in English, Frankish or Frisian missionary and monastic centres on the Continent. The Latin:Latin glossaries, on the other hand, survive in a considerable number of manuscripts from the eighth and ninth centuries and are apparently designed for Latin speakers and readers. The significance of this ubiquity of Latin:Latin glossaries in the Carolingian period is something to which I shall return below. Glossaries, therefore, are a new phenomenon in the early Middle Ages in terms of extant manuscripts, but they drew on classical and late antique precedent, which needs be explored a little further.

Glossary Manuscripts: The Leiden Examples

There are thirteen Carolingian manuscripts containing glossaries in Leiden alone, with other concentrations in Paris, the Vatican and elsewhere. The Leiden ones can be attributed to the interests of particular seventeenth-century scholars, notably Isaac Vossius, compiler of the *Etymologicon linguae latinae*, first published in 1695. These glossaries were categorized by late nineteenth and early twentieth century scholars according to their first words, so: *Abavus, Ab absens, Abba, Abolita, Abstrusa, Affatim* as in, for example, VLF 26, fol. 1r (Fig. 15/Plate 15), *Asbestos* and the like.[44] *Abstrusa* has sometimes been regarded as a nucleus for the others, though *Affatim* and *Abavus* (see VLF 24) were clearly also important repositories. Generally speaking, the Latin:

Latin glossaries offer explanations of unusual words to a greater degree than a basic vocabulary. Lindsay's suggestion that they offer a 'non-current' and a 'current' Latin word side by side, however, may only apply to the initial provision of the definitions, whenever that was.[45]

45. Lindsay, 'Note on the Use of Glossaries for the Dictionary of Medieval Latin'. See also below, p. 57.

Here are some examples of glossary definitions, taken from BPL 67 E and VLF 24, and see also the illustration of BPL 67 E, fol. 7r (Fig. 1/Plate 1):

> Abrogans: humilis
> Asfalto: bitumen
> Foedus: pax
> Gentibus: nationibus
> Hermafroditus: nec vir nec mulier
> Icarus: filius daedili
> Libertus: qui fuit servus
> Martyr: testis
> Monogamus: unius uxoris vir
> Rebecca: patientia
> Regimen: gubernatio
> Vigiles: urbis custodes

Mostly the definitions are single words (with the cases varying due to their being extracted originally from a literary text just as they were) but sometimes a phrase is added. Sometimes these definitions are straightforward and accurate. Others supplied are less like dictionary entries or synonyms and offer an encyclopaedia-like piece of information, such as the definitions of *hermafroditus*, *Icarus* and *vigiles*.

Still other definitions are allegorical, metaphorical or symbolic, such as these, extracted from VLF 24:

46. St Gallen, SB, MS 238, from 760-80 and thus the earliest witness to *Affatim*, which hitherto has been thought to be represented in the later VLF 26, s. viii/ix from Amiens.

47. Daly, *Contributions to a History of Alphabetization in Antiquity and the Middle Ages*.

48. Gerritsen, *Het alphabet als zoekinstrument*.

49. CLA, V, No. 611. See also Bishop, 'The Prototype of Liber glossarum' and Ganz, 'The "Liber Glossarum": A Carolingian Encyclopaedia'.

Ignis: spiritus sanctus
Ignis: caritas
Ignis: flammae eius
Ignis: tribulatio
Ignis: ira
Ignis: voluptas

All these glossaries appear to have spawned similar kinds of collections. Some compilers mixed the words in different glossaries into new composite versions. Some kept the words but abbreviated, or otherwise altered, the definitions in small ways. Some used a glossary but reorganized it, so that the same words occur but in a different order. Some even rationalized the word order. A prime example is the glossary *Affatim* which is in A-order in VLF 26 of the late eighth or early ninth century from Amiens, but Winithar of St Gallen c. 760-80 reorganized it most emphatically into AB order.[46] Alphabetisation existed in the ancient world, but it appears to have been these early medieval glossaries that marked a major phase in the development of this particular method of organizing information in western texts.[47] A later medieval phase of this has been charted by Wim Gerritsen in his Scaliger lecture.[48]

In addition there is the encyclopaedia-like dictionary, known as the *Liber glossarum* (*Glossarium Ansileubi*), produced at the end of the eighth century, and extant in what are now regarded as the original two huge volumes, BnF MSS lat. 11529 (A-E) and lat. 11530 (F-Z), compiled by scribes writing the peculiar script known as 'a-b' minuscule.[49] This text was established by Alan Bishop as undoubtedly having close links with Corbie. It was more probably written and compiled by a group of nuns in a different scriptorium, possibly Soissons. Chelles and Jouarre have also been suggested as candidates and the books themselves are also among those that have been associated with the court of Charlemagne.[50] It seems to be the outcome of a remarkable enterprise of selection, assembly and organization of a vast amount of material, presumably on slips or separate leaves of parchment, then sorted and copied painstakingly into the volumes we now see. The text itself drew on the glossaries available, especially *Abavus*, and on Isidore of Seville's *Etymologiae*, a text these same nuns also copied and used when putting the *Liber glossarum* together.[51] The *Liber glossarum* was almost in absolute alphabetical order and entries vary between one-word definitions and extended explanations and examples covering several columns of text. This vast work was copied in full in a number of other Frankish centres, such as Lorsch (Rome, BAV, MS Pal. lat. 1773) and Auxerre (BL, MS Harley 2735).[52] In its turn it spawned both slightly abbreviated versions, such as the *Collectio Salomonis* at St Gallen (St Gallen, SB, MS 905) which nevertheless still comprises 1070 pages, as well as much reduced epitomes, such as the generally overlooked BPL 67 D. This epitome was written on very poor quality parchment, some of it mere scraps, and looks as if the scribe excerpted as he went, often drastically misjudging the space he needed. One thing that caught his eye was the list of animal noises under *vox* in the *Liber glossarum*, for this scribe was moved to insert a far greater variety of birds than most other such lists, mostly ultimately based on Suetonius, extant from the early middle ages.[53]

The Sources of the Words in Early Medieval Glossaries

Scholars in the past have mostly been preoccupied with tracing the sources of the words in glossaries, often in the hope of recovering remnants of lost words from the archaic Latin of

50. See McKitterick, '"Nuns" Scriptoria in England and Francia in the Eighth Century', reprinted in McKitterick, *Books, Scribes and Learning in the Frankish Kingdoms*, Chapter VII. See also McKitterick, *Charlemagne: The Formation of a European Identity*, 362-3.

51. Brussels, KB, MS II 4856 and CLA, X, No. 1554.

52. See the ERC-funded project to produce a new edition of the *Liber Glossarum*, directed by Anne Grondeux, liber-glossarum.linguist.univ-paris-diderot.fr/node/13, accessed 9 November 2011.

53. Benediktson, 'Voces animantium'; Finch, 'Suetonius's Catalogue of Animal Sounds in Vat. lat. 6018', with reference to the older literature; Marcovich, 'Voces animantium and Suetonius'; and Lagorio, 'Three More Vatican Manuscripts of Suetonius's Catalogue of Animal Sounds'. For the use of such lists in poetry and fable see Ziolkowski, *Talking Animals: Medieval Latin Beast Poetry*, esp. 37-9 and 110-6.

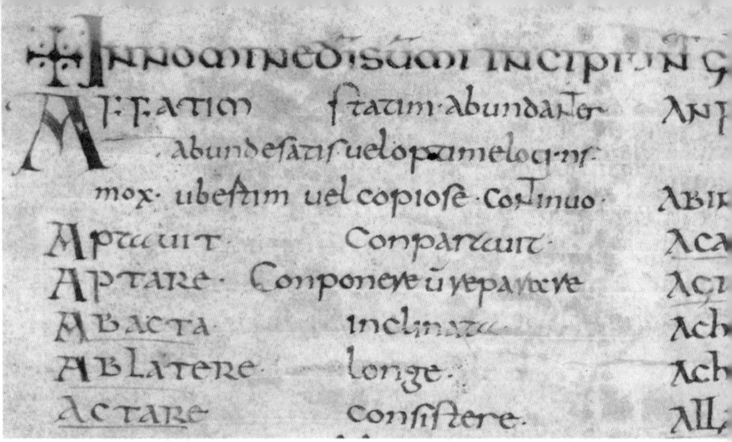

Fig. 15. Leiden, Universiteitsbibliotheek, MS VLF 26, fol. 1r (detail, enlarged). Latin glossary chrestomathy, Amiens, s. ix^(1/3) showing the beginning at *Affatim*.

Fig. 16. Leiden, Universiteitsbibliotheek, MS VLF 73, fol. 133v (detail, enlarged). *De Compendiosa Doctrina* of Nonius Marcellus, Tours s. ix^in, showing the section C-D.

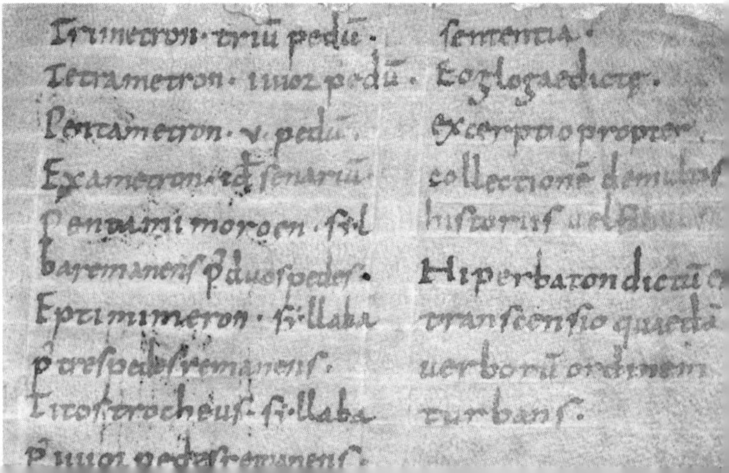

Fig. 17. Leiden, Universiteitsbibliotheek, MS BPL 67 D, fol. 1r (detail, enlarged). Added leaves (France, s. ix^ex) to an Epitome of the *Liber glossarum* (France, s. ix^(3/4)), showing a collection of Greek literary terms, transliterated into Roman script and explained in Latin.

Roman republican authors, let alone lost sections of larger works of the major Roman lexicographers of whom we now have at best early medieval epitomes. The form in which these sources of words were transmitted may have influenced how early medieval glossary scribes subsequently treated the physical layout of their texts. The best known of the latter is the epitome Paul the Deacon made of Festus' epitome of Verrius Flaccus' *De verborum significatu*, two ninth-century copies of which are in Leiden (VLQ 116 A-B and VLO 37).[54]

The *De compendiosa doctrina* of Nonius Marcellus (late fourth to early fifth century) was also an important repository of words, often in the order in which he had encountered them in his texts.[55] This too is represented in VLF 73, fol. 133v (Fig. 16/Plate 16) and VLQ 116. The Christian grammarian Placidus,[56] along with many Roman scholars and commentators, such as Servius on Virgil, grammarians, such as Donatus and Priscian and encyclopaedists, such as Pliny, offered still more treasures for glossary compilers. A set of definitions known as the *Sinonima* has been transmitted attached to Cicero though more likely to be a sixth-century text from Ravenna,[57] and another popular collection was that known as the Spiritual glosses attributed to Eucherius, the fifth-century bishop of Lyon, VLF 24, fol. 88r.[58]

There were also a number of classical and late antique discussions and compilations of specialized vocabulary in the fields of medicine, law and literature as well as biblical glosses.[59] BPL 67 D, fols 1r and 2r (Fig. 17/Plate 17) for example, contains a collection of Greek literary terms, transliterated into Roman script and explained in Latin. It is not in any systematized order and may simply have been compiled from a prose discussion of figures of speech. Similarly, VLQ 74, fols 146r-147r has a list of Greek and Latin grammatical terminology. Terms

54. Lindsay, ed., *Sexti Pompei Festi De verborum significatu quae supersunt cum Pauli Epitome* and the report of the AHRC Festus Lexicon project, directed by Fay Glinister, Michael Crawford, John North and Clare Woods, http://www.ucl.ac.uk/history2/research/festus/, accessed 31 December 2010.

55. Nonius Marcellus, *Nonius Marcellus' Dictionary of Republican Latin*, ed. Lindsay.

56. Placidus, *Liber glossarum*, ed. Goetz.

57. See Gatti, *Synonima Ciceronis*.

58. Eucherius, 'Glossae spiritales secundum Eucherium episcopum', ed. Wotke. Cf. Mandolfo, ed., *Eucherii Lugdunensis, Formulae Spiritalis intelligentiae, Instructionum libri duo*.

59. Vaciago, ed., *Glossae Biblicae, Pars I*. See also O'Sullivan, *Early Medieval Glosses on Prudentius Psychomachia*, 102-30.

60. Both found in De La-
garde, Morin and Adriaen,
eds., S. Hieronymi presbyteri
opera, Pars 1. Cf. Migne, ed.,
Patrologia Latina, Vol. 23,
cols 771-858. See also Kamesar, Jerome, Greek Scholarship
and the Hebrew Bible.

61. Alexander, 'The Etymology of Proper Names as an
Exegetical Device in Rab-
binic Literature', http://
www.pitts.emory.edu/hmp
ec/secdocs/Alexander
Etymol.pdf, accessed
14 June 2011.

62. Sweet, The Épinal Glossary, vii.

63. Philoxenus is part of
Scaliger 25, fols 3-73, from
the sixteenth century.

taken over into Latin texts when translated but still needing
clarification also prompted lexicographical or etymological
treatment. Jerome's tract on Hebrew names, the *Liber interpretationis hebraicorum nominum*, as well as his *Hebraicae quaestiones in
libro Geneseos*, are prime examples of this.[60] The list of Hebrew
names in VLF 24, fol. 108v (Fig. 18/Plate 18), for example, is clearly based on Jerome's.

Yet Jerome himself was manifestly drawing on an ancient
tradition of etymologizing, both Rabbinic etymology and even
older Babylonian and Hellenic 'science of names'.[61] Henry Sweet
long ago observed, moreover, that the number of names of animals and plants coming together in groups even in alphabetical
glossaries suggested the existence of what he called 'class glossaries', that is, specialized lists of beasts, birds, fish, minerals,
tools, or other natural objects collected in separate groups, and
most commonly in the nominative, whereas literary words
culled from a text are more often in an oblique case.[62] Further,
there are a number of Greco-Latin glossaries first compiled as
early as the second century for Romans needing to learn Greek.
One of these is called the Philoxenus glossary and another,
already mentioned with reference to VGQ 7 (see above, p. 41), has
material lumped together under the label of the *Hermeneumata* of
pseudo-Dositheus. I summarize the principal sources on which
early medieval compilers could draw as follows, all of which
except Philoxenus are represented among the early medieval
Leiden Universiteitsbibliotheek manuscript collections:[63]

Roman and late roman dictionaries and glossaries
Festus, *De verborum significatu*, in epitome by Paul the Deacon
Nonius Marcellus, *De compendiosa doctrina*
Servius on Virgil
Grammarians: Donatus, Priscian et al.

Roman encyclopaedists, e.g. Pliny.
Sinonima Ciceronis
Eucherius, Spiritual glosses
Jerome, Hebrew names
Philoxenus (Greek and Latin)
Hermeneumata of pseudo-Dositheus (Greek and Latin)

A wonderful resource, as well as an obvious model, was the seventh-century *Etymologiae* of Isidore of Seville. Not only was this work packed with words and Isidore's imaginative and often bizarre explanations thereof (some of which he owed to many of the sources I have already mentioned), but he devoted Book X of his *Etymologiae* to a discussion of words with a brief justification:

Isidore of Seville, *Etymologiae*, Book X, *De vocabulis*:
Origo quorundam nominum, id est unde veniant, non pene omnibus patet. Proinde quaedam noscendi gratia huic operi interiecimus.

People are for the most part unaware of the origin of certain terms. Consequently we have included a number in this work for their informational value.

Isidore then adds a glossary, set out in all the extant manuscripts I have seen so far as continuous prose rather than in glossary form. It starts as follows, in A-order:

Isidore of Seville, *Etymologiae*, Book X, A–
2 Aeros, vir fortis et sapiens. Auctor ab augendo dictus. Auctorem autem feminino genere dici non posse. Nam quaedam sunt quae in feminino flecti non possunt, ut cursor. Actor, ab agendo. 3 Alumnus ab alendo vocatus, licet et qui alit et qui alitur alumnus dici potest; id est et qui nutrit et qui

64. Isidore, *Etymologiae*, ed. Lindsay, X, 1-4. Translation: Barney et al., *Etymologies of Isidore of Seville*, 213.

65. See the invaluable survey by Dickey, *Ancient Greek Scholarship* and Lemerle, *Byzantine Humanism*, trans. Lindsay and Moffatt from the 1971 French edition, 309-46. See also the new online presentation of the 30,000 entries in the *Suda* (*Suidae lexicon*) in progress, ed. Whitehead, suda online and the stoa consortium, www.stoa.org, accessed 11 June 2011.

nutritur; sed melius tamen qui nutritur. 4 Amicus, per derivationem, quasi animi custos. 5 Dictus autem proprie: amator turpitudinis, quia amore torquetur libidinis: amicus ab hamo, id est, a catena caritatis; unde et hami quod teneant. Amabilis autem, quod sit amore dignus.

Aeros a strong and wise man. Author (auctor), so called from augmenting (augere). Moreover auctor cannot be used in the feminine gender for there are some terms which cannot be inflected in the feminine such as runner (cursor). Agent (actor) from acting (agere). Foster son (alumnus) from fostering (alere) although both he who fosters and he who is fostered can be called alumnus. i.e. he who nourishes and he who is nourished, but still the better use is for one who is nourished. Friend (amicus) by derivation as if from the phrase 'guardian of the spirit' animi custos. And amicus is appropriately derived; the term for someone tormented by carnal desire is amator turpitudinis, lover of wickedness, but amicus is from 'hook' hamus, that is, from the chain of charity, whence also hooks are things that hold. Lovable (amabilis), too because one is worthy of love (amor).[64]

There was thus a wealth of material available for would-be dictionary compilers and a long succession of lexicographical works in both the Roman and Greek worlds on which to draw. That the Bible became a major resource for glossary compilers is an obvious consequence of the process of Christianization in the late Roman and early medieval worlds. The Byzantine tradition so dramatically represented in the tenth-century *Suda* similarly developed from earlier Greek compilations such as Aristophanes, Harpocration, Aelius Dionysius and a lost second-century work of Diogenianus.[65] But from Byzantium there does not seem to be quite the same abundance and variety of early medieval glossaries, so diverse in their permutations and combinations, that survive from Western Europe in the eighth and ninth centuries.

It is certainly a source of wonder that so many scholars have spent decades successfully reducing these remarkable word hoards to some kind of order and suggesting the original authors and texts whence the words might have come. Important as such work is, the obvious further questions of course are: why, and in what context, were these new compilations put together as well as the Roman and late antique ones being recopied? The assembly of such collections of words in the early middle ages might suggest new readers of books with new requirements in relation to specific vocabularies they needed. Further, if these new glossaries are really a creation of the period from the late seventh to the late ninth centuries, even though so creatively drawing on older texts and guides as the extant manuscripts suggest, why did they appear when they did?

The Origin of the Glossaries: The Implications of the Earliest Manuscripts

The question of the origin of these glossaries, who first compiled them, and in what context, is notoriously difficult. For some of these glossaries, late seventh-century or even earlier origins *as collections*, that is, as already-formed and alphabetized word lists in Spain, Italy and Anglo-Saxon England, have been proposed. The arguments are difficult to sustain when there is such a dearth of examples from much earlier than the eighth century. The simplest solution would be to propose simple continuity and development from the Roman wordlists enumerated above to early medieval dictionaries, but this would be to duck certain problems. The gap between the first composition of any of the original Roman (or Greek) sources mentioned above and their earliest manuscripts means that

66. CLA, I, No. 15.

67. CLA, VII, No. 967a (CLA, VII, Nos 968-975). Codices Electronici Sangallenses (n. 7, above) and the accompanying description date it s. viii^{in}.

68. CLA, VII, No. 972.

69. CLA, VII, No. 967b.

70. Baesecke, Der Vocabularius Sti Galli in der angelsächsischen Mission. I cannot resist noting that my own copy of this work once belonged to W.M. Lindsay, who highlighted in pencil particular passages of Baesecke's text, and noted his agreement on palaeographical points throughout the book.

the new contexts for these texts and possible adaptations made to them need to be taken into account. The earliest extant glossary manuscripts are, as far as I can determine:

St Gallen, SB, MS 912 (Abba, Ababus ...), s. vii/viii (AB-order)

St Gallen, SB, MS 913 (Vocabularius Sancti Galli), s. viii^2 (topics)

St Gallen, SB, MS 238 (Ab ...), s. viii^2 (AB-order)

St Gallen, SB, MS 907 (... apostru(m)) (first section missing) (AB-order), s. viii^2

Vatican City, BAV, MS Vat. lat. 3321 (Abstrusa ...) (AB-order), s. viii^{med}

Épinal, BM, MS 72 (7) (Apodixen) (A-order), s. vii/viii-ix^{in}

Both MS Vat. lat. 3321 and St Gallen MS 912 have what might be counted as an 'author portrait', defined by Lowe as a 'teacher', at the beginning of the text, and both are from northern or central Italy.[66] St Gallen, SB, MS 912 was described by Bischoff and Lowe as 'written in north Italy, manifestly in a centre where many ancient texts existed', for as already noted, it is actually written on palimpsested leaves dating between the fifth and seventh centuries from seven different texts, including Donatus and the Vetus Latina.[67] There is besides what is described as an 'earlier rough draft' also palimpsested and reused for the final version.[68] The codex was certainly at St Gallen by the late eighth century for an attempted restoration in uncial was inserted at that stage.[69] St Gallen MS 913 (the word list is on pp. 181-206) appears to have been at St Gallen by the end of the eighth century, although its origin has been variously associated with Fulda, Murbach and other centres linked with missionary activity in the eighth century. Its words, however are grouped topically. These were established by Baesecke to be derived from the Hermeneumata tradition.[70] St Gallen MSS 238 and 907 from between 760 and 780 are the work of Winithar, who was most emphatic about his (re)organization of the words into AB-order.

The Épinal Glossary and the Question of the Insular Contribution

The Épinal Glossary is more problematic and merits fuller comment here.[71] The strongest English connections for any of the early medieval glossary manuscripts are those proposed for the Épinal glossary. The Épinal glossary is also the only one for which a late seventh-century date has been offered within a spectrum of opinion that includes a date as late as the ninth century, so it is potentially the earliest Latin:Latin glossary extant.[72] Yet the palaeographical and philological indications are far from straightforward. The seventh-century date proposed by Malcolm Parkes for the script, following Julian Brown's suggestion of a late seventh- or early eighth-century date though for different reasons, pushes back the date of the Old English glosses a little too far for the comfort of some Old English philologists, even though Sweet had already commentated on the glossary's many 'archaisms'. Pheifer thought that the archaic language of the glosses was consistent with a date in the first half of the eighth century, though for the Épinal glossary itself he suggested a date of c. 725.[73] The English gloss for piraticum, following the principle of 'cultural substitution', is uuincingasceadam, that is, 'destructive viking', or 'piracy', which might seem to place it into the very late eight or early ninth century, even on the Continent.[74] Lindsay, on the other hand, thought the likely context for the production of the manuscript was Willibrord's Continental mission.[75] The mistakes detectable in the Épinal glossary would also suggest its dependence on earlier lists or glosses of some kind. Nevertheless, the manuscript is currently favoured as a product of Anglo-Saxon England, even if

71. CLA, VI, No. 760 dates it s. viii[1].

72. Bischoff et al., The Epinal, Erfurt, Werden and Corpus Glossaries.

73. See the discussion by Pheifer, Old English Glosses in the Épinal and Erfurt Glossaries, xxxi-xxv and lxxxix-xci.

74. Épinal, BM, MS 72, fol. 9va, line 8, and Pheifer, Old English Glosses, 39. Cf. Sauer, 'Glosses, Glossaries and Dictionaries in the Medieval Period', 27, who notes this simply as puzzling, given the recorded destruction of Lindisfarne in 793 in relation to the date he offers for the Épinal glossary of c. 700. Pheifer observed (Old English Glosses, 108, line 736) that the Old English Exodus records saewicingas with the probable meaning of pirate.

75. Lindsay, The Corpus, Epinal, Erfurt and Leiden Glossaries, reprinted in Lindsay, Studies in Early Medieval Latin Glossaries, Chapter XI.

76. Originally dated to the eighth century by Hessels, *An Eighth-Century Latin-Anglo-Saxon Glossary* and to s. viii/ix in CLA, II, No. 122.

77. On Werden see Zechiel-Eckes, *Katalog der frühmittelalterlichen Fragmente der Universitäts- und Landesbibliothek Düsseldorf*, 62, who dates the manuscript to the first third of the ninth century and locates it in the Rhineland, near Cologne, though its provenance is Werden. See also Zechiel-Eckes, 'VII.42 Corpus glossarum', who regards these glossaries as 'der Typus einer rudimentären Enzyklopädie'.

it cannot be located more precisely on the linguistic evidence, and would seem to be not earlier than the beginning of the eighth century. The Épinal glossary is usually considered as part of a small group of glossaries, and consideration of its companions may throw more light on the Épinal glossary itself.

The so-called Erfurt I fragment, for example, is regarded as a Continental copy of the Épinal glossary, in A-order and AB-order, with some words omitted, perhaps completed c. 820 by a scribe unfamiliar with Old English. Cambridge, Corpus Christi College MS 144, now dated to the second quarter of the ninth century, is a rearranged and augmented version of the words in Épinal.[76] All these have 'related material' though it may be going too far to credit them as 'almost certainly' deriving from 'Anglo-Saxon originals' as stated by the authors of the most recent facsimile. Other scholars prefer to think in terms of multiple sources from which particular words might have been derived. Erfurt II and III, on the other hand, presenting a different alphabetically ordered (AB) glossary with some letter sets missing, is from the Cologne region. These also contain Old English, Old Saxon or even Frankish glosses indicated as '*sax*', or in Erfurt III by a long horizontal stroke bending back over the word. The Werden glossary, surviving in scattered leaves, appears to fill in gaps in Erfurt II and III, and to comprise three different alphabetical glossaries, also in AB-order. The scribe of the 'Werden glossary' also indicated Saxon vernacular words with the abbreviation '*sax*' or a horizontal line above the word, and others with the abbreviations *pop(ulariter)* and *mem(orande)*.[77] The Werden glossary at least also contains many quite rare Latin words as well as basic terms. *Baccula*, for example, is glossed as *vitula* and *cu caelf*. The gloss for *Buccula*, fol. 5v, the round boss in the middle of a shield, is glossed with Latin *umbo* and the word *randbaeg*. This word, because it is not exclusive to Old English but is also used in Frankish and Old Saxon, raises further questions about the role and identity of the vernacular glosses in these manuscripts.

The Werden, Erfurt II and Erfurt III glossaries may have links with sets of words devised in an Anglo-Saxon context. Sweet demonstrated over a century ago that the Erfurt and Épinal glossary compilers at least appear to have drawn on the same 'class glossaries' on a number of topics. He thought that they and the compiler of the Leiden glossary (discussed further below) also 'took their literary glosses partly from the same books'. Certainly the role of the English in the transmission and production of glossaries appears to have been as one strand of a complex range of lines of transmission. The initial uses appear to have been in classroom and missionary contexts, whether in England or on the Continent, and they made the most of whatever texts had become available to them in the course of the seventh century.

The Eighth-Century Legacy

These early Italian, Alemannic and Anglo-Saxon examples together suggest, moreover, that whatever the range of collection of specialized or more general collections of words, particular lists of words had coalesced by the late seventh or early eighth century and were subsequently redeployed in whole or in part by many new glossary compilers. Not only the content but also the format, in the familiar columns or words of mostly single-line or short-phrase definitions, each one on a new line, appear to have been settled at the same time. Eighth-century compilers can also be credited with introducing greater precision into the alphabetization of these glossaries. At what stage a judgement about what was perceived to be current or not current in the Latin *lemmata* selected could be applied depends

78. Murphy, *Pliny the Elder's Natural History*; Doody, *Pliny's Encyclopaedia*; Henderson, *The Medieval World of Isidore of Seville*; Wallis, 'Bede and Science', 116-9; Heyse, *Hrabanus Maurus Enzyklopädie De rerum naturis*; and Ribémont, *Les origines des encyclopédies médiévales d'Isidore de Séville aux Carolingiens*.

79. Uhlfelder, *De proprietate sermonum vel rerum: A Study and Critical Edition of a Set of Verbal Distinctions*.

80. For further comments see below, pp. 60-2.

in part on the assumptions one makes about possible exemplars and their extant eighth- and ninth-century representatives. It may make best sense to see the glossaries extant in the manuscripts from the eighth and ninth centuries as the first assembly and ordering of the words they contain and reflecting contemporary needs as well as aspirations.

The idea for such compilations may well have sprung from the Roman *differentiae* and *sinonima* collections already described, as well as the classical encyclopaedia tradition continued in the early middle ages by Isidore of Seville in seventh-century Spain, Bede in eighth-century England and Hrabanus Maurus in ninth-century Francia.[78] Yet Frankish, English and Alemannic scholars demonstrated a creative facility to draw on existing resources, whether in general format or precise details of content, to create something effectively new. In other words, the format may have been one inherited from older lists or handbooks, such as the Roman *differentiae*, *Hermeneumata*, or grammarians' paradigms, but new collections and selections were derived therefrom.[79] Small sets of words, or individual words arising from specific teaching contexts, may also have been introduced into existing glossaries. This may be the way to account for the fascinating survival of some of the interpretative or explanatory comments on particular words attributed to the oral teaching of Theodore and Hadrian of Canterbury which became established features of at least one Anglo-Saxon branch of the glossary manuscripts. Theodore and Hadrian themselves, of course, could also have been drawing on far older understandings which they imparted orally in their teaching but which are preserved independently in other written collections.[80]

The Implications of VLQ 69 (the 'Leiden Glossary') and its Possible Function

The focus in the discussion of origins of the early medieval glossaries hitherto has been on the transmission of particular lists of words that then simply got copied as sets into new manuscripts. Certainly parts of many compilations might be accounted for in this way. It may be more appropriate, as suggested above, to think in terms of an inherited format from antiquity that lent itself to adaptation (by more sophisticated alphabetization), classification (by thematic groupings of words) and selection (by the transfer of particular words or groups of words into new lists). Nevertheless, the question of how glossaries might have been compiled in particular centres and the implications of their inclusion in miscellanies of related material needs further consideration in the light of the famous Leiden Glossary, VLQ 69. This codex enables us to focus on how lists of words may have been chosen and compiled.[81]

Well over a century ago, Henry Bradshaw offered the notion of *glossae collectae* as a major stage before the compilation of a glossary in alphabetical order of any kind. W.M. Lindsay refined this description still further, imagining a process by which glosses, whether interlinear or marginal annotations made on a text, say, of Virgil, were then extracted and listed separately to form *glossae collectae* of Virgil, the Bible, Orosius and so on.[82] The next stage would be to organize these lists into alphabetical order. The stage after that would be to amalgamate these alphabetically ordered lists with those of other similarly alphabetically reordered *glossae collectae* to form the composite and varied glossaries which is what we see in the *Abavus*, *Affatim* and other collections.

An unfortunate consequence of this understanding of the process of glossary formation is that the idea of any *glossae col-*

81. See De Meyïer's description in *Codices Vossiani Latini*, Vol. 2, 157-63. See also the notes and full identification of texts accompanying the microfiche published by Bremmer and Dekker, *Anglo-Saxon Manuscripts in Microfiche Facsimile*, 89-105.

82. Lindsay, ed., *The Corpus, Épinal, Erfurt and Leyden Glossaries*, 1-16.

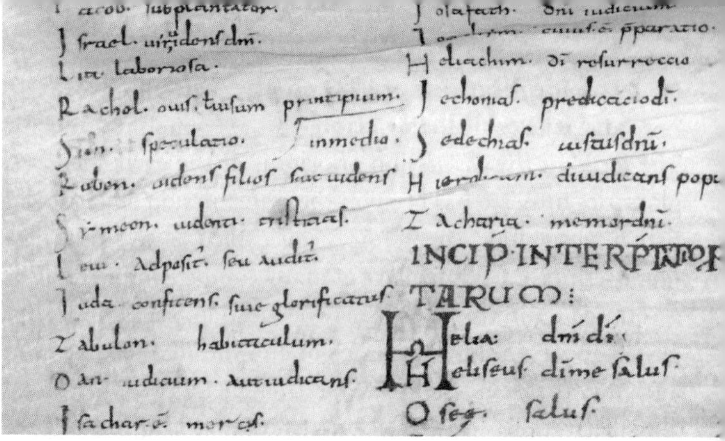

Fig. 18. Leiden, Universiteitsbibliotheek, MS VLF 24, fol. 108v (detail, enlarged). Latin glossary chrestomathy, Tours region s. ix²/⁴, showing a list of Hebrew names.

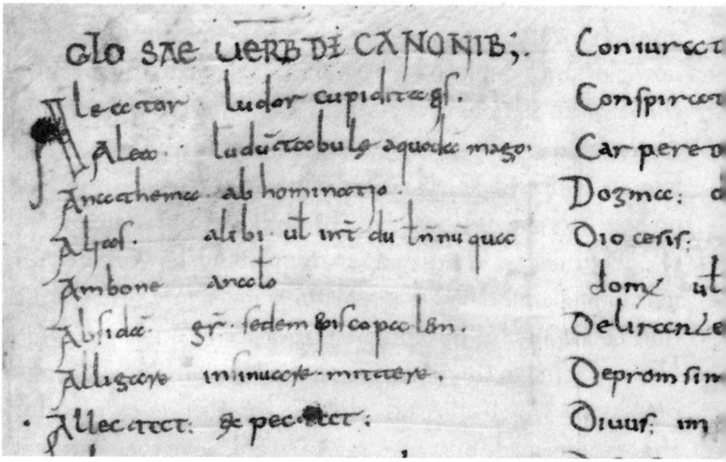

Fig. 19. Leiden, Universiteitsbibliotheek, MS VLQ 69, fol. 20r (detail, enlarged). Latin glossary chrestomathy ('Leiden Glossary'), St Gallen s. viii/ix, showing the *canones* glosses in A-order.

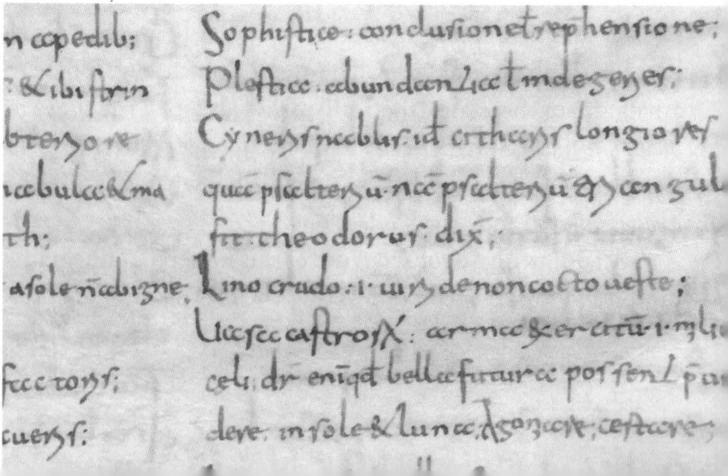

Fig. 20. Leiden, Universiteitsbibliotheek, MS VLQ 69, fol. 24vb lines 9-11 (detail, enlarged). Latin glossary chrestomathy ('Leiden Glossary'), St Gallen s. viii/ix, a gloss on *Cyneris* (harp) in the section on *Ecclesiasticus*

lectae being the direct record of someone reading a text and noting particular words is in danger of getting lost, as is the idea that *glossae collectae* might nevertheless preserve elements of direct classroom teaching. Instead, a notion of *glossae collectae* being circulated widely, alongside the composite glossaries, to serve as sources for word definitions, is in danger of reducing the role of the glossary compilers to that of mere copyists. Despite Lindsay's warning against 'the error of treating a glossary as if its items were *all* discovered by the compiler and not borrowed *in part* (my italics) from already existing glossaries', the *glossae collectae* themselves would then become simply witnesses to an extension of 'influence'. Rather than being a direct result of a reading process, therefore, these word lists, according to current understanding, would be only indirectly related either to reading in the past or to an anticipated future reading process. Because such glossaries are regarded as inherited from exemplars, they have lost any sense of the intended readers or whether they might be concerned with or derived from a specific category of text or even a specific text. Only in the case of the *glossae collectae*, which have retained the status of an intermediate stage between gloss and alphabetized glossary, might there still be a possibility of recapturing some of the immediate relationship between book and reader.

(XXXIX.20), showing where the definition supplied concludes with *Theodorus dixit* (Theodore said [so]).

This is one reason why the 'Leiden Glossary' is so important in the history of glossaries and glossary compilation. It preserves no fewer than forty-eight batches of *glossae collectae*, labelled as words taken from different texts.

The first two lists in the 'Leiden Glossary', VLQ 69, fol. 20r (Fig. 19/Plate 19) come from various church canons and papal decretals and the *Regula sancti Benedicti*. Unlike all the others in the collection these have been put into A-alphabetical order. The other *glossae collectae* appear to have been taken sequential-

83. Vaciago, ed., *Glossae Biblicae, Pars* II, 75-94.

ly from the texts. These remaining sets contain words from the major saints' lives such as Sulpicius Severus, *Vita* s. *Martini*, from history books such as the ecclesiastical history of Eusebius in the translation by Rufinus and Orosius' Seven books of history against the pagans. A harvest was garnered from Gildas, *De excidio Britanniae* and words were extracted from Isidore, *De ecclesiasticis officiis* and *De natura rerum*, and from the biblical exegesis of Cassiodorus and Jerome as well as Jerome's *De viris illustribus*. There are words taken from the *De ponderibus* of Eucherius, and from monastic texts such as Cassian's *De institutis coenobiorum*, the pseudo-Clementine *Recognitiones* translated by Rufinus, Gregory the Great's *Dialogues* and *Cura pastoralis*. There is a list of precious stones from the Book of Revelation (XXI.19-20). The bulk of the collection, however, comprises biblical glosses from Chronicles; Proverbs; Ecclesiastes; the Song of Songs; Ecclesiasticus; Isaiah; Jeremiah; and Lamentations; Ezekiel and Hosea; Daniel; the Minor Prophets; (Hosea again); Job; Tobias; Judith; Esther; Esdras and Nehemiah; the four Gospels. The selection ends with words from the grammarians Donatus and Phocas, the *Hermeneumata* of pseudo-Dositheus and more from Isidore's *De natura rerum* and Cassian.[83]

In an influential study, published twenty-five years ago, Michael Lapidge argued that a gloss on *Cyneris* (harp) in the section on *Ecclesiasticus* (XXXIX.20), one of the 48 batches of *glossae collectae* in the Leiden glossary VLQ 69, fol. 24vb lines 9-11 (Fig. 20/Plate 20) where the definition supplied concludes with '*Theodorus dixit*' (Theodore said [so]), indicated that this was a remnant of *viva voce* teaching and specifically the *viva voce* teaching of the Greek Theodore, archbishop of Canterbury in the later seventh century in England. *Dixit, ait* and such words are of course also used generally for citations of texts, and we do not know whether this '*Theodorus dixit*' was taken down at first hand, was a second-hand report, or derived from a written text. The *glossae collectae* in the Leiden glossary were then related by Lapidge to a large corpus of biblical glossaries 'mostly preserved in Continental manuscripts' but based on a proposed original corpus of English materials which similarly descended from the English Canterbury school. The entire set of 48 *glossae collectae* was judged similarly to be of English origin and to have been copied from an English exemplar at St Gallen. As such they provide 'a wonderful treasury of evidence for the books known and studied in early England'.[84]

This attractive suggestion is ostensibly given extra weight by the incidence of about 255 Old English or a mixed form of Old English and Old High German glosses added to some of the Latin definitions in the Leiden manuscript, usually indicated by the St Gallen scribe with either a little **v** above the word, or a stroke. These glosses are relatively sparse in the biblical section but more frequent in the extracts from Eusebius, *Historia ecclesiastica* and above all the *Hermeneumata* of pseudo-Dositheus. It is unclear whether they were taken over from the exemplar or added by the scribe of this manuscript. Neil Ker suggested for example, that a linguistic interest was uppermost as distinct from a native Englishman jotting down words.[85] It is also interesting that the glosses on *Ecclesiasticus* are different in character from all the others except those on the *Song of Songs*. In both these quite a lot of exegesis is incorporated. This qualitative difference, as well as the variations between the A-ordered selections for the *canones* and the Rule of Benedict (which have no Old English glosses), and the sections in which Old English glosses are concentrated, are more probably an indication that the collections in the Leiden glossary were taken from different sources. One of these sources may well have been material originally emanating from

84. Lapidge, 'The School of Theodore and Hadrian' and 'Old English Glossography: The Latin Context', reprinted in Lapidge, Anglo-Latin Literature. Cf. Baesecke, *Der Vocabularius Sti Galli in der angelsächsischen Mission*, 10, who also associated this gloss and other biblical glosses with Theodore of Tarsus and Abbot Hadrian at Canterbury.

85. Ker, *Catalogue of Manuscripts Containing Anglo-Saxon*, 478-9.

86. Sweet, *The Épinal Glossary*, vii.

87. Hessels, *An Eighth-Century Latin-Anglo-Saxon Glossary*, 50.

88. Sweet, *Épinal Glossary*, xi.

89. Porter, ed., *The Antwerp-London Glossaries* (quoted from the inside front flap of dust jacket, but this text is not to be found in the book itself). See also Porter, 'On the Antwerp-London Glossaries'.

Canterbury in some form. Even Sweet, after all, envisaged a scribe who 'evidently had before him a library of Latin books containing a number of scattered interlinear glosses, some in Latin some in English, which he copied out in parallel columns in the order of their occurrence. ... the heading *incipit ex diversis libris* seems to point to an earlier collection of glosses out of different books, which was copied straight off'.[86] The comment the compiler makes at the end of the second batch of lemmata from Cassian: *sicut inveni scripsi ne reputes scriptori* (which might be rendered: 'I wrote as I found it; don't blame it on the scribe') need not refer to the entire set of *glossae collectae*, let alone the entire codex.[87] Given the variety of sources suggested by the resultant compilation, it is unlikely that it does so.

A link of some kind with Anglo-Saxon England and Canterbury suggested by some at least of these glosses, first made by Henry Sweet in 1883,[88] has been readily accepted but has perhaps become both too direct and too entrenched. A recent edition of the eleventh-century Antwerp-London glossaries, for example, is confident in the blurb on the dust jacket at least (which alas will be discarded by most librarians) that these are the descendants of the 'earliest school text in the English language', that 'in their earliest form they played a central role at the seventh-century school of Canterbury' and that they 'contributed material to the fundamental texts, dated to the 600s, known as the Leiden glossary and the Épinal-Erfurt glossary'. These claims are then qualified with the statement that 'the glossaries have at their heart a late Latin encyclopaedia, the *Etymologies* of Isidore of Seville'.[89] But a further claim is made by the Editor of the series, Andy Orchard, on the back of the jacket, following the initial proposal made by Lapidge in 1986, namely that this is 'a collection of texts that originated in the seventh-century school at Canterbury'.

The Compilation of the 'Leiden Glossary' VLQ 69: The St Gallen Context

But, as *advocatus diaboli*, let me approach the contents of the Leiden *glossae collectae* from a different direction, and place the emphasis on process and the historical context of the compilation itself, rather than on the possible source of some of the definitions, choices of *lemmata*, or even sets of words. VLQ 69 was written at St Gallen in present-day Switzerland, then Carolingian Alemannia, at the end of the eighth century or very early ninth century. For the sake of the argument, let us suppose that not only was this book copied at St Gallen but that it was actually compiled there and that some at least of these *glossae collectae*, as well as some of the other collections of excerpts the manuscript contains, are St Gallen artefacts.[90] In other words, rather than solely witnessing to what might have been available in Canterbury in the seventh century, the glosses on particular texts also might, to adapt Michael Lapidge's phrase, 'provide a wonderful treasury of evidence for the books known and studied' in early Carolingian St Gallen.

Certainly there is a remarkable correspondence between the texts excerpted for the *glossae collectae* and manuscripts containing these very texts actually written, or known to have been, at St Gallen in the late eighth or early ninth century. If it is thought legitimate to consider some of the manuscripts copied at St Gallen from *c.* 810 onwards, as well as those recorded in the ninth-century catalogue St Gallen, SB, MS 728,[91] as possible witnesses to earlier manuscripts on the grounds that they may signal early exemplars or indicate early manuscripts now lost respectively, then the correspondence is even greater.

Of the forty-eight separate lists from specified texts in the Leiden Glossary only four, the anonymous *Vita Sanctae Eugeniae*, the pseudo-Clementine *Recognitiones*, Gildas' *De excidio Britan-*

90. On the extracts and the miscellany as a whole see Bremmer, 'Leiden, Universiteitsbibliotheek, Vossianus Latinus Q 69 (Part 2)'.

91. Lehmann, ed., *Mittelalterliche Bibliothekskataloge Deutschlands und der Schweiz.*

92. Baesecke, *Der Vocabularius Sti Galli in der angelsächsischen Mission*, 43.

93. Griffiths, 'The Leiden Glosses on the Regula S. Benedicti in Leiden, Vossianus Lat. Q. 69'.

niae, Phocas' *Ars de nomine et verbo*, cannot be identified among St Gallen codices still extant or known to have been at St Gallen (unless their use in the Leiden glossary itself could be regarded as such evidence). In addition, the *Hermeneumata* of pseudo-Dositheus is the basis also for the words in the *Vocabularius sancti Galli* in St Gallen, SB, MS 913, and there is some overlap between this word list and the one in VLQ 69.[92]

This is of course only a preliminary finding, at present interesting rather than conclusive, for what needs to follow is what Alan Griffiths has called a 'systematic sifting' of these *glossae collectae* in the Leiden Glossary in relation to the extant manuscripts, just as he has done for the pure and interpolated copies of the Rule of St Benedict.[93]

I list these correspondences below with the St Gallen early manuscripts marked in parentheses, and the later ones perhaps witnessing to exemplars or references in the library catalogue in bold italics. The first set concerns the biblical excerpts. Bibles were rarely transmitted in the early middle ages in a single volume, hence the need to discover particular volumes or small sets of biblical books and to register the different St Gallen early bible texts. The second set includes all the non-biblical texts except for those in the third small group of texts not now extant in a manuscript that can be linked with St Gallen at this early stage of its history.

I. Items 7-25 Glosses to biblical books in VLQ 69 available in St Gallen s. viii/ix

Chronicles (St Gallen, SB, MS 6, s. viii[4/4]);
Proverbs (St Gallen, SB, MS 12, s. viii[4/4]);
Ecclesiastes (St Gallen, SB, MS 30, c. 800);
Song of Songs (St Gallen, SB, MS 30, c. 800);
Ecclesiasticus (St Gallen, SB, MS 75, ix[in]);

Isaiah (St Gallen, SB, MS 40, c. 820);

Jeremiah (St Gallen, SB, MS 40, c. 820);

Lamentations (St Gallen, SB, MS 75, ix^{in});

Ezekiel (St Gallen, SB, MS 44, c. 780 and St Gallen MS 193);

Hosea (St Gallen, SB, MS 75, ix^{in});

Daniel (St Gallen, SB, MS 44, c. 780);

Minor Prophets (St Gallen, SB, MS 44, c. 780);

Job (St Gallen, SB, MS 12, s. viii$^{4/4}$);

Tobias (St Gallen, SB, MS 6, s. viii$^{4/4}$);

Judith (St Gallen, SB, MS 6, s. viii$^{4/4}$);

Esther (St Gallen, SB, MS 6, s. viii$^{4/4}$);

Esdras (St Gallen, SB, MS 12, s. viii$^{4/4}$);

Nehemiah (St Gallen, SB, MS 12, s. viii$^{4/4}$);

Matthew (St Gallen, SB, MS 51, c. 750);

Mark, Luke and John (St Gallen, SB, MS 51, c. 750);

Revelation (St Gallen, SB, MS 2, 760-80).

II. Leiden UB VLQ 69: non-biblical texts items 1-2 and 26-48

Various church canons and papal decretals (St Gallen, SB, MS 675, s. ix^{in} *Vetus gallica*);[94]

Regula s. Benedicti (St Gallen, SB, MS 914 (pure), s. ix$^{1/3}$ & MS 915 (interpolated) c. 800);

Sulpicius Severus, *Vita s. Martini* (St Gallen, SB, MS 552, s. viii/ix; St Gallen, SB, MS 567, s. viii^{ex}) and Sulpicius Severus *Dialogi* (if *Acta* then also these two);

Athanasius, *Vita S. Antonii* (trans. Evagrius) (St Gallen, SB, MS 558, c. 800);

Eusebius, *Historia ecclesiastica* trans. Rufinus (listed in library catalogue);

Isidore, *De ecclesiasticis officiis* (St Gallen, SB, MS 227, s. viii/ix, written in Verona);

94. Lapidge, 'School of Theodore and Hadrian', made the interesting observation that there was some overlap with words in the *Collectio Sanblasiana* collection. The earliest extant manuscripts of this Canon Law collection are Cologne, Diözesan-und Dombibliothek, MS 213, probably written at Cologne, and Sankt Paul im Lavanttal SB 7/1 from Italy. But there are St Gallen as well as insular links with both the *Sanblasiana* and the *Vetus Gallica* collections, see McKitterick, 'Knowledge of Canon Law in the Frankish Kingdoms Before 789'. For further comments on the Sanblasiana's Continental affiliations in relation to the words in VLQ 69, see Brett, 'Theodore and Latin Canon Law' and Elliott, 'Anglo-Saxon Canon Law: Collectio sanblasiana', http://individual.utoronto.ca /michaelelliot/manuscripts/ texts/sanblasiana.html, accessed 6 November 2011.

Isidore, *De natura rerum* (St Gallen, SB, MS 238, 760-80);
Athanasius, *Vita s. Antonii* (trans. Evagrius) (St Gallen, SB, MS
558, c. 800) and Cassiodorus, *Expositio psalmorum* (perhaps
Schaffhausen, Ministerialbibliothek, MS Min. 78, s. viii[2]);
Jerome, *Commentarium in evangelium Matthei* (perhaps St
Gallen, SB, MS 125, 770-80 or St Gallen, SB, MS 127);
Jerome, *De viris illustribus* (perhaps exemplar for St Gallen,
SB, MS 191, c. 830);
De ponderibus (perhaps Epiphanius/Jerome?);
De ponderibus from Eucherius, *Instructiones* (St Gallen, SB,
MS 238, 760-80);
Cassian, *De institutis coenobiorum* (perhaps exemplar for St
Gallen, SB, MSS 183 and 574);
Orosius, *Historiae adversus paganos* (perhaps exemplar for
St Gallen, SB, MS 621, s. ix);
Augustine, *Sermones* (St Gallen, SB, MS 213, s. viii);
Gregory, *Dialogi* (St Gallen, SB, MS 213, s. viii);
Gregory, *Cura pastoralis* (St Gallen, SB, MSS 216 and 217, s. ix[in]);
Donatus, *Ars maior* (St Gallen, SB, MS 876, s. viii/ix).

**III. *Glossae collectae* from texts not found among
existing manuscripts of St Gallen origin or
provenance s. viii/ix**
Anon, *Vita S. Eugeniae;*
Pseudo-Clement, *Recognitiones* (trans. Rufinus);
Gildas, *De excidio Britanniae;*
Phocas, *Ars de nomine et verbo;*
Pseudo-Dositheus, *Hermeneumata* (but cf. St Gallen, SB,
MS 913, s. viii[2]).

But this is not all. The rest of the Leiden manuscript, as Rolf
Bremmer has demonstrated, contains among a wealth of texts,

moralistic, devotional and didactic abecedarian poems, poems of Prudentius, epigrams and epitaphs, a discussion of the size of the ark, extracts from Pliny and late antique texts touching on matters of geography and the creation. That books already in the St Gallen library were the source for these extracts can only be surmised, for this Leiden compilation appears to be the witness to the availability of the text concerned at St Gallen.[95] The Leiden Glossary codex, which is also an encyclopaedic and moralistic compilation with some features of a topical glossary,[96] appears to be a culmination of an energetic engagement with words and a wide spectrum of knowledge, reassembled into new books at St Gallen in the later part of the eighth century. Specifically, these miscellanies were compiled under the guidance, and were often the personal creations, of the scribe Winithar and Abbot Werdo between c. 760 and c. 790. These new books comprise a remarkable number of glossaries, *etymologiae*, *florilegia* of biblical extracts, extracts from Isidore and grammatical texts and the like acquired (such as the early import from Fulda known as the *Vocabularius Sancti Galli*, St Gallen, SB, MS 913), or compiled at St Gallen. St Gallen, SB, MS 238, for example, is 494 pages long, and includes copious extracts from Isidore's *Etymologiae* as well as the *De natura rerum*, excerpts from biblical texts and a comment on translations, but nearly half its bulk comprises a glossary which Winithar says he has compiled. As I noted above, it is a re-organisation of the *Affatim* glossary into stricter alphabetical order. Another instance is St Gallen, SB, MS 294, one of the biblical glossaries.

This exuberant enthusiasm for words at St Gallen also produced Latin:German glossaries such as the famous *Abrogans Glossary* (St Gallen, SB, MS 911), a collection of sets of excerpts from patristic writers and no fewer than six different glossaries copied onto palimpsested leaves from nine different older

95. Bremmer, 'Schoolbook or Proto-Encyclopaedic Miscellany'.

96. Hüllen, *English Dictionaries 800-1700*, 60.

97. For a restatement of the conventional wisdom on the process of glossary formation see Sauer, 'Glosses, Glossaries and Dictionaries', 22-3.

98. For fuller details of this St Gallen enterprise, see McKitterick, *The Migration of Ideas in the Early Middle Ages*, forthcoming.

manuscripts (of Leo the Great, Psalms, the Epistles of Paul, liturgical texts, explanations of dreams, the poetry of Merobaudes, medicine, Junilius, all of the sixth century) now comprising St Gallen, SB, MS 908. Another collection of extracts and word lists is St Gallen, SB, MS 225, supplied with a table of contents for the whole book produced in this period, concerning exegesis, *computus*, synonyms, medicine and hagiography.

Glossae collectae are often assumed to be an intermediate stage between readers glossing texts, and the final amalgamation of words in alphabetical order. If this is so, why did so many collections of *glossae collectae*, quite apart from subject specific collections such as the *Notae iuris*, continue to be produced and circulated?[97] Should we abandon the notion that someone will only use a glossary like a dictionary and expect to have the process made easy by the alphabetization of the words, or should we also think of the *glossae collectae*, once the consequence of the reading process when first put together, thereafter remaining one form of reading aid? One might actually be guided through a particular text with these glosses of hard or unusual words to hand. The Leiden glossary compendium from St Gallen, therefore, may have been intended as a reading aid for the books available in the St Gallen library, compiled by someone from a number of different sources. These could have included alphabetical glossaries that he used as dictionaries.

Whether compiling glossaries from books already in house, books borrowed or acquired from elsewhere for the purpose, already prepared *glossae collectae*, or subject-specific compilations, St Gallen was a veritable glossary and miscellany factory, in a scriptorium energetically supplying the needs of a monastic church, library and school in a particularly focused way.[98]

Words and Knowledge: Glossary Chrestomathies

This accumulation of knowledge as an essential tool is the context in which not only the Leiden glossary, but also the other glossaries produced elsewhere in the Frankish realm need to be considered. St Gallen might be thought to be a special case, but we have to remember that it is one of the places left in Western Europe where the contents of both library and archive are still substantially intact from the early medieval period. It was not subject to the dispersal and disintegration with which we are familiar for so many other monastic and cathedral libraries in western Europe, and from which so many of the Leiden scholars of the seventeenth century benefitted. The St Gallen phenomenon, suggested by the probable origin of the scribe at least of the Leiden glossary collection, if not also the resources on which he drew, may be typical of a particular approach to language and knowledge that was widespread in the Carolingian world and the British Isles in the early middle ages.

As I noted above, many early medieval glossaries have been associated with places where Latin was learnt as a second language, notably in England and in areas east of the Rhine. The Old English and Old High German glosses some of these books contain apparently offer further faint traces of the men and women in the various centres producing these books in the early middle ages. But a substantial majority of these glossaries and glossarial and encyclopaedic collections was produced in North-western France and the Loire valley. Among the Leiden corpus in the BPL and Vossius collections, for example, only the Leiden glossary in VLQ 69 is from the Bodensee region; the others were written by scribes trained in France; at Reims, Paris, St Germain-des-Prés, Amiens, Fleury, Tours and other unidentified Frankish centres.

99. Vezin, 'L'emploi des notes tironiennes dans les manuscrits de la region parisienne'.

100. For late medieval examples see Elm, ed., *Literarische Formen des Mittelalters*.

These places were not just interested in the Latin language. We also find Greek:Latin, transliterated Greek:Latin, and Latin:Greek texts, such as VGQ 7 mentioned above. Many of these glossary manuscripts, moreover, such as VLF 26, fol. 49v, include Greek alphabets. There are also even more specialized compilations such as the list of legal abbreviations and their expansion in BPL 67 F, fol. 148v, and an extraordinary dictionary of tironian notes, VLO 94, written at Reims at the end of the ninth century. The latter was one of several tironian note lexicons extant from Carolingian Francia where the use of tironian notes, primarily by those trained for work in the royal writing office, continued late into the ninth century.[99]

Consideration of VLQ 69 and the other St Gallen compilations has also established that the form in which glossaries are most usually transmitted is as part of elaborate miscellanies, or in what could be called glossary chrestomathies. I use this word in an attempt to differentiate compilations centred on glossaries and illustrative excerpts from authors designed to enhance the knowledge of Latin in one way or another, namely chrestomathies, from miscellanies simply of a variety of material.[100] Of the eighth- and ninth-century glossaries I have so far consulted in the collections from Leiden, the Vatican, St Gallen and Karlsruhe, as well as among those in other modern libraries of which I am aware but have not yet seen, it is rare, except for the *Liber glossarum* itself, to find a single glossary presented in a single codex. Either glossaries form part of glossary collections, or one or more glossaries are accompanied by many other compilations of information. MS Vat. lat. 3321, for example, includes not only *Abstrusa* but also *Abolita* and Isidore's *Differentiae*. BPL 67 F, an even more elaborate example, contains the following items all written in the same hand:

Glossarium Affatim
Glossarium Ab absens ...zizanium
Glossarium Ababu ...zona
Glossarium vergilianae inc. Abector: exportatus
Glossae proprietatum inc. Arma: bellum
'Cicero' Sinonima (not organized alphabetically)
'Cicero' Sinonima, in abbreviated form, also not in
alphabetical sequence
Glosae Nonii (selections)
Glossae iuridicae
Eucherius glossae spirituales
Voces variae animantium
Expositiones Fidei (a collection of seven creeds)
Quaestiuncula sancti Augustini
Greek alphabet with the names of the letters written out
(A note is added in Greek letters: GAUSTMARUS FECIT
ISTO GRECO)

Other ninth-century Leiden manuscripts contain glossary chrestomathies, such as VLO 74, VLF 82, BPL 67 E and BPL 67 F. For example, VLO 74 contains three different glossaries; VLF 82 combines Isidore's *Etymologiae* Book X with the *Abavus* glossary (described as glosses from the Old and New Testaments), the *Sinonima Ciceronis* and Eucherius; BPL 67 E includes an AB-ordered glossary beginning *Abutere* and the *Sinonima Ciceronis*; BPL 67 F gathers together six different glossaries, including *Affatim*, and adds some of the *Sinonima Ciceronis*, of Nonius Marcellus, Eucherius, the specialist list of legal terms referred to above, Eucherius (again) and a collection of creeds. Extant Carolingian glossary chrestomathies in other modern collections in Paris, Rome, St Gallen and elsewhere, tell the same story.

101. See Bremmer and Dekker, eds., *Anglo-Saxon Manuscripts in Microfiche Facsimile*, 77-83; Tremp, Schmuki and Flury, *Karl der Grosse und seine Gelehrten*, with particular reference to St Gallen, SB, MSS 64, 75, 268, 271, 272, 275, 276 and 563.

The links between libraries and scholars in the Carolingian world are visible in the overlapping of texts in glossary chrestomathies from centres miles apart. VLF 24 from Tours, for example, shares many of the biblical and other *glossae collectae* with the St Gallen glossary in VLQ 69. The close Tours-St Gallen connection, moreover, can be corroborated by many other manuscripts from Tours or containing texts of Tours origin now in St Gallen.[101] The relationship between VLQ 69 and VLF 24 remains to be established by meticulous collation, but some samples I have taken suggest that the Tours compiler made a selection and slight abridgement from the sets in the Leiden glossary but also inserted some different words and omitted most of the Old English glosses.

In the list below the collections VLF 24 and VLQ 69 have in common are indicated in bold:

Glossae spiritales secundum Eucherium.
Synonyma, quae Ciceroni adtribuuntur.
Isidorus Hispalensis, *Etymologiae*, liber X
Glossae biblicae.
Glossae variae: de libro officiorum; de libro rotarum;
de libro Antonii; Interpretatio verborum;
de Catalogo Hieronymi in Prologo;
de Ponderibus. Glossae ad libros varios biblicos.
Glossae de Patristicis operibus.
Eucherius, *Instructiones*,
praefatio 'ad Salonium'.
Glossae variae: de Hebraeorum nominibus.
de Locis.
Voces variae animantium
Alcuin, *Disputatio Pippini cum Albino*

In the so-called Leiden glossary family of manuscripts which share parts of the word collections or texts to be found in VLQ 69, indeed, we have evidence not only of an extended network of communication across the empire, but also of a host of examples of individual enterprise and choice, selection and compilation.

Glossary readers

Together, moreover, these books raise the issue of how they might have been used and what they were for.[102] Dictionary users need particular literate skills.[103] I mentioned above how many glossary manuscripts still survive. The number originally produced, in itself a significant indication of the assumptions about the basic metalinguistic skills of the users, may well have been so great as to mean that all groups of men or women who were reading and copying texts possessed a glossary or glossary chrestomathy of some kind. But why are there quite so many glossary chrestomathies? These books have more than one function. Generally they served as a didactic tool, assisting a process of acquisition of Latin vocabulary for those needing both to understand and to communicate in Latin. Given the intellectual activity that can be documented at many of the places to which these glossaries can be located, they were undoubtedly aids for honing the skills of rhetoric and eloquence as well. Was there any way of sifting the bizarre and fanciful information they often supply? They were not only used as we might use a dictionary, detached from the texts that needed explanation.[104] Early medieval dictionaries, however, were not just repositories of explanations of the unfamiliar, and were not designed only to serve bilingualism. They were also not compiled with the primary aim of documenting the total vocabulary of the language, unlike such modern

102. For a discussion of 'who uses dictionaries, and what for', see Béjoint, The Lexicography of English from Origins to Present, 224-61.

103. For literacy in the eighth and ninth centuries, see McKitterick, The Carolingians and the Written Word and McKitterick, ed., The Uses of Literacy in Early Mediaeval Europe, esp. 1-10 and 318-33.

104. Hüllen, English Dictionaries, 44.

105. Hüllen, *English Dictionaries*, 6.

106. Hüllen, *English Dictionaries*, 44. See also Dionisotti, 'On the Nature and Transmission of Latin Glossaries'.

107. See McKitterick, *Charlemagne*, 292-380 and McKitterick, ed., *Carolingian Culture*.

108. See Holtz, *Donat et la tradition de l'enseignement grammatical*; Law, *Grammar and Grammarians in the Early Middle Ages*; Alcuin, *De Orthographia*, ed. Bruni; and Cassiodorus, *De Orthographia*, ed. Stoppacci.

enterprises as that of James Murray in England, the brothers Grimm in Germany, or Paul Robert in France. To some extent they fulfil what Hüllen has described as a 'mediating position for language use. ... They serve language-in-performance by providing linguistic knowledge'.[105] But the glossaries were also encyclopaedic dictionaries in their inclusion of explanations of the subject matter of the words as well as meanings. Thus they become treasuries of knowledge. As Hüllen puts it, they 'can represent the world'.[106] Similarly, glossary chrestomathies often include encyclopaedic sections as well as linguistic sections. They represent codifications of knowledge according to special conventions. It is this assembly of lexical and encyclopaedic knowledge in distinctive codices containing elaborate word hoards – glossary chrestomathies – that represents the innovative element of Carolingian book production. The glossary compilers of the eighth and ninth centuries drew on many varieties of text, not least the glossaries, to form these extraordinary new forms of book.

Conclusion

All these glossary collections are manifestations of an interest in words, the imperative to understand texts, and the practical consequences of the Carolingian insistence on correct texts and right understanding that are such a prominent aspect of the phenomenon described as the Carolingian renaissance.[107] The glossaries and glossary chrestomathies need to be seen alongside the Carolingian copies of Paul the Deacon's epitome of Festus and of Nonius Marcellus, the Greek:Latin Dictionaries, the production of the *Liber glossarum* and the dictionaries of tironian notes. They complement, moreover, the interest in grammar and orthography also represented in so many extant Carolingian manuscripts and newly-composed texts.[108] These glossary chrestomathies also reflect a sheer fascination with words and their layers of meaning. VLF 24, as we have seen above, not only includes in its assemblage of word lists the Spiritual glosses of Eucherius, and a list of animal and bird noises, but also the famous *Disputatio* between Alcuin and Pippin which is practically all in the form of riddles about the meanings of words.[109]

Above all the glossary chrestomathies are a collective statement of cultural affiliation. They offered a bridge to the Latin past constructed from the most basic elements of the textual inheritance of the compilers, designed to enhance literate communication in the present as well as for future generations. I have emphasized the vital importance of the relationship between the physical features of manuscripts and the texts they contain. I have explored some of the fascinating questions raised by the richness and diversity of the books produced in the Carolingian period, so remarkably well represented in the collections in Leiden Universiteitsbibliotheek. These have concerned not only the relationship between a book and its scribes and readers, but also of the ways in which older practices in the presentations of texts could be adopted, adapted, abandoned, or further developed in the ninth century as much as in the twelfth. I have suggested both that particular needs played a large role in determining the contents of books and the particular formats of texts, and that scribes proved marvellously creative in accommodating those needs to their expected readers. The subsequent copying and continued use of specific texts throughout the middle ages needs to be explored further. The particular examples discussed in this chapter, namely, the *Chronicon* of Eusebius-Jerome and the glossaries, were incorporated into other larger works – medieval world chronicles in the case of Eusebius-Jerome; glossary

109. *Disputatio regalis et nobilissimi iuvenis Pippini cum Albino scholastico*, ed. Daly and Suchier, 137-43. For a translation, see Dutton, *Carolingian Civilization*, 139-46. See also Bayless, 'Alcuin's *Disputatio Pippini* and the Early Medieval Riddle Tradition'.

110. First of all may I thank Erik Kwakkel for asking me to give the second Lieftinck lecture in Leiden in November 2010 in association with his project 'Turning over a New Leaf: Manuscript Innovation in the Twelfth-Century Renaissance', on which this chapter is based. I am particularly grateful to Harm Beukers and Kasper van Ommen for their suggestion that this be combined with a Scaliger lecture as part of my tenure of a Scaliger Fellowship in Leiden Universiteitsbibliotheek in the autumn of 2010. I should also like to take this opportunity to thank André Bouwman of Western Manuscripts and all the staff in Special Collections of Leiden Universiteitsbibliotheek for their help during my months in Leiden.

chrestomathies and the dictionaries of Papias, Huguccio of Pisa and finally the *Catholicon* in the case of the glossaries and *Liber glossarum*. Only close work with the manuscripts will enable us to understand the precise contributions of both Carolingian and twelfth-century scribes to the presentation of texts for contemporary and subsequent readers, and the degree of innovation they represent.[110]

INCIPIT PLOGV MAGIST HV
DIDASCALOr
VE·PRECIP

R es sunt. quibus quisq; ·
instruit. lectio uidelicz & m
equib lectio pore indoctrina
Et de hoc tctat lib iste: dando pc

Tria aut st pcepta magis lectioni n
pmu. ut sciat qsq; qd legere debeat. scdm q ordin
debeat. id est qd prius. qd postea: terciu. quom le
De his trib psingla agit in hoc libro. Instruit aut
qua diuinax scpturax lectore. Vnde & induas pa
quax una queq; tres habet distinctioes. In pma par
lectore artiu: in scda parte diuinu lectore. Docet.
do. ostendendo scilicz pmo qd legendu sit: deinde q
qm legendu sit. Vt q sciri possit qd legendu sit.
pcipue legendu sit. in pma parte pmum enume
ne omniu artiu: deinde desceptione & particione
qm una queq; otineat alia. uel otineat ab alia: sec
sophia asumo usq; ad ultima menbra. Post modu
rat auctores artiu. & ostendit que ex his uidelicet
prius & pcipue legende sint: deinde etia quo ordin
legende sint apit: postremo. legentibus uite sue
p scribit: & sic finitur pma pars. In scda parte

Biting, Kissing and the Treatment of Feet: The Transitional Script of the Long Twelfth Century

Erik Kwakkel

This essay is concerned with manuscripts produced during 'the long twelfth century', an era that is sometimes addressed as the 'Twelfth-Century Renaissance' (1075-1225). While the latter term may not do full justice to the events that occurred during this century and a half, the notion it covers (a single cultural movement that united scholars in different fields and geographical locations) is useful in that it brings under one umbrella a number of related historical developments in Europe. These can be summarized as the birth of scholasticism, the establishment of universities, a revival of jurisprudence and the introduction of Greek and Arabic philosophy.[1] The label 'renaissance of letters' is sometimes used to highlight the fact that the cultural movement was driven by scholars and the texts they produced, first those in Northern France, Belgium and Northern Italy, followed by kindred spirits in Southern Italy, Germany and Spain.[2] These intellectuals – who lacked cohesion other than a shared back-

* I wish to thank Francis Newton (Duke University) for his very useful suggestions to an earlier version of this essay.

1. Starting points for exploring the period are Benson and Constable, eds., *Renaissance and Renewal in the Twelfth Century*; Haskins, *The Renaissance of the Twelfth Century*; Swanson, *The Twelfth-Century Renaissance*; and Luscombe, 'Thought and Learning'. A fuller bibliography is provided in Jaeger, 'Pessimism in the Twelfth-Century 'Renaissance', 1151 n. 1. See also the latter for some reconsiderations about optimism and Thomson's review, 'Richard Southern on the Twelfth-Century Intellectual World'.

2. See for example Haskins, *Renaissance*, 153 and Damian-Grint, *The New Historians of the Twelfth-Century Renaissance*, 1.

3. Haskins, *The Renaissance of the Twelfth Century*, 70.

4. Derolez, *The Palaeography of Gothic Manuscript Books*, Chapter 2 (Caroline minuscule) and Chapters 3-5 (various stages and presentations of the Gothic bookhand). Note that the traditional starting date of developed Gothic, which is placed by Derolez (at 72) to c. 1200, is disputed below.

5. Some physical aspects of the evolving twelfth-century manuscript are discussed in Ker, *English Manuscripts in the Century after the Norman Conquest*. For the emergence of new reading aids see Rouse and Rouse, 'Statim Invenire'.

ground in higher education and a deep yearning for knowledge – exchanged ideas through intellectual compositions, translations and letters, which were disseminated through such intellectual centres as monasteries, cathedral schools and, near the end of the period, universities. Here the new voices, presenting new ideas in a new language of eloquence, were read and heard, and contradicted and expanded upon.

If we regard texts as an important thrust behind the Twelfth-Century Renaissance, then their carrier, the book, must be valued as equally significant, as has indeed already been emphasized in the pioneering study of the period by Charles Homer Haskins.[3] Such attention is warranted because the years between the late eleventh and early thirteenth century saw significant shifts in the physical presentation of manuscripts. During this century and a half we witness on the one hand the waning and ultimate disappearance of many of the characteristics of Carolingian book production that had dominated much of Europe for almost 300 years; and on the other hand the emergence of features that were to become standard elements of the Gothic codex, another widely-disseminated book format, that had reached its final (i.e. recognizably Gothic) form by the first quarter of the thirteenth century and would dominate book culture until well into the sixteenth century.[4] This transition from one type of manuscript to the other not only entailed the introduction of a new script, the subject of the present study, but it also produced modifications in the manner in which texts were presented on the page (*mise en page*), and it increased the available reading tools, most notably aids to find information more quickly.[5]

It is the modification, even disappearance, of established conventions and the appearance of new ones that is the focus of the present study, which examines one material dynamic of this transformational process, namely the script used for the production of books. The issue of how the Gothic bookhand differs from its Carolingian counterpart is no stranger to the scholar of the medieval book. The palaeographical features of the two are the subject of a broad range of studies and from these it becomes quickly apparent just how different they are in appearance.[6] The present study attempts to break new ground, however, firstly in that it deduces how Caroline minuscule evolved into Gothic script over the period 1075-1225.[7] It does so by querying, among other things, when and where the Gothic features are first encountered, in what order the new palaeographical traits were introduced and when the process of transformation was completed. The other way in which the present study seeks to add to existing scholarship is the means through which these issues are approached, namely through a quantitative study of dated manuscripts. Before we turn to the manuscript evidence, however, and discuss such features as biting, kissing and the treatment of feet, it is important briefly to present some general considerations regarding the notion of change in the domain of the medieval manuscript.

Transformations in the Material Book

While manuscript culture in the long twelfth century may have witnessed a more than usual amount of change, material developments as such are quite common in the history of the codex. The physical book was modified continuously throughout the medieval period, usually at a modest pace but at times surprisingly fast. These modifications occurred in different material dynamics, most notably in the object's script and physical construction, and they were implemented for a variety of reasons, from the availability of new materials (such as paper in thirteenth-century Europe) to occupation by a foreign

6. Many of these studies are mentioned in Derolez, The Palaeography of Gothic Manuscript Books. Publications devoted specifically to the transition from Caroline minuscule to Littera pregothica are listed in Derolez, The Palaeography of Gothic Manuscript Books, 68 n. 69.

7. This essay covers the period in between what is regarded to be the end of Caroline minuscule (late 11th century) and the moment at which Gothic script is established (c. 1200), as discussed below.

8. For ninth-century examples of monastic house styles, involving ligatures, the shapes of graphs, preparation of parchment, see Ganz, 'Book Production in the Carolingian Empire and the Spread of Carolingian Minuscule', 790-1 and McKitterick, 'Carolingian Book Production: Some Problems', reprinted in her *Books, Scribes and Learning*, Chapter XII. For unusually-styled catchwords in manuscripts from the Franciscan house of Assisi, see Mercati, 'Codici del convento di S. Francesco in Assisi nella Biblioteca Vaticana', 85-6.

9. Municipal chanceries in thirteenth-century Holland, for example, had their own palaeographical peculiarities, as noted in Burgers, *De paleografie van documentaire bronnen in Holland en Zeeland in de dertiende eeuw*, Vol. 1, 308-10 (Dordrecht). A well-known example is that in the chancery of King Roger of Sicily paper was

culture (note for example the impact of the Norman Conquest on the development of the English manuscript).

Changes in the palaeography and codicology of the book could be implemented on various scribal levels. An individual scribe, for example, may do something different from the people around him, either in the execution of a graph, the positioning of the catchword, or pricking of the page. On a higher level, groups of scribes associated with an institution may also exhibit peculiarities that were anything but mainstream. Religious houses, especially those in the early Middle Ages, frequently adopted their own palaeographical or codicological house style, expressed in such features as the shape of letters, the creation of particular ligatures, the preparation of parchment or the appearance of quire marks.[8] The same goes for other writing centres, such as municipal and royal chanceries, many of which developed their own style of writing or even adopted unusual codicological traits.[9]

Still larger bodies of scribes could do things differently, as is shown by the existence of regional and national script styles. The *littera praegothica* and *littera textualis* in manuscripts from Southern France, for example, look distinctly different from the same scripts found in manuscripts made in other parts of France; and books from England, Italy and Spain (to take some very pronounced cases) can frequently be distinguished by their palaeographical or codicological peculiarities, including the manner of ruling and the shape of graphs and ligatures.[10] Also note, in this respect, that Derolez's handbook of Gothic scripts divides the analysis of *Littera textualis* into two sections, called 'Northern Textualis' (Germanic countries, Scandinavia) and 'Southern Textualis' (Italy, Spain, Portugal, Southern France),[11] which shows how a single script may be subdivided into distinctly different subtypes based on the geographical location of scribes – or, more to the point, the location where the individuals learned to write.

Most of these deviations from established conventions had little impact on the broader scheme of medieval book production. A peculiarity applied by an individual hand or a small group of scribes in a single institution had generally little chance to become broadly adopted on a regional or national scale. However, it must be emphasized that change, perhaps any change, ultimately originated in the practice of a small group of scribes, occasionally maybe even in the behaviour of a single individual. After all, the alternative, that a new feature was independently introduced at several locations around the same time, seems far less attractive. Consequently, small groups of individuals working within the same milieu may potentially have had a major influence on the broader course of development of the material book. Perhaps the peculiarities of such 'conglomerations' of scribes became mainstream because they inhabited an important house within a monastic order. After all, from the Cistercian mother-house of Cîteaux certain manuscript features were disseminated throughout the order.[12] Alternatively, new features may have become established because the individuals who first applied them inhabited a key intellectual centre, an influential school perhaps. Or they may become mainstream simply because the newly acquired practice made more sense than the one it ultimately replaced.

However they came to be, for the scholar interested in the development of the material book these 'moments' which new conventions appear on the radar screen are of obvious importance. Here we may not only observe a mere deviation from an existing practice, but potentially also the start of a new codicological or palaeographical convention (and thus, likewise, the phasing out of an existing habit). Tracing such 'switches' in

used very early in the twelfth century, at which point parchment was generally still the standard material for documents.

10. A useful source for tracing national and regional styles of script is Derolez, *The Palaeography of Gothic Manuscript Books* (Southern France at 116-7). Some codicological peculiarities of English manuscripts are discussed in Ker, *English Manuscripts in the Century after the Norman Conquest*.

11. Derolez, *The Palaeography of Gothic Manuscript Books*, Chapters 4 and 5.

12. This concerns punctuation, see Parkes, *Pause and Effect*, 38-9. See for Cistercian punctuation Palmer, 'Simul cantemus, simul pausemus'.

13. In the handbooks the start of this transition is placed in the eleventh century, often in the last quarter. See for example Derolez, *The Palaeography of Gothic Manuscript Books*, 56 (in the 'eleventh century' changes in the book 'seem to amount to a new era'); Brown, *A Guide to Western Historical Scripts from Antiquity to 1600*, 73 (late 11th century); and Schneider, *Paläographie und Handschriftenkunde für Germanisten: Eine Einführung*, 28 (late 11th century/early 12th century).

register is not easy because material transformations are commonly slow to develop. Indeed, they may take decades to materialize to the extent that we recognize them as a new mannerism, as will become clear shortly. Moreover, material change usually entails a limited number of modifications at the same time, which means that such moments of change can be missed quite easily. In sum, developments in the material book of the Middle Ages are not likely to constitute a paradigm shift.

By contrast, at other times the material features of manuscripts evolve more rapidly and cover a considerable number of traits that seem to evolve almost simultaneously. In some cases the speed and severity of these developments are such that it may even become difficult to see what is convention and what may be designated as individual, institutional or regional variation. The age covered by this essay is such a period in which change was swift, intense and invasive.

The Transitional Script of the Long Twelfth Century

Studying the transition from Caroline minuscule to Gothic script presents unique problems to the book historian, the most significant of which resonates prominently on these pages and needs to be addressed even before a single manuscript is invited to enter the stage: that of terminology and definition. While the formal differences between Caroline minuscule and Gothic are recognized and well established, a significant complication emerges when one tries to simply ascertain to what periods the two are connected. If, as is normally assumed, Caroline minuscule starts to give way to something new in the eleventh century, most probably towards the end of the century,[13] and if the fully developed Gothic script is a creature that is in existence from the early thirteenth century onwards, then how are we to understand the handwriting produced in the hundred-and-fifty or so years in between? How does it fit into the scheme of the waning Caroline minuscule and emerging Gothic? Are we to regard this object in transition as part of the one or the other? And, most elementary, what do we call it?

Judging from the terms used by palaeographers, the script written between c. 1075 and c. 1225 is either regarded as waning Caroline minuscule (considering the application of such terms as 'Late Caroline' and 'Post-Caroline'), as a precursor of Gothic (reflected in the use of such terms as 'Primitive Gothic', 'Proto-Gothic' and 'Pregothic'), or as a hybrid that has one leg in each side of the divide ('Carolino-Gothica', 'caroline gothicisante', 'minuscola di transizione' and 'Übergangsschrift').[14] Considering that the script in question exhibits (throughout the entire period and in various mixtures) features that are from Caroline minuscule and those that will become part of Gothic script, as will be discussed shortly, the last perspective seems to me the most appropriate. As will become clear shortly, it is worthwhile studying the transitional script written between the late eleventh and early thirteenth centuries as a category of handwriting in its own right, different in physical appearance from both Caroline minuscule and Gothic, yet closely related to both. In the following I shall therefore use the neutral term 'transitional script'. While it may perhaps lack precision, the term does justice to the fact that twelfth-century handwriting includes elements of two great scripts, as opposed to such alternative terms as 'pregothic' and 'postcaroline', which hide its hybrid nature and reduce the script to a mere phase, either as aftermath of Caroline minuscule or the precursor of Gothic. Moreover, understanding the script written between c. 1075 and c. 1225 as an entity in transition also highlights that it is in a state of flux, that its physical form is in permanent migration from Caroline minuscule to Gothic, developing rapidly – and consequently hard to pin down.

14. For these designations by various paleographers, see Derolez, *The Palaeography of Gothic Manuscript Books*, 57. Derolez rejects some other terms, including Romanesque. The term 'Übergangsschrift' is found in Schneider, *Paläographie und Handschriftenkunde*, 30-1.

15. Derolez, *The Palaeo-graphy of Gothic Manuscript Books*, 56-9.

16. Letter forms are presented in bold throughout this chapter.

The existence of such a transitional script prompts important questions. How did Caroline minuscule evolve into Gothic? What features were in play? When were signature features of Caroline minuscule first replaced with traits we now call Gothic? And where in Europe did this process start? The already-mentioned palaeographical handbook by Albert Derolez is a suitable starting point for tackling these queries. The assessments it contains enable us to trace what changed in the physical appearance of letters, which will be the main focus here – I am focusing exclusively on individual letter forms in this chapter, which does not take into account such palaeographical features as ligatures, abbreviations and punctuation. First of all, in his chapter on 'Praegothica', Derolez distinguishes six general trends in handwriting during the transition from Caroline minuscule to Gothic, all of which are influencing the shape of individual letter forms:

1. Letters became narrower;
2. Fusions were introduced, namely the joining or slight overlapping of two adjacent letters (also called 'biting');
3. Shortening of ascenders and descenders;
4. Some parts of traditionally round strokes were given an angular appearance (a phenomenon called 'angularity');
5. Broadening of the strokes;
6. Feet on minims curved to the right (also sometimes observed at the top of ascenders).[15]

In addition, Derolez identifies the following developments in individual letter forms (I continue my count):

7. Shaft of **a** becomes upright (sloping in Caroline minuscule);[16]

8. Introduction of uncial **d** that complemented the existing straight type (Caroline minuscule exclusively used the latter);

9. 'Tongue' stroke at **e** sloped upwards (horizontal in Caroline minuscule);

10. Placement on baseline of **f** and (long-stemmed) **s** (through baseline in Caroline minuscule);

11. Lower lobe of **g** becomes closed (open in Caroline minuscule);

12. Limb of **h** is extended below the line (placed on the line in Caroline minuscule);

13. Strokes appeared on **i**, and the second **i** in **ii** was sometimes extended, producing a **j** (not present in Caroline minuscule);

14. The use of uncial **m** at the end of lines (not present in Caroline minuscule);

15. Adaptation of round **r** (in the shape of '2') from the old, long-established ligature ('-orum') to the letter **r**, which came to complement the straight **r**;

16. Continuation of straight **r** extending below the line;

17. Introduction of uncial (or round) **s**, complementing the straight **s** in Caroline minuscule;

18. Stem of **t** is turned into a minim that 'pricks' through the horizontal bar (flat top in Caroline minuscule);

19. Introduction of **w** written as two **v**'s;

20. Reduction of **x**, its two legs placed on baseline (in some cases the second stroke was broken);

21. Dotting of **y**, although undotted in some cases (as in Caroline minuscule).[17]

17. Derolez, *The Palaeography of Gothic Manuscript Books*, 60-5. In some cases the development of a letter form took its own turn in a given region. I have not specified these regional tendencies in this enumeration. Derolez discusses the dotting of i and lengthening of the second i as general tendencies. I have opted to present them as developments in the shape of individual letters. Derolez (at 93) places the second modification in t (projection of shaft above headstroke) in the middle of the thirteenth century, but this modification is, in fact, encountered in numerous dated manuscripts of the twelfth century as well.

These twenty-one traits indicate that there are different 'modes' of development in the transitional script investigated here. First of all, some letters kept their Carolingian appearance, namely those that are not included in Derolez's list of individual letter shapes that underwent change: **b, c, k, l, o, p, q, u** and **z**. Some of these were altered slightly under the influence of the six general trends of the changing script, as identified by Derolez. The **o**, for example, became oval-shaped under the influence of the general compression introduced to the transitional script. Similarly, the appearance of the **c** was influenced by the emerging tendency towards angularity, which flattened the upper part of the letter, as will be discussed. Apart from such superficial modifications, however, the overall shape of these nine letters did not change much.

Second, other letter forms from Caroline minuscule were modified, in part, again, under the influence of the general trends. These are, for example, the **f, r** and **s**. In all three cases the minim would ultimately be placed on the baseline rather than being extended below it. Similarly, the slight change in angle of the tongue stroke in **e** and the shaft of **a** (both of which became more elevated) may be seen as a modification of Carolingian practice.

Lastly, some letters received an entirely new shape and were written with a different ductus. The new presentation of a letter would commonly be used in addition to the Caroline form, at least in the period under investigation. Some of the older forms would disappear beyond the temporal scope of this paper. The long-stemmed **s** in final position, for example, which was complemented by a round form in the age of transition, disappeared over the course of the fourteenth century. In Northern Textualis, straight **d** disappeared *c*. 1300. The letters used complementary to Caroline are the uncial **d, m** (used at end of line) and **s**, as well as the round **r** in the '2' shape. The introduction of uncial **d** may potentially be connected to a general tendency as well because it encouraged fusion (biting), for example in **de** and **do** (discussed below).

Thus Derolez's handbook not only shows us what palaeographical traits are changing but also that these modifications were implemented in different ways: through continuation of existing practices (many letter forms of Caroline minuscule enjoyed a safe passage through to fully developed Gothic); modification of letter forms (usually changing the features of Caroline minuscule only modestly); and the introduction of new features (in large part by borrowing from uncial). What Derolez's study does not provide, however, and what is generally not addressed in palaeographical handbooks, is a sense of when the new features were introduced and how long it took for new traits to take shape and to become established.[18] In sum, we know what changed but are more or less in the dark about chronological progression.

There is a tool available, however, that may provide clarification in this matter: the *Catalogues des manuscrits datés* (CMD).[19] After all, if we regard dated manuscripts as a good statistical sample, an assumption to which this paper subscribes, such codices allow us to track with some level of precision how (future) Gothic features were treated by scribes over the course of the long twelfth century. Less clear-cut may seem the application of the CMD for getting a sense of the geographical spread of script developments, resulting from the fact that the catalogues are built up with current (rather than medieval) national boundaries as geographical dividers. However, following the modern boundaries has little impact on the present study.[20] To get a sense of when and where the first new traits were introduced I have analysed 342 manuscripts from the CMD, the oldest one dating from 1075 and the youngest from 1224 (cf. Appendix, Table 3). Due to limitations of space the main focus here will be on the general trends identified by Derolez, principally because these form the major thrust

18. This is reflected in the varying dates connected to the end of Caroline minuscule and beginning of Gothic script found in secondary literature, as discussed in n. 13, above.

19. A brief introduction to the CMD is provided in Derolez, *The Palaeography of Gothic Manuscript Books*, 11-2. See about the series also Grand, ed., *Les manuscrits datés: Premier bilan et perspectives*.

20. When the discussion demands that the medieval division of states is followed, I have done so. See the assessment of biting and the shape of minims in Austria, Germany and Switzerland, discussed below.

21. The data used here is derived from a database that tracks the development of palaeographical and codicological features over the course of 1075-1225. This database is currently produced in the research project 'Turning Over a New

Leaf: Manuscript Innovation in the Twelfth-Century Renaissance', of which I am principal investigator (Leiden University Institute of Cultural Disciplines, 2010-15), http://www.hum.leiden.edu/icd/turning-over-a-new-leaf/, accessed 4 November 2011.

22. For this phenomenon, which is related to the 'breaking' of shafts, see Bischoff, *Paläographie des römischen Altertums und des abendländischen Mittelalters*, 173-4.

23. These manuscripts are Appendix, Table 3, Nos 32 (It.), 84 (Eng.), 104 (unknown origins), 156 (Fr.), 169 (Eng.), 207 (Eng.), 209 (English scribe in Paris), 214 (idem.), 235 (It.), 246 (Eng.), 249 (Eng.), 255 (Germ.), 268 (Eng.), 298 (Eng.), 303 (Eng.), 325 (Belg.), 326 (Aust.), 327 (Eng.), 331 (Eng.), 351 (Eng.) and 365 (Eng.).

24. The data for this Graph are found in Appendix, Table 1 at 105-7, below. I

behind the new script, as is evident, for example, from their influence on the appearance of so many individual letter forms.[21] More precisely, I have traced how three of these general tendencies developed, namely those that can be clearly measured and quantified with the photographs provided by the CMD: the treatment of the feet on minims, the emergence of angularity and the introduction of biting.

To start with the minims, a good litmus test for how scribes treated their feet are the letters **m** and **n** because their shapes consist of multiple minims.[22] The essential difference between Caroline minuscule and Gothic is that in the latter the feet are all turning to the right, although their formation is not as pronounced in every manuscript because in some cases the right-turn of the feet can be barely observed. In Caroline minuscule, by contrast, we encounter a variety of 'systems'. Quite frequently the first two feet of the **m** turn left, while the third turns right. Treatment of the feet in the Gothic manner (with all three turning right) is generally not observed in Caroline minuscule. In addition to these two treatments, we encounter manuscripts throughout the period 1075-1225 with feet that turn neither left or right but that go straight down and culminate in either a small horizontal line placed on the baseline (a 'flat foot', so to speak) or a small 'diamond' (what may be called a 'club foot'). These manuscripts, twenty-two in all, are predominantly produced by English scribes and the script in which flat and club feet occur is usually somewhat larger and of higher quality.[23] Feet fashioned in this way seem to form a separate category, independent of the development described here and these will therefore be no part of this discussion – they are marked as 'No Turns' (cf. Graph 1 at p. 206, below).[24]

The data in Appendix, Table 1 show that three groups of manuscripts may be distinguished, roughly representing the three different stages of development in the treatment of feet. The first group comprises manuscripts that are in effect written in pure Caroline minuscule. As expected, this group decreases in size as the period progresses. However, the treatment of feet in Caroline minuscule never fully disappears from sight, primarily because this style remains popular among scribes tied to locations in modern Austria, Germany and Switzerland – in other words, copyists from the German empire north of the Alps (Fig. 21/Plate 21). It is telling, in this respect, that twelve of the fifteen manuscripts from these countries that are made after 1150 (when the trait had been well established as a new norm in much of Europe) follow Caroline minuscule in the treatment of their minims. These countries evidently form a 'Kulturraum' that hangs on longer to this particular established palaeographical mannerism.[25] Just how much they stand out becomes clear when we compare this cultural space with the two countries from which we have the highest volumes of manuscripts, France and England. As shown in Graph 2 at p. 206, below, while the line representing the latter countries is above the 50% marker for much of the years 1075-1225, the one representing Austria and Germany, by contrast, stays below this marker for much of this period.[26]

A second group of manuscripts is united in that they all show a remarkable mix. The scribes who made these books may at times treat the feet of **m** in the Caroline manner, while at other times within the same codex, sometimes even within the same line or word, they opt for the Gothic presentation – but they never opt for one or the other all the time. These mixed manuscripts are present throughout the period, although after 1120-34 they almost never represent more than 20% of the manuscripts. Apparently, the transition from one practice to another led scribes to use both the older and younger forms simulta-

wish to thank Ms. Julie Somers (Leiden) for her help in producing Tables 1-2 and the graphs derived from them.

25. These fifteen manuscripts are Appendix, Table 3, Nos 162 (Aust.), 182 (Aust.), 183 (Aust.), 188 (Switz.), 190 (Switz.), 221 (Fr.), 223 (Aust.), 227 (Germ.), 228 (Germ.), 240 (unknown origins), 251 (Germ.), 287 (Aust.), 315 (Fr.) and 338 (Aust.?).

26. The data for this Graph are found in Appendix, Table 2. Note that the line representing Austria, Germany and Switzerland is produced by only forty-nine manuscripts. The lower end in particular may potentially present a slightly distorted picture.

Fig. 21. Leiden, Universiteitsbibliotheek, MS Vulcanius 46 (dated 1176-77), fol. 130v (detail, enlarged). This manuscript from Fulda presents minims as in Caroline minuscule, as is still common in manuscripts from Austria, Germany and Switzerland. The r descends below baseline, a feature that by this time has disappeared in much of the rest of Europe.

Fig. 22. Leiden, Universiteitsbibliotheek, MS BPL 20 (dated 1138-39), fol. 22v, col. B (detail, enlarged). This manuscript consistently shows angularity in round letter forms, as visible, for example, in the first words on the page: in ipso exordio (the e and o show one or more 'flat' sides, the round part at the top of n is slanted and angular, as is the case in r).

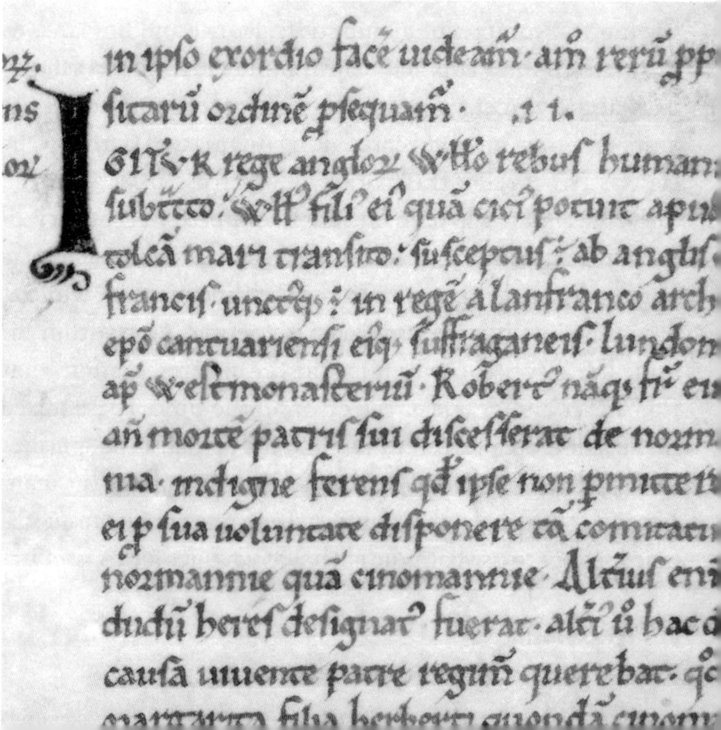

neously for some time. We will encounter this phenomenon again below and it may well be a broader practice in developing medieval scripts. A similar situation is encountered in the transformation from Cursiva Antiquior to Cursiva Recentior over the course of the fourteenth century.[27]

A third group, finally, is formed by manuscripts in which the minims are consistently executed in the Gothic style. As expected, this group increases in size throughout the period. Graph 1 suggests that the introduction of the new presentation may slightly predate the period covered by this essay. After all, in the first segment of Graph 1 (covering the years 1075-89) little over a quarter of the corpus already shows minims in the Gothic fashion (27%). It seems quite likely, then, that the novelty was introduced earlier in the second half of the eleventh century, perhaps in the third quarter. The biggest jump in the application of minims in the Gothic style is seen shortly after 1100: whereas in 1090-1104 only 14% of manuscripts consistently show minims in the Gothic style, a small dip compared to the previous period, in 1105-19 this number has increased dramatically to 74%. Throughout much of the remaining years the number hovers around 70%, peaking lightly at 82% in 1210-24. On the basis of these numbers we may conclude that the Gothic treatment of feet established itself in the first two decades of the twelfth century. That their number never hits 100% is due to the presence of manuscripts from the Germanic regions, as discussed. Excluding these manuscripts would bring the numbers for the periods 1150-64, 1180-94 and 1210-24 to 100%, suggesting that apart from a regional exception the first of the three general trends in Gothic script is fully established by 1225, the end of the long twelfth century.

While it is not possible to say with certainty where the first manuscripts with Gothic-styled minims were made, one

27. I plan to publish a quantitative palaeographical study of this transformation.

28. Webber, 'Script and Manuscript Production at Christ Church, Canterbury, After the Norman Conquest'.

29. See for example Derolez, *The Palaeography of Gothic Manuscript Books*, 70 and Schneider, *Paläographie und Handschriftenkunde*, 28.

30. The data for this Graph are found in Appendix, Table 1.

region jumps out in that the three earliest manuscripts to exhibit this feature were produced there: Normandy. The manuscripts in question are Rouen, BM, MSS 1406 and 1409, made respectively in 1072-92 in the Abbey of St Ouen and in 1078-95 in the abbey of Jumièges (Appendix, Table 3, Nos 7-8); and Le Mans, BM, MS 23, produced in 1081-94 in the Norman abbey of Nogent-le-Rotrou (No. 9). In addition to these, the fourth manuscript in the chronological list of books to exhibit minims in the Gothic style also shows a Norman link because it was copied in Christ Church, Canterbury (CUL MS Ii 3.33: No. 14). In the eleventh century this monastery was inhabited by a large contingent of Normans and the script that developed there shortly before *c.* 1100, the so-called 'Christ-Church type', was a modified version of Norman script.[28] The first feature observed here seems to confirm suggestions presented elsewhere that the transitional script of the twelfth century may have originated in the Anglo-Norman kingdom.[29]

The second general feature, the angular shape given to parts of curved strokes, is more difficult to define than the treatment of feet. According to Derolez, angularity is most clearly observed in the **c**, **e** and **o**, as well as in the limb of **h** and the headstroke of **r** (Fig. 22/Plate 22). This appearance was caused by the alternative manner in which a curved stroke was executed: rather than 'rounding' the entire stroke, part of it is made straight, which produces an 'angle' (a flattened part of a round stroke). The graphic representation of the development of angularity shows some interesting parallels with the treatment of minims (cf. Graph 3 at p. 207, below).[30]

Mirroring the treatment of minims, the development of angularity shows that we may distinguish three categories of manuscripts: those in which none of the letter forms are given an angular appearance; those that present a mix of both systems in that a scribe in a single manuscript may at one point opt for giving a certain letter form an angular appearance, while at other times in the same manuscript he will not do so, even if it concerns the same graph (Fig. 23/Plate 23); and finally those manuscripts in which all letter forms subject to angularity are indeed always given an angular appearance.

Also in parallel with what we have observed in the treatment of minims is that at the outset of the period, the years 1075-89, some scribes are already consistently adding angularity in the manuscripts they produce. It is possible that this feature was also introduced slightly earlier in the second half of the eleventh century. Again, the biggest jump in the application of this novelty is encountered just after the turn of the century: while in 1090-1104 only 14% of the manuscripts contained in the corpus show consistent angularity (i.e. in all relevant letter forms, at all times), in 1105-19 this number has increased to 70%. This is another dramatic change, which is comparable to the sharp shift observed in the treatment of minims during the same period, as observed – in fact, the numbers are exactly the same. Throughout the remaining years to 1225 this number will keep on increasing until it hits 100% in 1210-24. The same conclusions as for the treatment of feet can be drawn: angularity established itself as the norm in the first two decades of the twelfth century, and by 1225 the transition process was probably fully completed. A very striking observation with respect to the two sharp shifts observed in 1105-19 (i.e. that both the Gothic-style minims and angularity increase from 14% to 70% in these years) is that with only two exceptions these changes occur in the same manuscripts.[31] In other words, the introduction of these Gothic features is related in that scribes generally introduce them simultaneously.

Another parallel with the treatment of minims is encoun-

31. These are Appendix, Table 3, Nos 34 (Gothic minims but no angularity) and 51 (angularity but minims as in Caroline minuscule). Manuscripts with a mix in either of these features are not taken into account here.

32. Another early manu-
script to show consistent
angularity (but whose feet
show a mix of Caroline minuscule and Gothic) is Bodl.
MS Lat. th. d. 20, which was
produced somewhere in
Normandy in 1091 (Appen-
dix, Table 3, No. 17).

33. Parkes, *Their Hands*
before Our Eyes, 149.

tered in the potential origins of angularity. The three earliest cases to show full angularity, all dating from well before the big jump in 1105-19, are the Norman manuscripts already mentioned above (Rouen MSS 1406 and 1409, and Le Mans MS 23). The fourth manuscript, CUL MS Ii 3.33 from Christ Church, Canterbury, sometimes shows angularity, but not consistently so. Apparently, these Norman scribes had augmented their repertoire of letter forms in more than one way, which adds to the argument that Normandy may be the birthplace of the transitional script.[32] Nevertheless, Gothic as we know it was not exclusively shaped here, as will be discussed at the end of this study. Given the early application of Gothic features in Normandy it is interesting to observe that some Norman scribes did not change their ways at all. Some scribes in Norman houses kept on treating their feet in the Carolingian manner and did not add any angularity, such as the scribe of Rouen, BM, MS 477 (produced in Fécamp, c. 1075). Other Norman scribes went the new way with one of these features, but not both, as demonstrated by Cambridge, Corpus Christi College, MS 415 (Normandy, 1095-1109: Table 3, No. 29), which does show angularity but not the Gothic presentation of the feet on minims.

The development of the third general trend under investigation here – fusion, biting or *Bogenverbindung* – follows quite a different track. For this study of biting I have ignored letters that are part of abbreviations because in such cases letter forms may in my experience be shaped differently. Malcolm Parkes defines biting as 'the coalescence of two contrary curves in adjacent letters that follow **b**, round-backed **d**, **h**, **o** and **p**.'[33] These five letters are in play, then, when studying the development of biting over the course of the period 1075-1225. The most common combinations of biting with the letters **b**, **d**, **h** and **p** are the letters **e** and **o** (producing such pairs as **be** and **po**), while the o most commonly bites with **c**, **d** and **q** (**op**, **od** and **oq**). In addition to these five, it is worthwhile assessing how scribes treated the combination **pp** and **bb**. While these pairs do not represent biting according to Parkes' definition (the connecting curves are, after all, not contrary), the pairs do show overlap and they are recognized as important novelties of the period – indeed, Derolez labels them as biting.[34] When studying how the phenomenon of biting progressed chronologically it quickly becomes apparent how important it is to study the five letters identified by Parkes separately. As it turns out, not every type of biting was introduced around the same time, nor did they all progress in the same fashion (cf. Graph 4 at p. 207, below).[35]

Graph 4 shows that the first cases of biting are encountered in 1135-49. They all concern **bb/pp** and there are only three manuscripts in this period (or 12%) in which these pairs consistently show fusion: the oldest is of unknown origins and was made in 1139 (Appendix, Table 3, No. 109), the second was copied in 1148 in the Premonstratensian abbey of Parc near Leuven (No. 134) and the third was made in the Cistercian abbey of Belval in 1149 (No. 138). Evidently, the third general trend had a much later start than the previous two. However, from 1150 fusion in **bb/pp** quickly picks up speed. In 1150-64 biting has increased to 40% and in 1165-79 even further, to 70% – which places it among the quickest developments presented in this essay. Fusion in these pairs, we may carefully conclude, is rare before the middle of the twelfth century and seems to have become quickly established in the third quarter.

In the period 1150-64 a second type of biting starts to occur, namely in pairs with (round or uncial) **d** (**de/do**). The increase in biting involving the round **d** is slow to gain momentum: it is only in 1195-1209 that we pass the 20% line (21% of manuscripts in this period have consistent fusion). In

34. Derolez, *The Palaeography of Gothic Manuscript Books*, 57. Bischoff regards 'bb' and 'pp' as precursors ('Vorläufer') of the slightly later *Bogenverbindung* (see his *Paläographie*, 174).

35. The data for this Graph are found in Appendix, Table 1. Graph 4 includes only those manuscripts that present consistent biting throughout for a given combination. I have excluded those that present biting in a mixed form, namely where pairs within an individual manuscript sometimes bite but at other times do not. This concerns a very small group of books that does not alter the general patterns observed here.

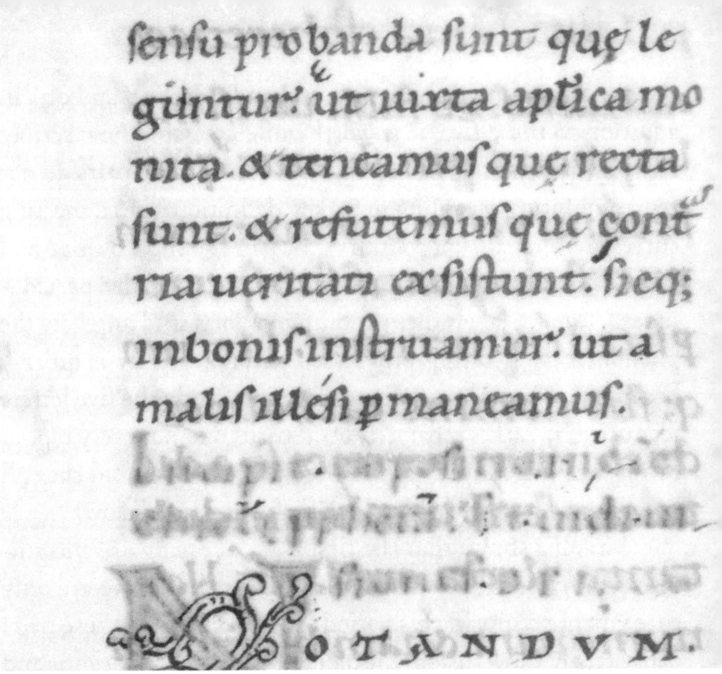
sensu probanda sunt que le
guntur: ut iuxta aplica mo
nita. & teneamus que recta
sunt. & refutemus que cont
ria ueritati exsistunt. sicq;
inbonis instruamur: ut a
malis illesi pmaneamus.

Fig. 23. Leiden, Universiteitsbibliotheek, MS BPL 196 (dated 1145-49), fol. 129v (detail, enlarged). Angularity is often observed here, for example in the **b**, **p**, **r** and **o** (*probanda*, line 1). The round parts of **m** and **n** are often also given an angular appearance (*teneamus*, line 3; *sunt* in line 4), but at times these do not show this trait (*probanda*, line 1; *instruamur*, line 6; *permaneamus*, line 7). The **b** may also lack clear angularity, as seen in the word *bonis* (line 6).

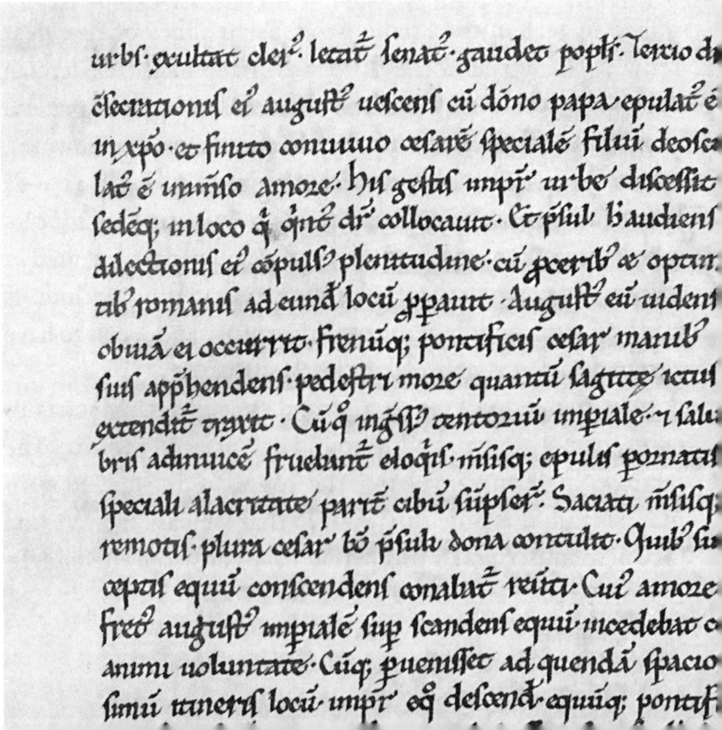

Fig. 24. Leiden, Universiteitsbibliotheek, MS VLF 8 (dated 1130), fol. 17v col. A (detail, enlarged). In this manuscript we observe 'kissing', as visible in for example lines 3 (**pe** in *specialem*), 4 (**be** in *urbe*), 5 (**oc** in *loco*) and 13 (**do** in *dona*).

the years 1165-79 the remaining letters (**b, h, o** and **p**) start to fuse, following a similar slow ascent to that of the letter **d**. In sum, apart from one form of biting (**bb/pp**) the third general trend is not in play during the first seventy-five years under investigation here: it is not at the forefront of the developing script but follows in the wake of other trends. (Where this feature stands among the three general features not studied here remains to be seen). Moreover, apart from **bb/pp**, biting is hardly established as a Gothic feature by 1225. While consistent fusing of **bb/pp** occurs in 81% of the manuscripts by the close of our period, most other combinations are by that time still stuck between 19% (**he/ho**) and 33% (**pe/po**). Only fusion involving round **d** has reached a comfortable 52% in the period 1210-24, which means that about half of the scribes apply the feature.

As in the previously studied general trends, we encounter a mixed category in biting as well. However, one cannot simply distinguish between Caroline minuscule (no fusion), Gothic (fusion) and a mix (sometimes fusion, sometimes not), as has been done so far. Fusion is made possible, perhaps even encouraged, because letters were placed together more closely as the twelfth century progressed. Derolez calls this phenomenon 'lateral compression', stating that it 'was enhanced by the introduction of fusions'.[36] In other words, fusions enabled, in his opinion, lateral compression. However, as fusions appear quite late in the period, as shown, I am inclined to turn the order around and suggest that lateral compression encouraged the appearance of fusion. Parkes suggests that fusion was 'originally adopted as a space-saving device during the twelfth century', which shows just how much biting is related to lateral compression, which also allowed for more text on the page.[37]

As the letters were placed more closely together we start to observe different relationships between adjacent letters, not just

36. Derolez, *The Palaeography of Gothic Manuscript Books*, 57.

37. Parkes, *Their Hands before Our Eyes*, 149.

38. For this purpose I
scanned the CMD plates at
400 dpi and studied the
graphs heavily enlarged on
a 27-inch monitor. There is
no official term for this
phenomenon, as far as I am
aware, although Malcolm
Parkes apparently used
'kissing' in his palaeography courses (personal communication David Rundle,
Oxford, with whom I dis-
cussed this feature).

39. The data for this Graph
are found in Appendix,
Table 1.

fusion. Apart from pure biting, where a letter pair shares a central stroke (forming, as it were, a Siamese twin), another common
phase can be distinguished, an earlier one as it appears, which I
will call 'kissing'. Here we see the connecting strokes of two adjacent forms *touch* one another, without fusing (Fig. 24/Plate 24).
That is to say, when the letters are dramatically increased in size
on a computer screen, one observes that there is no stroke reduction or overlap but merely that two strokes are placed right next
to one another so that it appears as though they are one.[38]
'Kissing' pairs can often be recognized by the increased thickness
of the central stroke, which is applied twice.

Taking the round **d** as an example, we observe that kissing
(first cases encountered in 1120-34) predates actual biting (first
cases in 1165-79) by some four decades (cf. Graph 5 at p. 208,
below).[39] In the remaining letters this honeymoon period – where
first kissing becomes first biting – is even longer, up to some sixty
years. For all of these the first cases of fusion are encountered in
1180-94, while the first kissing pairs are observed as early as 1105-
19 (pairs involving either **b** or **o**) and 1120-34 (pairs involving
either **h** or **p**). Evidently, true biting takes a long time to catch on,
much longer than some other Gothic traits, as we have seen.
Perhaps the lateral compression was not advanced enough in the
first half of the century for biting to be possible or encouraged,
but needed the letters to move closer still for this process to start.

Graph 5 shows that the mix we encountered in the treatment of minims and angularity – where scribes within a single
manuscript would sometimes opt for the Caroline presentation
and at other times for Gothic – is encountered in both kissing
and biting. When kissing is becoming more common, we
encounter manuscripts in which scribes present the pairs **do**
and **de** as kissing, while in the same book (on the same page, or
even in the same sentence) these forms may actually still be pre-

sented separately, as in Caroline minuscule. The same goes for the other letters that will ultimately show biting (cf. Appendix, Table 1). Similarly, biting may also be presented as a mix, always with kissing as the other component of the mix. These cases show that scribes tend to mix two connecting stages in the process of fusion (separated/kissing, kissing/biting), but they do generally not blend forms from non-adjacent stages. The manuscript corpus suggests that codices with a mix of separated/biting are unusual. This phenomenon is also seen in the other letters that will ultimately show biting (cf. Appendix, Table 1).

40. The data for this Graph are found in Appendix, Table 1.

By the end of our period, in 1210-24, quite a lot of manuscripts do not show any kissing or biting but present the letter pairs in question still as separate forms. For round **d** this number is 33%, the remaining letters range between 43-74%. By that time both mixed forms have disappeared, although manuscripts with consistent kissing are present in 1210-24. In other words, the Gothic feature of biting is now beyond its infant stages but has by no means established itself as a new standard. This observation is even more evident in other adjacent letters with contrary strokes, in which the number of manuscripts that show consistent biting is considerably lower (cf. Appendix, Table 1). For example, by 1210-24 the number of codices in which the pairs **be/bo** consistently overlap is only 2% (cf. Graph 6 at p. 208, below).[40] Here we see, by contrast, that by the end of the period of this investigation separation is still the standard (43%) and that when the pairs are no longer presented as separate letters, it is kissing (and not biting) that is most common (24%). The remaining pairs follow the pattern of **be/bo** which shows just how unestablished biting – a signature feature of Gothic – actually is by 1225.

As far as the location where biting was introduced, there is far less clarity in this matter than in the previous two features

41. Appendix, Table 3, No.
302 (Admont?, c. 1197). Consistent kissing is equally
rare and is limited to four
cases (Nos 153, 226, 231 and
308). Additionally, a total of
five manuscripts from these
countries have consistent
biting in bb/pp (Nos 223,
231, 267, 308 and 323), which
is also very low.

that have been examined. In fact, the introduction of biting is literally all over the map: the earliest cases of **bb/pp** almost simultaneously appear in the Low Countries (Appendix, Table 3, No. 134, made in 1148), France (Nos 138 and 144, from 1149 and c. 1151, respectively) and England (No. 148, made in 1150-3); while early cases of biting with round **d** occur around the same time in both France (Nos 211 and 224, from 1164-70 and 1171, respectively) and England (No. 225, likely made in 1171). The only pattern we can establish here is not one of origins but of absence. In a second example of how scribes in Austria, Germany and Switzerland hang on to established (that is, Caroline) mannerisms, there is from the entire period 1075-1225 only one manuscript from these countries that shows biting in two adjacent letters with contrary strokes.[41]

In Conclusion

The introduction of new scripts is a common topic of discussion in palaeography. After all, recognizing that a given script is different from what was used before, and in what way these two are different, lies at the core of constructing the evolution of medieval scripts, an important task of the discipline. What is less commonly encountered, however, are studies of how the actual transition process from one script to another took place over time – that is, how particular features of the disappearing script evolve into palaeographical peculiarities of an emerging script, and when these transitions took place. The study presented here, which has focused on only a modest segment of the birth of one such new script, shows why this may be: it is time-consuming to chart how individual letter forms evolved and in the process all sort of problems are encountered. (The existence of an earlier phase of biting, dubbed 'kissing', may serve as an example of the latter). Moreover, not all conclusions are necessarily satisfying. Even if their existence can be proven quantifiably, it may not be possible to explain why certain phenomena occurred, as shown by the observation that scribes in Austria, Germany and Switzerland are less *en vogue* in the application of new features than their colleagues in, for example, France.

In spite of such difficulties, the quantitative study presented here does add to our understanding of the birth of Gothic. What is apparent above all is that by 1225 it is hardly the case that scribes all over Europe wrote their manuscripts consistently in the new script. In fact, of the three individual general features observed here, only the trait of angularity scores 100% on the Gothic scale. The treatment of minims is still occasionally done in the Carolingian fashion (4%) or shows a mix of both (11%), suggesting that a segment of scribes is still in transitional mode as far as this feature is concerned. For biting these numbers are much higher. While scribes in Europe are getting accustomed to this feature, it is by no means broadly accepted by 1225. The most accepted form of biting in 1210-24 is **bb/pp** (only 29% of manuscripts do *not* show biting for these pairs), while the least accepted form is **he/ho** (81% of manuscripts do not show consistent fusion here). However, the conclusion that the transition to Gothic has by no means been fully completed around 1225 is most dramatically illuminated by the observation that only three of the twenty-eight manuscripts from 1210-24 apply the Gothic presentation for all eight features tracked in this paper, namely angularity, minims and six manners of biting (including **bb/pp**).[42] Consequently, we need to adjust the accepted starting date of Gothic script. After all, in Derolez's handbook this moment is placed as early as *c.* 1200: '[W]e may conveniently accept the year 1200 as the conventional beginning of the period of fully developed Gothic script'.[43] The data in this paper, however, suggests a likely beginning in the second quarter of the thirteenth century.

42. These are Appendix, Table 3, Nos 356 (a manuscript of unknown origins made in 1216-27, provenance Cîteaux), 349 (Fr., 1218) and 362 (It., Novara, 1223-24). No. 356 contains sermons by Pope Honorius III and may have been sent to Cîteaux by the pope himself (cf. Powell, 'Pastor Bonus', 525). This would place the manuscript's likely origins in Rome. These three are the only codices in the corpus of 342 used for this study to show all Gothic features studied here.

43. Derolez, *The Palaeography of Gothic Manuscript Books*, 72. Derolez acknowledges that the transitional script continues after 1200, for he continues, 'Nevertheless quite a number of hands of the thirteenth century should still be considered representatives of Gothic script'. My argument to push the date of fully-developed Gothic is prompted by the importance of biting

for the identity of Gothic
(which was, as shown, by no
means accepted as standard
around 1225) as well as a
small number of manu-
scripts in which all Gothic
features are displayed at all
times in 1210-24.

44. Compare in this respect
also Derolez, 'Observations
on the Aesthetics of the
Gothic Manuscript', 3,
where the author urges us
to regard the Gothic manuscript as a European phe-
nomenon.

What this study has also shown is that the transition from one script to another is not only a long process, which is well known, but that the evolution occurred in stages. The first wave of change has actually remained out of sight here and may well be placed in the third quarter of the eleventh century, when scribes probably started to give new direction to their minims and introduced angularity – features we now call 'Gothic'. The biggest wave made visible in the present study relates to the same two features and occurs in the period 1100-25, when the new treatment of feet and the angularity of some round letter forms became established as common practice within a very short period of time. Moreover, it appears that scribes introduced these two simultaneously in their manuscripts, making this the most significant push forward towards Gothic script. A third wave can be seen in the period 1150-75, when 'true' biting was introduced, namely in all five letter forms with contrary curves (**bb/pp** had already started a few decades earlier).

Thus, much of the script that we now call Gothic was born in three major pushes, spanning around a century in total, with significant periods of inactivity in between. Normandy may be the cradle of the initial wave, but where the other thrusts may be located remains, for now, unclear. There are, at any rate, no particular regions that may be flagged with the help of dated manuscripts. What is evident, however, is that we cannot simply state that Gothic script originated in Normandy (or indeed any single location), as is sometimes done. The script was crafted over a long period of time and thus it probably received input from individuals and communities in very different geographical locations. If a location is to be credited with the composition of Gothic it seems we may best define this script, in parallel with other cultural movements in the Twelfth-Century Renaissance, as a joint European product.[44]

Appendix

Table 1: Script Development 1075-1225

An asterisk marks the number of manuscripts ignored for a calculation because the feature in question does not appear on the sample photographs used for this study.

Feature										
Presentation	1075-89	1090-1104	1105-19	1120-34	1135-49	1150-64	1165-79	1180-94	1195-1209	1210-24
Minims										
Total	11	14	23	41	41	59	52	35	38	28
Caroline min.	6 (55%)	7 (50%)	4 (17%)	3 (7%)	4 (10%)	6 (10%)	6 (12%)	1 (3%)	1 (3%)	1 (4%)
Gothic	3 (27%)	2 (14%)	17 (74%)	28 (68%)	29 (71%)	42 (71%)	36 (69%)	24 (69%)	26 (68%)	23 (82%)
Mix	2 (18%)	4 (29%)	2 (9%)	9 (22%)	7 (17%)	9 (15%)	3 (6%)	9 (26%)	4 (11%)	3 (11%)
No turns	0	1 (7%)	0	1 (2%)	1 (2%)	2 (3%)	7 (13%)	1 (3%)	7 (18%)	1 (4%)
Angularity										
Total	11	14	23	41	41	59	52	35	38	28
Caroline min.	8 (73%)	11 (79%)	2 (9%)	1 (2%)	1 (2%)	1 (2%)	0	0	0	0
Gothic	3 (27%)	2 (14%)	16 (70%)	31 (76%)	35 (85%)	54 (92%)	51 (98%)	34 (97%)	36 (95%)	28 (100%)
Mix	0	1 (7%)	5 (22%)	9 (22%)	5 (12%)	4 (7%)	1 (2%)	1 (3%)	2 (5%)	0
be/bo										
Total	10 (1*)	14	18 (5*)	34 (7*)	28 (13*)	47 (12*)	40 (12*)	34 (1*)	28 (10*)	21 (7*)
Separated	10 (100%)	14 (100%)	16 (89%)	32 (94%)	26 (93%)	36 (77%)	30 (75%)	22 (65%)	17 (61%)	9 (43%)
Biting	0	0	0	0	0	0	0	2 (6%)	4 (14%)	6 (29%)
Kissing	0	0	2 (11%)	2 (6%)	2 (7%)	5 (12%)	1 (3%)	5 (15%)	1 (4%)	5 (24%)
Sep./Kissing	0	0	0	0	0	6 (13%)	7 (18%)	4 (12%)	4 (14%)	1 (5%)
Kissing/Biting	0	0	0	0	0	0	2 (5%)	1 (3%)	2 (7%)	0

Feature Presentation	1075-89	1090-1104	1105-19	1120-34	1135-49	1150-64	1165-79	1180-94	1195-1209	1210-24
de/do										
Total	11	14	23	41	40 (1*)	58 (1*)	49 (3*)	35	38	27 (1*)
Separated	11 (100%)	14 (100%)	23 (100%)	38 (93%)	35 (88%)	46 (79%)	35 (71%)	18 (51%)	21 (55%)	9 (33%)
Biting	0	0	0	0	0	0	3 (6%)	5 (14%)	8 (21%)	14 (52%)
Kissing	0	0	0	3 (7%)	3 (8%)	8 (14%)	2 (4%)	3 (9%)	2 (5%)	4 (15%)
Sep./Kissing	0	0	0	0	1 (3%)	4 (7%)	6 (12%)	7 (20%)	5 (13%)	0
Kissing/Biting	0	0	0	0	1 (3%)	0	3 (6%)	2 (6%)	2 (5%)	0
he/ho										
Total	10 (1*)	10 (4*)	22 (1*)	34 (7*)	30 (11*)	53 (6*)	46 (6*)	25 (10*)	32 (6*)	26 (2*)
Separated	10 (100%)	10 (100%)	22 (100%)	31 (91%)	29 (97%)	40 (75%)	39 (85%)	18 (72%)	21 (66%)	19 (73%)
Biting	0	0	0	0	0	0	0	2 (8%)	3 (9%)	5 (19%)
Kissing	0	0	0	2 (6%)	0	7 (13%)	3 (7%)	2 (8%)	7 (22%)	2 (8%)
Sep./Kissing	0	0	0	1 (3%)	1 (3%)	5 (9%)	4 (9%)	3 (12%)	1 (3%)	0
Kissing/Biting	0	0	0	0	0	1 (2%)	0	0	0	0
oc (and od, oe, oq)										
Total	8 (3*)	12 (2*)	20 (3*)	35 (6*)	31 (10*)	48 (11*)	41 (11*)	27 (8*)	34 (4*)	20 (8*)
Separated	8 (100%)	12 (100%)	19 (95%)	28 (80%)	28 (90%)	36 (75%)	29 (71%)	19 (70%)	23 (68%)	10 (50%)
Biting	0	0	0	0	0	0	0	3 (11%)	4 (12%)	4 (20%)
Kissing	0	0	1 (5%)	7 (20%)	3 (10%)	9 (19%)	5 (12%)	3 (11%)	6 (18 %)	6 (30%)
Sep./Kissing	0	0	0	0	0	2 (4%)	7 (17%)	1 (4%)	1 (3%)	0
Kissing/Biting	0	0	0	0	0	1 (2%)	0	1 (4%)	0	0

Presentation	1075-89	1090-1104	1105-19	1120-34	1135-49	1150-64	1165-79	1180-94	1195-1209	1210-24
pe/po										
Total	11	13 (1*)	22 (1*)	36 (5*)	38 (3*)	50 (9*)	47 (5*)	28 (7*)	31 (7*)	21 (7*)
Separated	11 (100%)	13 (100%)	22 (100%)	35 (97%)	35 (92%)	35 (70%)	37 (79%)	15 (54%)	17 (55%)	9 (43%)
Biting	0	0	0	0	0	0	0	3 (11%)	5 (16%)	7 (33%)
Kissing	0	0	0	1 (3%)	2 (5%)	9 (18%)	6 (13%)	6 (21%)	5 (16%)	4 (19%)
Sep./Kissing	0	0	0	0	1 (3%)	6 (12%)	3 (6%)	3 (11%)	4 (13%)	0
Kissing/Biting	0	0	0	0	0	0	1 (2%)	1 (4%)	0	1 (5%)
bb/pp										
Total	8 (3*)	10 (4*)	14 (9*)	29 (12*)	25 (16*)	35 (24*)	33 (19*)	17 (18*)	22 (16*)	16 (12*)
Separated	8 (100%)	10 (100%)	14 (100%)	29 (100%)	20 (80%)	17 (49%)	7 (21%)	2 (12%)	2 (9%)	2 (13%)
Biting	0	0	0	0	3 (12%)	14 (40%)	23 (70%)	10 (59%)	17 (77%)	13 (81%)
Mix	0	0	0	0	2 (8%)	4 (11%)	3 (9%)	5 (29%)	3 (14%)	1 (6%)

Table 2: Script Development by Region 1075-1225

Feature

Presentation	1075-89	1090-1104	1105-19	1120-34	1135-49	1150-64	1165-79	1180-94	1195-1209	1210-24
Minims France										
Total	7	5	11	16	16	23	24	15	16	11
Caroline min.	4 (57%)	3 (60%)	2 (18%)	1 (6%)	0	0	1 (4%)	0	1 (6%)	0
Gothic	3 (43%)	0	8 (73%)	8 (50%)	13 (81%)	17 (74%)	21 (88%)	15 (100%)	14 (88%)	10 (91%)
Mix	0	2 (40%)	1 (9%)	5 (31%)	3 (19%)	5 (22%)	0	0	1 (6%)	1 (9%)
No turns	0	0	0	0	0	1 (4%)	2 (8%)	0	0	0

Feature

Presentation	1075-89	1090-1104	1105-19	1120-34	1135-49	1150-64	1165-79	1180-94	1195-1209	1210-24
Minims England										
Total	1	4	7	18	10	16	15	11	11	10
Caroline min.	1 (100%)	1 (25%)	0	0	0	0	0	0	0	0
Gothic	0	1 (25%)	7 (100%)	16 (89%)	10 (100%)	15 (94%)	12 (80%)	8 (73%)	6 (55%)	9 (90%)
Mix	0	2 (50%)	0	1 (6%)	0	0	0	2 (18%)	0	0
No turns	0	0	0	1 (6%)	0	1 (6%)	3 (20%)	1 (9%)	5 (45%)	1 (10%)
Minims Austria, Germany and Switzerland										
Total	1	0	2	3	8	12	9	6	5	3
Caroline min.	1 (100%)	0	1 (50%)	1 (33%)	3 (38%)	6 (50%)	4 (44%)	1 (17%)	0	1 (33%)
Gothic	0	0	0	1 (33%)	3 (38%)	4 (33%)	1 (11%)	0	2 (40%)	2 (66%)
Mix	0	0	1 (50%)	1 (33%)	2 (25%)	2 (17%)	3 (33%)	5 (83%)	2 (40%)	0
No turns	0	0	0	0	0	0	1 (11%)	0	1 (20%)	0
Angularity France										
Total	7	5	11	16	16	23	24	15	16	11
Caroline min.	4 (57%)	3 (60%)	1 (9%)	1 (6%)	0	1 (4%)	0	0	0	0
Gothic	3 (43%)	2 (40%)	9 (82%)	12 (75%)	13 (81%)	20 (87%)	24 (100%)	15 (100%)	16 (100%)	11 (100%)
Mix	0	0	1 (9%)	3 (19%)	3 (19%)	2 (9%)	0	0	0	0
Angularity England										
Total	1	4	7	18	10	16	15	11	11	10
Caroline min.	1 (100%)	4 (100%)	1 (14%)	0	0	0	0	0	0	0
Gothic	0	0	5 (71%)	15 (83%)	9 (90%)	16 (100%)	15 (100%)	11 (100%)	11 (100%)	10 (100%)
Mix	0	0	1 (14%)	3 (17%)	1 (10%)	0	0	0	0	0

Feature

Presentation	1075-89	1090-1104	1105-19	1120-34	1135-49	1150-64	1165-79	1180-94	1195-1209	1210-24

Angularity Austria, Germany and Switzerland

	1075-89	1090-1104	1105-19	1120-34	1135-49	1150-64	1165-79	1180-94	1195-1209	1210-24
Total	1	0	2	3	8	12	9	6	5	3
Caroline min.	1 (100%)	0	0	0	1 (13%)	0	0	0	0	0
Gothic	0	0	0	3 (100%)	6 (75%)	11 (92%)	8 (89%)	5 (83%)	5 (100%)	3 (100%)
Mix	0	0	2 (100%)	0	1 (13%)	1 (8%)	1(11%)	1 (17%)	0	0

Biting de/do France

	1075-89	1090-1104	1105-19	1120-34	1135-49	1150-64	1165-79	1180-94	1195-1209	1210-24
Total	7	5	11	16	16	23	24	15	16	11
Yes	0	0	0	0	0	0	2 (8%)	2 (13%)	4 (25%)	5 (45%
No	7 (100%)	5 (100%)	11 (100%)	16 (100%)	16 (100%)	23 (100%)	22 (92%)	13 (87%)	12 (75%)	6 (55%)
Mix	0	0	0	0	0	0	0	0	0	0

Biting de/do England

	1075-89	1090-1104	1105-19	1120-34	1135-49	1150-64	1165-79	1180-94	1195-1209	1210-24
Total	1	4	7	18	10	16	15	11	11	10
Yes	0	0	0	0	0	0	1 (7%)	2 (18)	4 (36%)	6 (60%)
No	1 (100%)	4 (100%)	7 (100%)	18 (100%)	10 (100%)	16 (100%)	14 (93%)	9 (82)	7 (64%)	4 (40%)
Mix	0	0	0	0	0	0	0	0	0	0

Biting de/do Austria, Germany and Switzerland

	1075-89	1090-1104	1105-19	1120-34	1135-49	1150-64	1165-79	1180-94	1195-1209	1210-24
Total	1	0	2	3	8	12	9	6	5	3
Yes	0	0	0	0	0	0	0	0	0	
No	1 (100%)	0	2 (100%)	3 (100%)	8 (100%)	12 (100%)	9 (100%)	6 (100%)	5 (100%)	3 (100%)
Mix	0	0	0	0	0	0	0	0	0	0

Table 2: Script Development by Region 1075-1225

Feature

Presentation	1075-89	1090-1104	1105-19	1120-34	1135-49	1150-64	1165-79	1180-94	1195-1209	1210-24
Minims France										
Total	7	5	11	16	16	23	24	15	16	11
Caroline min.	4 (57%)	3 (60%)	2 (18%)	1 (6%)	0	0	1 (4%)	0	1 (6%)	0
Gothic	3 (43%)	0	8 (73%)	8 (50%)	13 (81%)	17 (74%)	21 (88%)	15 (100%)	14 (88%)	10 (91%)
Mix	0	2 (40%)	1 (9%)	5 (31%)	3 (19%)	5 (22%)	0	0	1 (6%)	1 (9%)
No turns	0	0	0	0	0	1 (4%)	2 (8%)	0	0	0
Minims England										
Total	1	4	7	18	10	16	15	11	11	10
Caroline min.	1 (100%)	1 (25%)	0	0	0	0	0	0	0	0
Gothic	0	1 (25%)	7 (100%)	16 (89%)	10 (100%)	15 (94%)	12 (80%)	8 (73%)	6 (55%)	9 (90%)
Mix	0	2 (50%)	0	1 (6%)	0	0	0	2 (18%)	0	0
No turns	0	0	0	1 (6%)	0	1 (6%)	3 (20%)	1 (9%)	5 (45%)	1 (10%)
Minims Austria, Germany and Switzerland										
Total	1	0	2	3	8	12	9	6	5	3
Caroline min.	1 (100%)	0	1 (50%)	1 (33%)	3 (38%)	6 (50%)	4 (44%)	1 (17%)	0	1 (33%)
Gothic	0	0	0	1 (33%)	3 (38%)	4 (33%)	1 (11%)	0	2 (40%)	2 (66%)
Mix	0	0	1 (50%)	1 (33%)	2 (25%)	2 (17%)	3 (33%)	5 (83%)	2 (40%)	0
No turns	0	0	0	0	0	0	1 (11%)	0	1 (20%)	0
Angularity France										
Total	7	5	11	16	16	23	24	15	16	11
Caroline min.	4 (57%)	3 (60%)	1 (9%)	1 (6%)	0	1 (4%)	0	0	0	0
Gothic	3 (43%)	2 (40%)	9 (82%)	12 (75%)	13 (81%)	20 (87%)	24 (100%)	15 (100%)	16 (100%)	11 (100%)
Mix	0	0	1 (9%)	3 (19%)	3 (19%)	2 (9%)	0	0	0	0

Feature Presentation	1075-89	1090-1104	1105-19	1120-34	1135-49	1150-64	1165-79	1180-94	1195-1209	1210-24
Angularity England										
Total	1	4	7	18	10	16	15	11	11	10
Caroline min.	1 (100%)	4 (100%)	1 (14%)	0	0	0	0	0	0	0
Gothic	0	0	5 (71%)	15 (83%)	9 (90%)	16 (100%)	15 (100%)	11 (100%)	11 (100%)	10 (100%)
Mix	0	0	1 (14%)	3 (17%)	1 (10%)	0	0	0	0	0
Angularity Austria, Germany and Switzerland										
Total	1	0	2	3	8	12	9	6	5	3
Caroline min.	1 (100%)	0	0	0	1 (13%)	0	0	0	0	0
Gothic	0	0	0	3 (100%)	6 (75%)	11 (92%)	8 (89%)	5 (83%)	5 (100%)	3 (100%)
Mix	0	0	2 (100%)	0	1 (13%)	1 (8%)	1(11%)	1 (17%)	0	0
Biting de/do France										
Total	7	5	11	16	16	23	24	15	16	11
Yes	0	0	0	0	0	0	2 (8%)	2 (13%)	4 (25%)	5 (45%)
No	7 (100%)	5 (100%)	11 (100%)	16 (100%)	16 (100%)	23 (100%)	22 (92%)	13 (87%)	12 (75%)	6 (55%
Mix	0	0	0	0	0	0	0	0	0	0
Biting de/do England										
Total	1	4	7	18	10	16	15	11	11	10
Yes	0	0	0	0	0	0	1 (7%)	2 (18)	4 (36%)	6 (60%)
No	1 (100%)	4 (100%)	7 (100%)	18 (100%)	10 (100%)	16 (100%)	14 (93%)	9 (82)	7 (64%)	4 (40%)
Mix	0	0	0	0	0	0	0	0	0	0
Biting de/do Austria, Germany and Switzerland										
Total	1	0	2	3	8	12	9	6	5	3
Yes	0	0	0	0	0	0	0	0	0	0
No	1 (100%)	0	2 (100%)	3 (100%)	8 (100%)	12 (100%)	9 (100%)	6 (100%)	5 (100%)	3 (100%)
Mix	0	0	0	0	0	0	0	0	0	0

(CMD), the former of which
I have followed. For an
analysis of the potential dating, see the the essay 'Location and Dating' under
'Background Essays',
http://digital.library.mcgill.
ca/ms-17/index.htm,
accessed 29 August 2011.

Table 3: Corpus of Dated Manuscripts

The corpus used for this study consists of all manuscripts dated between 1075 up to (but not including) 1225 as present in all volumes of the CMD except the Cambrai volume. For these, see http://www.palaeographia.org/cipl/cmd.htm, accessed 15 August 2011; the abbreviations used in col. 12 below are also found here. To construct this corpus I excluded manuscripts dated 'Before...' or 'After...'; those of which the date is in dispute in secondary sources;[45] some of those whose date is not certain ('?'); and those whose date exceeds a quarter century (e.g. '1125-68'). This resulted in a corpus of the 367 manuscripts, which form the primary corpus of the research project this study stems from (see n. 18, above).

For this particular study of how script evolved between 1075-1225 I omitted eighteen codices, mostly because they are written in a so-called national script (Beneventan, Insular and Visigothic) and in some cases because the image in the CMD is not suitable for a palaeographical study of this kind (image not clear enough, selected page contains numbers only). These rejected manuscripts are marked with an asterisk in column 1 and the data boxes are simply left blank.

Of manuscripts whose date covers multiple years the average year is taken as criterion for placing the codex in question in a time segment. No. 9, for example, is dated 1081-94, the median of which is 1088, and so it is placed in 1075-89 and not 1090-1104. The median year is placed between parentheses behind the date in column 3.

This study is based on the images provided in the CMD, which are supplemented by those from other sources. When the CMD provides images of multiple hands, the hand used for the survey is identified by listing the folium on which it appears between square brackets after the shelfmark in column 2. If the CMD presents multiple plates displaying the hand in question, only one is listed here for reasons of brevity.

For the abbreviations used in the shelfmarks, consult the list at p. 13, above.

Columns:

1= Number in this table;

2= Manuscript (city, shelfmark, for clarity sometimes institution);

3= Date (median date of manuscripts whose date cover multiple years is placed between parentheses);

4= Origins (A= Austria; B= Belgium; E= England; F= France; G= Germany; Ir= Ireland; Is= Israel; It= Italy; S= Switzerland; Sw= Sweden; Y= Yugoslavia; W= Wales; ? = unknown);

5= Angularity;

6= Minims (Ca= manner of Caroline minuscule; Go= Gothic manner; nt= No turns observed in feet, as discussed above, p. 90);

7= Biting following **b**;

8= Biting following **d**;

9= Biting following **o**;

10= Biting following **p**;

11= Biting in **bb/pp**;

12= Plate in CMD.

Abbreviations in columns 7-12:

b= Biting;

s= Separated (no biting);

m= Mix (biting and not);

k=Kissing;

sk= Separated and kissing (mix);

kb= Kissing and biting (mix);

?= Feature in question not found in available photographs

1	2	3	4	5	6	7	8	9	10	11	12
1	Bodl. Bodley 309	1075	F	No	Ca	?	s	?	s	?	GB Ox II 31
2	Rouen BM 477	1075, c.	F	No	Ca	s	s	s	s	s	F 7 II XXIV
3	ÖNB Cod. 1247 [f. 17r]	1079	G	No	Ca	s	s	?	s	s	A 1 II 21-23
4	Tournai Seminar 1	1084	B	No	Mix	s	s	s	s	s	B I 2
5*	Bodl. Canon . Bibl. Lat. 61	1081-86 (1083)	Y								GB Ox II 32
6	Orléans BM 229 [p. 29]	1080-87 (1083)	F	No	Ca	s	s	s	s	s	F 7 II XXV
7	Rouen BM 1406 (Y. 41)	1079-92 (1085)	F	Yes	Go	s	s	s	s	s	F 7 II XXVII
8	Rouen BM 1409 (Y. 189)	1078-95 (1086)	F	Yes	Go	s	s	s	s	s	F 7 II XXVII
9	Le Mans BM 23 [f. 117v]	1081-94 (1087)	F	Yes	Go	s	s	s	s	s	F 7 II XXVIII
10	Uppsala University Libr. C 88	1085-89 (1087)	I	No	Mix	s	s	s	s	?	S I 2
11	TNA, PRO E31/1 [f. 33r]	1086-88? (1087)	E	No	Ca	s	s	?	s	?	GB Lond II 4-7
12*	Cambridge Corpus Christi 199	1085-91 (1088)	W								GB Ca II 33
13	Angers BM 187	1083-93 (1088)	F	No	Ca	s	s	s	s	s	F 7 II XXVI
14	CUL Ii 3.33	1079-1101 (1090)	E	Mix	Go	s	s	s	s	s	
15	Tours BM 90	1084-96 (1090)	F	No	Ca	s	s	s	s	?	F 7 II XXVIII
16	Rouen BM 32 (A. 21) [f. 1v]	1084-97 (1090)	E	No	Ca	s	s	s	s	s	F 7 II XXIX
17	Bodl. Lat. th. d. 20 [f. 76r]	1091	F	Yes	Mix	s	s	s	?	?	GB Ox II 34
18*	Bodl. Rawl. B. 503	1093	Ir								GB Ox II 36
19*	Évreux BM 60 L	1093 c.	F								F 7 II XXX
20	BnF nouv. acq. lat. 348	1093-94	F	No	Ca	s	s	s	s	s	F 4 II XVII
21	BL Add. 28106 & 28107	1094-97 (1095)	B	No	Ca	s	s	s	s	s	GB BL II 52
22	Cambridge Corpus Christi 270	1091-1100 (1095)	E	No	Mix	s	s	s	s	s	GB Ca II 34
23	BnF nouv. acq. lat. 2246 [f. 79v]	1090-1100, c. (1095)	F	No	Mix	s	s	s	s	s	F 4 II XVI
24	BL Cotton Tiberius A.XIII [f. 103r]	1096, c.	E	No	Mix	s	s	s	s	s	GB BL II 53
25	BAV Barb. lat. 587	1097	It	No	Ca	s	s	?	s	s	ITBAV 1 II 1
26*	BL Arundel 60	1099	E								GB BL II 55
27*	BL Add. 40000	1100, c.	E								GB BL II 56
28	BL Harley 3904 [f. 13r]	1100, c.	?	No	Go	s	s	s	s	?	GB BL II 57
29	Cambridge Corpus Christi 415 [p. 265]	1095-1109 (1100)	F	Yes	Ca	s	s	s	s	s	GB Ca II 35
30	Rome BNC Farf. 2 [f. 348r]	1103	It	No	Ca	s	s	s	s	s	It Roma II 22-23
31	Paris Mazarine 364	1099-1105 (1103)	It								F 1 II VI

32	Cesena Bibl. Malatestiana 3.210	1104	It	No	nt	s	s	?	s	?	It 13 1
33	BnF nouv. acq. lat. 2195	1105	B	Yes	Go	s	s	s	s	?	F 4 II XVII
34	BL Cotton Nero C.V [f. 76v]	1105, c.	E	No	Go	s	s	s	s	?	GB BL II 59
35	BL Cotton Vitellius C.XII	1100-1110 (1105)	E	Yes	Go	s	s	s	s	s	GB BL II 58
36	The Hague KB 128 E 14	1106-11 (1108)	F	Yes	Go	s	s	s	s	s	NL 2 II 956
37	Chantilly Mus. Condé 16 [f. 45v]	1105-13 (1108)	G	Mix	Mix	s	s	s	s	s	F 1 II X
38	Dijon BM 12, 13, 14 and 15	1109	F	Yes	Go	s	s	s	s	?	F 6 II IX
39	Rouen BM 1174 (Y. 14)	1109-10	F	Mix	Mix	s	s	s	s	s	F 7 II XXXIV
40	Oxford St John 17	1110-11	E	Yes	Go	s	s	s	s	s	GB Ox II 33
41	Dijon BM 168, 169 and 170	1111	F	Yes	Go	s	s	?	s	?	F 6 II X
42	BL Royal 6 C.VI	1108-14 (1111)	E	Yes	Go	s	s	s	s	s	GB BL II 61
43	Admont SB Cod. 735	1106-18 (1112)	A	Mix	Ca	s	s	?	s	?	A 7 II 1-2
44	BnF lat. 10062	1113, c.	F	Yes	Go	?	s	s	s	s	F 3 II XXVI
45	BnF lat. 17767	1102-23 (1113)	F	No	Ca	?	s	s	s	s	F 3 II XXV
46	BNC Farf. 1 [f. 363r]	1105-19 (1113)	It	Mix	Ca	s	s	s	s	?	It Rome II 24-25
47	BnF lat. 1918	1107-21 (1114)	F	Yes	Go	s	s	s	s	s	F 2 II XIII
48	Auxerre BM 212	1109-24 (1116)	F	Yes	Go	?	s	s	s	?	F 6 II IX
49	Avranches BM 211 [f. 68r]	1117, c.	F	Yes	Go	?	s	?	?	s	F 7 II XXXVI
50	Bodl. e Mus. 112	1108 & 26 (1117)	E	Mix	Go	s	s	s	s	s	GB Ox II 37
51	Amsterdam UB 89	1109-25 (1117)	B?	Yes	Ca	s	s	s	s	?	NL 1 II 55-56
52	BnF nouv. acq. lat. 1496	1109-25 (1117)	F	Yes	Go	s	s	s	s	s	F 4 II XVIII
53	Leiden UB BPL 114 B	1118, c.	E	Yes	Go	s	s	s	s	s	NL 1 II 57
54	BnF lat. 2500 [f. 49r]	1113-24 (1118)	F	Yes	Go	?	s	s	s	?	F 2 II XII
55	Cambridge St John's D. 19 (94)	1112-26 (1119)	E	Yes	Go	s	s	s	s	?	GB Ca II 39
56	Vendôme BM 44	1120, c.	F	No	Ca	s	s	s	s	?	F 7 II XXXIX
57	BL Cotton Nero D.II	1120, c.	E	Yes	Go	s	s	s	?	s	GB BL II 64
58*	Leiden UB BPL 2505, a-f	1113-27 (1120)	F								NL 1 II 104-109
59	Cambridge Corpus Christi 373	1114-25 (1120)	F	Yes	Mix	s	s	s	s	s	GB Ca II 41
60*	Leiden UB BPL 2505	1113-27 (1120)	F								NL 2 II 957-960
61	BL Royal 5 D.II	1115-24 (1120)	E	Yes	Go	s	s	s	s	s	GB BL II 62
62*	Bodl. Laud misc. 636	1121	E								GB Ox II 39
63	Cambridge Corpus Christi 371	1113? & 1130 (1121)	E	Yes	Go	s	s	s	s	s	GB Ca II 40

64	Oxford Jesus 26	1119-24 (1121)	E	Yes	Go	s	s	s	s	?	GB Ox II 38
65	BnF lat. 2502	1120-24 (1122)	F	Yes	Go	s	s	s	s	?	F 2 II XIV
66	BnF lat. 2900	1120-24 (1122)	F	Yes	Go	s	s	s	s	s	F 2 II XIV
67	BnF nouv. acq. lat. 1064	1114-33 (1123)	F	Yes	Go	?	s	s	s	?	F 4 II XVIII
68	Oxford Lincoln lat. 100	1125	E	Yes	Go	s	s	s	s	s	GB Ox II 45
69	Heerenberg Huis Bergh Inv. 25 ['fr. b']	1125	B	Yes	Mix	s	s	s	s	s	NL 1 II 58-59
70	Bergamo Bibl. Capitolare 1047	1125	It	Mix	Mix	s	s	?	s	s	It 6 1
71	Dijon BM 130	1125, c.	F	Yes	Go	s	s	s	s	?	F 6 II XI
72	Oxford Magdalen lat. 172	1125, c.	E	Mix	Go	s	s	s	s	s	GB Ox II 46
73	Alençon BM 26	1113-37 (1125)	F	Yes	Mix	s	s	s	s	s	F 7 II XXXIII
74	Rouen BM 1343 (U. 43)	1113-37 (1125)	F	Mix	Go	s	s	s	s	s	F 7 II XXXIV
75	Cambridge Corpus Christi 393	1116-35 (1125)	E	Yes	Go	s	s	s	s	s	GB Ca II 42
76	Paris Mazarine 2013 [f. 136r]	1120-31 (1125)	F?	Mix	Go	?	s	s	s	s	F 1 II VIII
77	Cambridge Corpus Christi 452	1122-30, c. (1126)	E	Yes	Go	s	s	s	s	s	GB Ca II 47
78	BnF lat. 1793	1127, c.	B	Yes	Go	s	s	s	s	?	F 2 II XV
79	BL Cotton Tiberius C.I & Harley 3667	1122-35? (1128)	E	Yes	Mix	?	s	s	s	s	GB BL II 67
80	Bodl. Bodley 561	1124-33 (1128)	E	Yes	Go	s	s	s	s	?	GB Ox II 43
81	BL Add. 16979	1129	F	Yes	Mix	s	s	s	s	s	GB BL II 68
82	Bodl. Arch. Selden b. 16	1129	E	Yes	Go	s	s	s	s	s	GB Ox II 48
83	BnF lat. 13779	1129, c.	F	Yes	Mix	s	s	s	?	s	F 4 II XIX
84	Cambridge Corpus Christi 2	1121-38 (1129)	E	Mix	nt	s	s	s	s	s	GB Ca II 45-46
85	Leiden UB VLF 8 [f. 17v]	1130, c.	F?	Yes	Mix	s	s	s	s	?	NL 1 II 60-62
86	BL Add. 16918	1130, c.	F	Yes	Mix	s	s	s	s	s	GB BL II 69
87	Cambridge Trinity R. 7. 28 (770)	1120-40 (1130)	E	Mix	Go	s	s	s	s	?	GB Ca II 44
88	Vendôme BM 193	1129-32 (1130)	F	Yes	Go	s	s	?	s	s	F 7 II XL
89	London Lambeth Palace 224	1120-43 (1131)	E	Yes	Go	s	s	s	s	s	GB Lond II 8
90	BL Cotton Vespasian A.IX	1131?	E	Yes	Go	?	s	s	?	?	GB BL II 70
91	Rome BNC Farf. 3	1132, c.	It	Mix	Ca	s	s	s	s	s	It Roma II XXVI
92	Cambridge St John's A.22 (22)	1132, c.	E	Yes	Go	s	s	?	?	?	GB Ca II 58
93	BnF lat. 5506	1123-41 (1132)	F	Mix	Go	s	s	s	s	s	F 2 II XV
94	Bodl. Bodley 297 [f. 145r]	1131-34 (1132)	E	Yes	Go	s	s	?	s	s	GB Ox II 50
95	BnF lat. 12055	1133	G?	Yes	Go	?	s	?	?	?	F 3 II XXVII

#	Shelfmark	Date									Class
96	Brussels KB II 2524 [f. 137v]	1132-35 (1133)	B	Yes	Go	?	s	s	s	s	B I 3
97	ÖNB Cod. 1063	1134	A	Yes	Ca	s	s	?	s	s	A 1 II 27
98	BL Harley 3099 [f. 152v]	1134	B	Mix	Go	s	s	s	s	s	GB BL II 72
99	Cambridge Trinity O.5.20 (1301)	1125-43 (1134)	E	Yes	Go	?	s	s	s	s	GB Ca II 52
100	BL Harley 2660 [f. 33r]	1136-38 (1137)	G	Yes	Ca	s	s	s	s	s	GB BL II 73
101	CUL Kk. 4. 6	1130-45 (1137)	E	Yes	Mix	s	s	s	s	?	GB Ca II 57
102	Oxford Lincoln lat. 63 [f. 139r]	1136-38 (1137)	E	Yes	Go	s	s	s	s	?	GB Ox II 66
103	BL Egerton 1139	1131-43 (1137)	Is	Yes	Go	?	s	?	s	?	GB BL II 71
104	BnF lat. 3790	1138	?	Yes	nt	?	s	?	s	?	F 2 II XVI
105*	BL Harley 1802	1138	Ir								GB BL II 74
106	Fitzwilliam Museum McClean 49	1128-49 (1138)	Is	Yes	Mix	?	s	s	s	?	GB Ca II 54
107	Leiden UB BPL 20 [f. 22v]	1138-39	F	Yes	Go	s	s	s	s	s	NL 1 II 63-68
108	Brussels KB 104-05 [f. 131v]	1139	?	Yes	Go	s	s	?	?	s	B I 4
109	Brussels KB II 1065	1139	?	Yes	Go	s	s	s	s	b	B I 5
110	BnF lat. 11851 [f. 214r]	1139, c.	G?	Yes	Go	s	s	s	?	s	F 3 II XXIX
111	Oxford Corpus Christi 157 [f. 1r]	1135-43 (1139)	E	Mix	Go	s	s	s	s	s	GB Ox II 52
112	Cambridge St John's B.20 (42)	1140, c.	E	Yes	Go	s	s	s	s	s	GB Ca II 61
113	BL Cotton Nero C.VII	1140?	E	Yes	Go	s	s	s	?	s	GB BL II 76
114	BL Add. 14250	1140?	E	Yes	Go	s	s	?	s	s	GB BL II 75
115	Blois BM 44 [f. 9r]	1140-41, c.	F	Yes	Go	s	s	s	s	s	F 7 II XLI
116	BnF lat. 10913	1141, c.	F	Mix	Go	s	s	s	s	?	F 3 II XXIX
117	ÖNB Cod. 375	1142	A	Yes	Ca	?	s	s	s	s	A 1 II 28
118	BL Add. 15722	1142	F	Yes	Go	s	s	s	s	s	GB BL II 77
119	BnF lat. 1654	1134-50 (1142)	F	Yes	Go	s	sk	?	s	?	F 2 II XVI
120	BnF lat. 11577	1134-50 (1142)	F	Yes	Go	s	s	s	s	s	F 3 II XXVII
121	BnF lat. 12072	1134-50 (1142)	F	Yes	Go	s	s	?	s	?	F 3 II XXVIII
122	BnF lat. 17545	1137-47 (1142)	F	Yes	Go	s	s	s	s	s	F 3 II XXVIII
123	ÖNB Cod. 275	1143 c.	G	Yes	Mix	?	s	s	s	?	A 1 II 30
124	BnF nouv. acq. lat. 706	1143-44, c.	F	Yes	Go	?	s	s	sk	s	F 4 II XX
125	Bern Burgerbibliothek 226	1143-44	G	No	Go	s	s	s	s	s	Sch 2 II 16-17
126	Rouen BM 470 (A. 291) [f. 41r]	1144, c.	F	Yes	Mix	?	s	s	s	?	F 7 II XLII
127	Bodl. Canon. Pat. Lat. 148	1145	It	Yes	Ca	s	s	?	s	m	GB Ox II 54

#	Manuscript	Date									Ref
128*	Angers BM 827	1137-54 (1145)	F								F 7 II XLI
129	BL Add. 46487	1146, c.	E	Yes	Go	s	s	s	s	s	GB BL II 78
130	Charleville BM 114 [f. 24v]	1145-48 (1146)	F	Yes	Go	?	s	s	s	?	F 5 II X
131	Bodl. Digby 40	1147	F	Yes	Go	s	kb	s	s	?	GB Ox II 55
132	Leiden UB BPL 196	1145-49 (1147)	G	Mix	Mix	s	s	s	s	s	NL 1 II 73-74
133	Charleville BM 26 (1)	1148	F	Yes	Go	s	s	s	s	s	F 5 II XII
134	BL Add. 14788	1148	B	Yes	Go	?	s	s	s	b	GB BL II 81
135	BL Harley 2803 & 2804	1148	G	Yes	Go	s	s	s	s	s	GB BL II 82
136	BnF lat. 1663	1148, c.	F	Mix	Mix	?	s	s	s	s	F 2 II XVIII
137	London Soc. of Antiquaries 154	1148, c.	E	Yes	Go	?	s	s	s	?	GB Lond II 13
138	Charleville BM 12	1149	F	Mix	Go	s	s	?	s	b	F 5 II XII
139*	Charleville BM 26 (2)	1149	F								F 5 II XII
140	Bodl. Auct. D. 2. 6	1139-58 (1149)	E	Yes	Go	?	?	s	s	?	GB Ox II 53
141	BnF lat. 5064	1143-56 (1149)	F	Yes	Mix	s	s	?	s	?	F 2 II XVII
142	BnF lat. 5129 [f. 6r]	1145-53 (1149)	F	Yes	Go	s	s	s	s	m	F 2 II XVIII
143	London Univ. College Germ. 16	1145-53 (1149)	G	Yes	Ca	?	s	?	s	?	GB Lond II 12
144	BnF nouv. acq. lat. 214	1151, c.	F	Mix	Mix	s	s	s	s	b	F 4 II XXI
145	Udine Bibl. Arcivescovile 82 [f. 66r]	1152	It	Yes	Mix	s	s	kb	s	m	It Friulane II 5
146	BnF lat. 14314 [f. 208v]	1152, c.	F?	Yes	Go	s	sk	s	s	b	F 3 II XXX
147	Auxerre BM 142	1152, c.	F	Yes	Go	?	s	s	s	?	F 6 II XII
148	BL Cotton Vitellius A.XVII	1150-53 (1152)	E	Yes	Go	s	s	s	s	b	GB BL II 83
149	BnF lat. 14802 [f. 45v]	1153	?	Yes	Mix	s	sk	?	?	b	F 3 II XXX
150	BnF nouv. acq. lat. 429	1151-56 (1153)	F	Yes	Mix	s	s	s	?	?	F 4 II XXII
151	Leiden UB BPL 30 [f. 91v]	1153-54	F	Yes	Go	s	s	s	s	s	NL 1 II 75-80
152	Leiden UB VLF 67 [f. 33r]	1153-54	G	Yes	Go	s	s	s	?	b	NL 1 II 81-83
153	Chantilly Mus. Condé 121 [f. 107v]	1154	G	Yes	Go	s	s	s	sk	b	F 1 II IX
154	Strasbourg Grand Séminaire 37	1154	G	Yes	Go	s	s	s	s	s	F 5 II XV
155	BnF lat. 3853 [f. 120r]	1154, c.	F	Yes	Go	?	s	s	s	?	F 2 II XIX
156	BnF lat. 7561 [p. 71]	1153-55 (1154)	F	No	nt	s	s	s	s	b	F 4 II XXIII
157	Mons Bib. de la Ville 333/352 [f. 116v]	1155	B	Yes	Go	s	s	s	s	b	B I 6
158	BL Add. 17737 and 17738	1155, c.	B	Yes	Go	sk	s	s	s	b	GB BL II 86
159	Cambridge Trinity B. 15. 10 (346)	1155, c.	E	Yes	Go	sk	s	sk	s	s	GB Ca II 67

160	Lambeth Palace 109	1155, c. (& 1176?)	E	Yes	Go	s	s	s	s	m	GB Lond II 14
161	Admont SB Cod. 36 [f. 36r]	1147-64 (1155)	A	Yes	Mix	?	s	?	s	?	A 7 II 3
162	Admont SB Cod. 52	1147-64 (1155)	A	Yes	Ca	?	s	s	s	?	A 7 II 4
163	Brussels KB II 1635 [f. 29r]	1156	?	Yes	Go	s	s	s	s	?	B I 7
164	Avranches BM 210 [f. 18v]	1154-58 (1156)	F	Mix	Mix	s	s	s	s	s	F 7 II XLIV
165	Charleville BM 246 B	1156-57	F	Yes	Go	sk	s	sk	s	m	F 5 II XVI
166	Avranches BM 159	1156-57	F	Yes	Go	s	s	s	sk	s	F 7 II XLIV
167	Charleville BM 2	1157	F	Yes	Go	s	s	s	s	s	F 5 II XVI
168	Metz BM 1154	1157	It	Yes	Go	s	s	s	s	s	F 5 II XVII
169	Cambridge Trinity R.17.1 (987)	1145-70 (1157)	E	Yes	nt	s	s	?	s	?	GB Ca II 63-64
170	BnF nouv. acq. lat. 1772	1155-60 (1157)	It	Mix	Go	s	s	s	s	b	F 4 II XXIV
171	BnF lat. 13779	1160, c.	F	Yes	Mix	s	s	s	?	?	F 4 II XXV
172	Reims BM 452	1145-74? (1160)	F	Yes	Go	s	s	s	s	?	F 5 II XI
173	BL Royal 2 A.X	1161	E	Yes	Go	s	s	s	s	s	GB BL II 88
174	Oxford Corpus Christi 134	1161?	E	Yes	Go	s	s	?	?	s	GB Ox II 67
175	BL Royal 3 A.XII	1147-76 (1161)	E	Yes	Go	s	s	s	s	s	GB BL II 79
176	BL Royal 7 F.VI	1147-76 (1161)	E	Yes	Go	s	s	s	s	s	GB BL II 80
177	Oxford Jesus 53	1147-76 (1161)	E	Yes	Go	s	s	s	?	s	GB Ox II 56
178	Oxford Jesus 68	1147-76 (1161)	E	Yes	Go	s	s	s	s	?	GB Ox II 57
179	Bodl. Auct. D. 4. 6	1158-64 (1161)	E	Yes	Go	s	sk	?	?	?	GB Ox II 64
180	Charleville BM 197 A, t. 2	1148-74? (1161)	F	Yes	Go	s	s	?	s	b	F 5 II XIII
181	BnF lat. 2444	1162	F?	Yes	Mix	?	s	s	s	?	F 2 II XX
182	Admont SB Cod. 221 [f. 1r]	1162	A	Mix	Ca	s	s	?	?	?	A 7 II 9-10
183	Vorau SB Cod. 255 [f. 1r]	1162, c.	A	Yes	Ca	?	s	s	s	?	A 7 II 5-8
184	Oxford Jesus 52	1149-76 (1162)	E	Yes	Go	?	s	s	s	?	GB Ox II 58
185	Oxford Jesus 63	1149-76 (1162)	E	Yes	Go	s	s	?	?	?	GB Ox II 59
186	Oxford Jesus 67	1149-76 (1162)	E	Yes	Go	?	s	?	s	?	GB Ox II 60
187	Cambridge St John's C.18 (68)	1152-73 (1162)	E	Yes	Go	s	s	?	s	?	GB Ca II 65
188	Engelberg SB 3-5 [f. 2v]	1147-78 (1162)	S	Yes	Ca	s	s	s	s	m	Sch 2 II 18-23
189	Engelberg SB 12 [f. 24r]	1147-78 (1162)	S	Yes	Ca	s	s	s	s	b	Sch 2 II 26-27
190	Engelberg SB 13 [f. 83r]	1147-78 (1162)	S	Yes	Ca	?	s	s	s	b	Sch 2 II 28
191	BL Add. 15307 [f. 143r]	1163	B	Yes	Go	s	s	?	s	?	GB BL II 89

No.	Manuscript	Date									Code
192	Troyes Médiathèque 1484 [f. 57r]	1152-74 (1163)	F?	Yes	Go	s	s	s	sk	s	F 5 II XIII
193	Troyes Médiathèque 799 [f. 19r]	1152-74 (1163)	F?	Yes	Go	sk	s	s	s	s	F 5 II XIV
194	Troyes Médiathèque 1176 [f. 24r]	1152-74 (1163)	F?	Yes	Go	s	s	s	sk	s	F 5 II XIV
195	Troyes Médiathèque 426 [f. 51v]	1152-74 (1163)	F?	Yes	Go	s	s	s	s	s	F 5 II XV
196	Dijon BM 658 [f. 103r, col. A]	1152-74 (1163)	F?	Yes	Go	?	sk	s	sk	?	F 6 II XIII
197	Oxford St John's 49	1158-69 (1163)	F	Yes	Go	?	s	s	s	?	GB Ox II 65
198	Saint-Brieuc BM 7 [f. 68r]	1153-72 (1163)	F?	Yes	Go	sk	s	?	s	?	F 7 II XLIII
199	BnF lat. 11575 [and 11576]	1164	F	Yes	Go	sk	s	s	s	?	F 3 II XXXI
200	Bodl. Canon. Liturg. 297 [f. 145r]	1154-73 (1164)	G	Yes	Go	?	s	?	sk	s	GB Ox II 61
201	Cambridge Corpus Christi 46 [f. 184r]	1159-70 (1164)	E	Yes	Go	s	s	s	s	b	GB Ca II 68
202	Leiden UB Periz. quarto 17	1160-68 (1164)	G	Yes	Mix	?	s	s	s	?	NL 1 II 87
203	Bodl. Digby 56	1164-68 (1166)	EW	Yes	Go	s	?	?	s	b	GB Ox II 73
204	BnF lat. 9688	1167	F	Yes	Go	s	s	s	s	b	F 3 II XXXII
205	BnF lat. 2702	1167	F?	Yes	Go	?	sk	s	s	b	F 4 II XXV
206	Charleville BM 246 D	1167	F	Yes	Go	?	s	s	?	m	F 5 II XVIII
207	Oxford Christ Church lat. 88	1167	E	Yes	nt	s	s	s	?	s	GB Ox II 75
208*	Bodl. Auct. D. 2. 4	1161-73 (1167)	E								GB Ox II 70
209	Cambridge Trinity B. 3. 11 (90)	1164-70 (1167)	F	Yes	nt	sk	kb	s	s	b	GB Ca II 69
210	Cambridge Trinity B. 3. 30 (109)	1164-70 (1167)	F	Yes	Go	s	s	?	sk	s	GB Ca II 70
211	Cambridge Trinity B. 5. 5 (151)	1164-70 (1167)	F	Yes	Go	kb	b	s	kb	?	GB Ca II 71
212	Cambridge Trinity R. 4. 4 (637)	1164-70 (1167)	F	Yes	Go	sk	kb	sk	sk	b	GB Ca II 72
213	Cambridge Trinity B. 16. 17 (391)	1164-70 (1167)	F	Yes	Go	s	s	s	s	b	GB Ca II 73
214	Bodl. Auct. E. inf. 7	1164-70 (1167)	F	Yes	nt	kb	kb	s	s	b	GB Ox II 71
215	Bodl. Bodley 345	1164-70 (1167)	F	Yes	Go	s	s	s	s	b	GB Ox II 72
216	Admont SB Cod. 434 [f. 200r]	1166?-69 (1167)	A	Yes	Mix	?	s	s	s	m	A 7 II 11-26
217	Bodl. Auct. E. inf. 1	1167-71 (1169)	E	Yes	Go	s	s	?	s	?	GB Ox II 76
218	Leiden UB VLF 70 III [f. 107r]	1159-79 (1169)	F	Yes	Go	s	s	s	s	b	NL 1 II 84-86
219	BL Egerton 3668	1169?	E	Yes	Go	s	s	s	s	s	GB BL II 92
220	Charleville BM 264	1170	F	Yes	Go	sk	s	s	s	m	F 5 II XIX
221	Nîmes BM 14	1170	F	Yes	Ca	s	s	s	s	b	F 6 II XV
222	Cambridge Corpus Christi 139 [f. 85r]	1164-75 (1170)	E	Yes	Go	?	sk	s	s	s	GB Ca II 74
223	Admont SB Cod. 686a	1169-71 (1170)	A	Yes	Ca	s	s	s	s	b	A 7 II 27-28

224	BnF lat. 8314	1171	F	Yes	Go	sk	b	s	s	b	F 3 II XXXIV
225	BL Cotton Claudius C.IX	1171?	E	Yes	Go	?	b	s	s	b	GB BL II 93
226	BL Harley 2798 and 2799	1172	G	Yes	Go	sk	sk	s	s	b	GB BL II 94
227	Frankfurt UBi Barth. 41	1172	G	Yes	Ca	s	s	s	s	?	G 1 2
228	Stuttgart WLB I 236	1172	G	Yes	Ca	s	s	s	s	?	G 3 15
229	BL Harley 2800	1172, c.	G	Yes	Mix	sk	s	sk	sk	b	GB BL II 95
230	BnF nouv. acq. lat. 583	1172, c.	F	Yes	Go	?	s	?	s	?	F 4 II XXVI
231	BL Harley 3045	1172, c.	G	Yes	Mix	s	s	sk	s	b	GB BL II 96
232	Rouen BM 209 and 210	1173, c.	F	Yes	Go	s	s	s	s	?	F 7 II XLVII
233	Cambridge Trinity B. 5. 6 (153)	1170-77? (1173)	F	Yes	Go	?	s	sk	s	?	GB Ca II 83
234	BnF lat. 12583	1172-74, c. (1173)	F	Yes	Go	s	s	?	s	?	F 3 II XXXII
235	Padova Bibl. Antoniana 498	1174	It	Yes	nt	s	s	s	s	b	It 4 1
236	Évreux BM 17 L	1174, c.	E	Yes	Go	?	s	?	s	?	F 7 II XLVIII
237	Évreux BM 92 L	1165-83 (1174)	F	Yes	Go	s	s	s	?	?	F 7 II XLV
238	Bodl. Rawl. Q. f. 8	1171-77 (1174)	E	Yes	Go	s	sk	sk	?	?	GB Ox II 77
239	Bodl. Auct. E. inf. 6	1173-76 (1174)	F	Yes	Go	s	s	?	s	b	GB Ox II 78
240	ÖNB Cod. 568	1175	?	Yes	Ca	s	?	?	s	?	A 1 II 37
241	Fitzwilliam Mus. McClean 165	1175, c.	B	Yes	Go	s	s	s	s	b	GB Ca II 89
242	Cambridge Trinity B. 5. 4 (150)	1173-77 (1175)	F	Yes	Go	?	s	?	s	b	GB Ca II 84
243	BnF lat. 946	1167-83 (1175)	F	Yes	Go	s	?	?	s	b	F 2 II XX
244	BL Royal 13 D.IV [f. 7v]	1167-83 (1175)	E	Yes	Go	s	s	s	s	s	GB BL II 90
245	Cambridge St John's G. 15 (183)	1167-83 (1175)	E	Yes	Go	sk	sk	sk	s	?	GB Ca II 80
246	Cambridge Trinity Hall 2	1167-83 (1175)	E	Yes	nt	s	s	s	s	?	GB Ca II 81
247	BnF lat. 11564	1174-78 (1176)	F	Yes	Go	s	s	s	s	?	F 3 II XXXIV
248	Cambridge Trinity O.7.13 (1341)	1167-83? (1175)	E	Yes	Go	s	s	s	s	b	GB Ca II 82
249	BL Harley 3038	1176	E	Yes	nt	s	s	s	s	?	GB BL II 104
250	Bodl. Digby 40	1176	E	Yes	Go	?	s	s	s	b	GB Ox II 83
251	Leiden UB Vulc. 46 [f. 130v]	1176-77	G	Mix	Ca	s	sk	sk	?	s	NL 1 II 88-92
252	Bodl. e Mus. 249 [f. 9v]	1177, c.	E	Yes	Go	?	s	s	s	?	GB Ox II 82
253	Bodl. Bodley 509	1176-78 (1177)	E	Yes	Go	s	s	s	s	?	GB Ox II 80
254	BnF lat. 11700	1179	F	Yes	Go	?	s	?	s	?	F 3 II XXXV
255	BL Lansdowne 381	1168-89 (1179)	G	Yes	nt	s	s	s	s	?	GB BL II 91

No.	Manuscript	Date									Reference
256	Admont SB Cod. 18 [f. 257r]	1180	A	Yes	Mix	s	s	s	s	?	A 7 II 35-38
257	Udine Bibl. Comunale 142	1180	It	Yes	Mix	s	s	s	s	?	It Friulane II [6]
258	BnF lat. 17768	1173-87 (1180)	F	Yes	Go	s	kb	?	s	m	F 3 II XXXIII
259	The Hague KB 76 E 15 [f. 54v]	1178-83 (1180)	B	Yes	Go	s	s	s	s	b	NL 1 II 93-100
260	ÖNB Cod. 340	1181	A	Yes	Mix	s	s	s	s	m	A 1 II 39
261	Cambridge Trinity O. 2. 1 (1105)	1173-89 (1181)	E	Yes	Go	s	sk	s	?	?	GB Ca II 85
262	ÖNB Cod. 363	1180-83 (1181)	A	Yes	Mix	s	sk	?	s	b	A 1 II 38
263	BL Cotton Tiberius E.IV	1181-82	E	Yes	Go	s	s	s	s	?	GB BL II 106
264	BnF lat. 16729	1182	F	Yes	Go	sk	sk	?	s	?	F 3 II XXXVI
265	BnF lat. 10477	1182	F	Yes	Go	s	kb	s	s	?	F 3 II XXXVI
266	BnF lat. 5411	1182, c.	F	Yes	Go	kb	sk	sk	?	s	F 2 II XXI
267	Bodl. Laud misc. 633	1182, c.	G	Yes	Mix	sk	sk	s	sk	b	GB Ox II 85
268	BL Add. 46203	1173-92 (1182)	E	Yes	nt	s	s	s	s	?	GB BL II 99
269	BnF lat. 16943	1183	F	Yes	Go	?	s	s	sk	?	F 3 II XXXVII
270	BnF nouv. acq. lat. 1543	1184, c.	F	Yes	Go	s	s	s	s	b	F 4 II XXVI
271	BL Egerton 2951	1181-87 (1184)	E	Yes	Go	s	s	?	s	?	GB BL II 107
272	Tours BM 344	1185	F	Yes	Go	s	b	s	s	b	F 7 II LI
273	BnF lat. 8898	1180-90 (1185)	F	Yes	Go	s	s	s	?	?	F 3 II XXXV
274	Dijon BM 114	1183-88 (1185)	F	Yes	Go	s	s	kb	s	?	F 6 II XVII
275	Tours BM 308	1186	F	Yes	Go	s	sk	s	s	?	F 7 II LI
276	Bodl. Canon. Liturg. 325	1173-1200 (1186)	G	Yes	Mix	s	?	s		?	GB Ox II 79
277	Auxerre BM 227	1187, c.	F	Yes	Go	s	s	?	?	?	F 6 II XVIII
278	BnF lat. 16528	1188	F	Yes	Go	b	b	b	?	?	F 3 II XXXVIII
279	Auxerre BM 145	1182-97 (1189)	F	Yes	Go	sk	s	s	s	?	F 6 II XVI
280	Cambridge Trinity R. 14. 9 (884)	1188-91 (1189)	E	Yes	Mix	s	sk	s	?	m	GB Ca II 93
281	Leiden UB VLQ 12	1190, c.	F	Yes	Go	s	s	s	s	b	NL 1 II 101
282	BL Royal 7 F.III	1191 or 1192	E	Yes	Go	s	s	s	b	b	GB BL II 109
283*	Oxford Balliol 256	1191, c.	E?								GB Ox II 88
284*	BL Add. 35109	1192	?								GB BL II 110
285	BL Egerton 3031 [f. 13r, not in CMD]	1190-95 (1192)	E	Yes	Go	s	b	b	kb	m	GB BL II 108
286	Bodl. Tanner 169*	1192-93	E	Yes	Go	s	s	?	sk	b	GB Ox II 89
287	Vorau SB Cod. 276 [f. 136v]	1185-1202 (1193)	A	Mix	Ca	s	s	?	s	?	A 7 II 39-40

288	Rome BNC Sess. 2 [f. 352r]	1193?	It	Yes	Mix	b	b	b	b	s	It Roma II 27-28
289	Cambridge Gonville & Caius 427/427	1193-94	E	Yes	Go	s	s	s	s	m	GB Ca II 96
290	Dijon BM 601	1194, c.	F	Yes	Go	s	s	s	?	?	F 6 II XVIII
291	London Lambeth Palace 8	1188-1201 (1194)	E	Yes	Mix	s	b	s	b	b	GB Lond II 17
292	Bodl. Bodley 672	1194?	E	Yes	Go	sk	s	s	s	b	GB Ox II 90
293	BnF lat. 994	1195	F?	Yes	Mix	s	s	s	s	?	F 2 II XXI
294	BnF nouv. acq. lat. 264	1195, c.	F	Yes	Go	s	sk	s	?	?	F 4 II XXVIII
295	BL Add. 40007	1195, c.	E	Yes	Go	b	b	s	b	m	GB BL II 112
296	BnF lat. 17801	1184-1207 (1195)	F?	Yes	Go	sk	sk	sk	s	b	F 3 II XXXVII
297	Cambridge Corpus Christi 339	1192-98 (1195)	E	Yes	Go	sk	sk	s	sk	m	GB Ca II 95
298	Bodl. Barlow 6	1187-1205 (1196)	E	Yes	nt	s	s	s	s	?	GB Ox II 87
299*	Oxford Christ Church fr. 341	1196 or 97	E								GB Ox II 92
300	BnF lat. 11949	1196, c.	F	Yes	Go	s	s	s	s	b	F 3 II XXXIX
301	BnF nouv. acq. lat. 1145	1191-1201 (1196)	F	Yes	Go	s	s	s	?	b	F 4 II XXVII
302	Vorau SB Cod. 33	1197, c.	A	Yes	Mix	b	s	s	sk	?	A 7 II 41
303	BL Harley 1229	1192-1202 (1197)	E	Yes	nt	s	s	s	s	b	GB BL II 111
304	ÖNB Cod. 373	1197-98	A	Yes	Mix	s	s	s	s	m	A 1 II 40
305	Stockholm Statens Historiska Mus. 21288 [f. 31r]	1198, c.	Sw	Yes	Go	s	s	s	?	?	S 2 2-3
306	BL Cotton Claudius E.III [f. 10r]	1198?	E	Yes	Go	?	s	s	s	s	GB BL II 113
307	Bodl. Rawl. C. 819	1199	F	Yes	Go	b	b	b	?	?	GB Ox II 93
308	Udine Bibl. Arcivescovile 75	1199	A	Yes	Go	kb	kb	b	s	b	It Friulane II [7]
309	BnF nouv. acq. lat. 349	1191-1210 (1199)	F	Yes	Go	s	s	s	s	?	F 4 II XXVII
310	Reims BM 248	1200, c.	F	Yes	Go	?	s	s	s	?	F 5 II XVIII
311	Le Mans BM 224	1201, c.	F	Yes	Go	?	kb	s	s	?	F 7 II LIII
312	BnF lat. 2770	1198-1205 (1201)	F	Yes	Go	kb	b	b	s	b	F 2 II XXII
313	BnF lat. 2406	1202	F	Yes	Go	s	s	s	?	b	F 2 II XXIII
314	BL Royal 5 B.XII	1202	E	Yes	Go	?	b	b	b	b	GB BL II 115
315	BnF lat. 2428	1202, c.	F	Yes	Ca	s	s	s	s	?	F 2 II XXIII
316	BnF lat. 1835	1202, c.	F	Yes	Go	s	s	s	s	?	F 2 II XXIV
317	BnF lat. 14853	1202, c.	F	Yes	Go	?	b	s	b	s	F 3 II XXXIX
318	BnF lat. 6191	1200-1203, c. (1202)	F	Yes	Go	?	b	s	s	b	F 2 II XXIV

#	Manuscript	Date									Ref
319	BnF lat. 3549	1198-1207 (1202)	F	Yes	Go	?	s	?	s	b	F 2 II XXII
320	London Lambeth Palace 415	1201-05 (1203)	E	Yes	Go	s	s	s	s	b	GB Lond II 20
321	Fitzwilliam Mus. 24	1204	It	Yes	Go	s	s	s	s	b	GB Ca II 100
322	Bodl. Canon. Misc. 230	1204	It	Mix	Mix	sk	sk	s	s	?	GB Ox II 96
323	Admont SB Cod. 501 [f. 27v]	1205	A	Yes	Go	?	sk	s	?	b	A 7 II 43-44
324	BL Royal 4 D.VII	1195-1214 (1205)	E	Yes	Go	?	b	s	b	?	GB BL II 121
325	BL Add. 16952	1200-11 (1205)	B	Mix	nt	sk	s	?	sk	b	GB BL II 114
326	Admont SB Cod. 184	1202-08 (1205)	A	Yes	nt	s	s	?	s	?	A 7 II 42
327	BL Cotton Faustina A.VIII	1202-07 (1205)	E	Yes	nt	b	b	s	b	?	GB BL II 116
328*	Bodl. Canon. Liturg. 340	1200-16? (1207)	It								GB Ox II 94
329	Bodl. e Mus. 185	1208?	E	Yes	nt	s	s	?	s	?	GB Ox II 97
330	Friulane Mus. arch. naz. CXXXVII	1200-17 (1208)	It	Yes	Go	s	s	s	sk	b	It Friulane II [8]
331	London Victoria Albert 404-1916	1197?-1220 (1209)	E	Yes	nt	s	s	s	s	b	GB Lond II 18
332	BL Add. 17396	1207-12 (1209)	B	Yes	Go	?	s	s	?	b	GB BL II 117
333	Bodl. Add. A. 197	1203-18 (1210)	It	Yes	Mix	s	s	s	s	?	GB Ox II 95
334	London Lambeth Palace 51	1200-21 (1211)	E	Yes	Go	?	b	s	s	s	GB Lond II 19
335	Rouen BM 74 (A. 183)	1203-20 (1211)	F	Yes	Go	?	s	b	b	?	F 7 II LIII
336	BL Cotton Faustina B.VII	1208-15 (1211)	E	Yes	Go	b	b	s	kb	b	GB BL II 118
337	Avranches BM 214	1210-12 (1211)	F	Yes	Go	s	s	s	?	b	F 7 II LIV
338	ÖNB Cod. 1028	1212	A?	Yes	Ca	s	s	?	?	?	A 1 II 41
339	Cambridge Corpus Christi 313	1209-16 (1212)	E	Yes	Go	s	b	?	s	?	GB Ca II 101
340	Stuttgart WLB II 24	1211-13 (1212)	G	Yes	Go	s	s	?	s	?	G 3 16
341	BL Harley 447	1212?	E	Yes	Go	?	b	s	b	b	GB BL II 119
342	BnF lat. 3237	1213	F	Yes	Go	s	s	?	s	b	F 2 II XXV
343	BL Cotton Vespasian A.XXII	1214 or 1215	E	Yes	Go	s	?	s	?	m	GB BL II 120
344	Cambridge Corpus Christi 425 vol. I	1209-23 (1215)	E	Yes	Go	s	s	s	s	b	GB Ca II 102
345	Graz UBi 713 [f. 301v]	1216	A	Yes	Go	s	s	s	s	s	A 6 II 1-2
346	BL Egerton 3661	1216?	A	Yes	Go	s	s	?	?	b	GB BL II 122
347	BL Cotton Faustina B.VII	1217, c.	E	Yes	Go	s	s	s	b	?	GB BL II 124
348	Paris Arsenal 887	1218	F?	Yes	Go	s	s	s	s	b	F 1 II XI
349	BL Add. 17742	1218	F	Yes	Go	b	b	b	b	b	GB BL II 125
350	BnF nouv. acq. lat. 1741	1218, c.	F	Yes	Go	?	s	?	s	b	F 4 II XXIX

351	London Soc. of Antiquaries 59	1214-22 (1218)	E	Yes	nt	s	s	?	s	?	GB Lond II 21
352	BnF lat. 12833	1216-20 (1218)	F	Yes	Go	?	b	?	?	b	F 3 II XL
353	Cambridge Trinity R. 3. 29 (609)	1219	F	Yes	Mix	s	b	s	s	b	GB Ca II 105
354	Bodl. Lat. liturg. f. 1	1219	F	Yes	Go	sk	b	s	s	?	GB Ox II 98
355	Rome BNC Sess. 51 [f. 1r]	1216-26 (1221)	It	Yes	Mix	?	b	s	s	?	It Roma II 35-36
356	Troyes Médiathèque 597	1216-27 (1221)	?	Yes	Go	b	b	b	b	b	F 5 II XX
357	BnF nouv. acq. lat. 605	1218-24 (1221)	F?	Yes	Go	s	s	s	?	b	F 4 II XXIX
358	Troyes Médiathèque 1158	1218-24 (1221)	F	Yes	Go	b	b	s	b	?	F 5 II XX
359	BL Cotton Tiberius B.II	1221-22	E	Yes	Go	?	b	?	?	?	GB BL II 128
360*	Admont SB Cod. 714	1223	It?								A 7 II 45
361	London Lambeth Palace 236	1215-33 (1223)	E	Yes	Go	b	b	s	?	?	GB Lond II 22
362	Tours BM 1	1223-24	It	Yes	Go	b	b	b	b	b	F 7 II LVI
363	Angers BM 7	1225	F?	Yes	Go	b	b	s	b	b	F 7 II LVI
364*	Graz UBi 1703/137	1225	It								A 6 II 3
365	Bodl. Douce 270	1225-26?	E	Yes	nt	s	kb	?	s	b	GB Ox II 99
366	London Gray's Inn 14	1221-31 (1226)	E	Yes	Go	b	b	s	b	?	GB Lond II 23
367	Orléans BM 129 [f. 1r]	1218-38 (1228)	F	Yes	Go	s	b	s	b	?	F 7 II LV

Hi libri hic habent. Liber regum. A geographa .i. u. Ysido
Canones .i. u. xx. omelie. Lib ppfetarum. Glossa psalt. Te
ria de ueri testamto. Passiones aplorum. Passionariu. Apl
aplorum. Pastorat cura. Regula solitarioru. Roman ordo.
Penitentialis. Dialogi .n. uet znouus. Missat snellonis. O
n. breuiat. n. estiuat. Sinonima ysidori. Missat .i. Lec
Gradat .iii. quartu cu sequent. Sequentiarii .iii. Offic
Antaphonar .n. Ymnar .iii. Scoru urte cu omt .i. u. M
n. u. Psalt .n. tertiu cu ymnar. Regula monach. Vit
Prudentius ymnor. Glosse .iii. sup uet znouu testamt.
anat .n. Ius noricoru. Cronica. Priscian maior zmino
Donati .iii. Donat maior zminor cu corrito remigii .i. u.
ritu remigii. Isagoge porphirii cu comtario boetii maio
zminore. Cathegorie aristotilis. F. su. n. Oratius. Stat
Terentii .n. Iuuenalis. Alcim. Maximiad. Homeri.
Virgilii .n. in .iiii. diuisi. Macrobius. Iuuencus. Com
sup Statiu. Aratores .n. Plperi .iii. Sedulii .n. Salusti
Catilinarius .i. u. Psichimachie libri .n. Auiani .n. C
Boetii .n. Seruius sup uirg. Ionarius. Dedlu .u. Lul
Martianus. Albuinus.   Came

The Place of Germany in the Twelfth-Century Renaissance: Books, Scriptoria and Libraries

Rodney Thomson

1. Thomson, 'The Place of Germany in the Twelfth-Century Renaissance'. For the Twelfth-Century Renaissance in general, see the literature at 79 n. 1, above.

In recent years I have been attempting to grapple with the great problem of Germany's place in the Twelfth-Century Renaissance, a problem, as I have suggested elsewhere, not much addressed by modern scholarship, perhaps because it has been taken for granted that Germany lagged behind, followed in the wake of, or did not even try to emulate the achievements associated with the schools of Paris and early 'scholasticism'. According to this school of thought, Germany was 'off the pace', not 'at the cutting edge'. In a recent article I tried to offer some correctives to this view, and to characterize German cultural and intellectual life over the course of the long twelfth century.[1]

In this paper I wish to address what might seem at first sight a simpler and narrower issue; yet it must be clarified and understood before further progress can be made on the larger one. From the late eleventh century Germany – by which I mean the Empire north of the Alps – experienced a prodigious growth in the revival and reform of religious communities and the founding of new ones. A fundamental component of this process was the expansion of ancient libraries and the making of new ones, both tasks

2. Heinzer, *Klosterreform und mittelalterliche Buchkultur in deutschen Südwesten*, 388.

3. See Appendix, pp. 141-4 below.

involving the copying of large – indeed astonishing – numbers of books, to a high standard of workmanship. Scholars in Germany and elsewhere have studied individual instances of this growth in the output of scriptoria and expansion of collections, but no-one, as far as I know, has drawn attention to the impressive scale and character of the phenomenon as a whole. Germany was perhaps in the forefront of the whole of Western Europe in book-production during the twelfth century, both quantitatively and qualitatively. The aim of this paper is to provide a 'panorama' of this production in order to validate these large generalizations, and to encourage further work in the field.

As I have already hinted, the motor was reform of the Church, along monastic or quasi-monastic lines: whether manifested in native movements such as those which radiated from Gorze and Hirsau, or imported like the Augustinian canons, Premonstratensians and Cistercians. Old houses were reformed and new ones founded. New books, for the liturgy and for meditative learnings were necessary in both cases. Networks of communities and individals were formed to facilitate this. With respect to just one of these networks, that which radiated from Hirsau, Felix Heinzer has written: 'Schrift und Buch beanspruchen ... einen hervorragenden Stellenwert'[2], a judgement that could be applied generally. In this movement an important contribution was made by literate, aristocratic women, both as members of self-standing nunneries and of the female community in double houses. No role was played by the emperors and only a little by the cathedrals and less by the lay aristocracy.

The evidence for the phenomenon is abundant in some localities, but overall extremely patchy and problematic. It falls into three categories. First, there are the booklists dating from the 'long' twelfth century (that is, between the late eleventh and early thirteenth centuries): not many overall, only some sixty-one from forty-six centres.[3] They are of different kinds, and very few of them are library-catalogues in the full sense, that is, listing all of a community's books for study and meditation: some are of liturgical books only, some list the donations of a particular individual, others the books used for the monastic or cathedral school. Not all are accessible in modern editions: Austria is fully covered, but only eleven of the forty-odd medieval dioceses of the remainder of the Reich north of the Alps. None of these editions, old or new, includes commentary identifying the titles or matching them with surviving volumes.[4]

Next come the surviving books, in numbers that vary hugely from place to place, the variation bearing almost no relation to the size, importance or longevity of the particular foundation. The need to identify the medieval provenances of as many extant books as possible is paramount for our enquiry, but this is not easily done. Fundamental are the lists in Sigrid Krämer's *Handschriftenerbe des deutschen Mittelalters*, but this was inevitably dependent upon information supplied by other printed material, often of indifferent accuracy.[5] Very many relevant manuscript-collections still do not have up-to-date descriptive catalogues, without which accurate data as to dates, contents and provenance can hardly be collected. In addition, Krämer's definition of 'Germany' does not correspond to any medieval, let alone twelfth-century boundaries, but to those established in 1812.[6] The German part of Switzerland, as well as Austria, are thus omitted from her inquiry.

Finally, there are in-depth studies of individual scriptoria and libraries, of which a number have been published in recent years, but still not many in comparison with all the localities that provide the requisite material.[7] An exception is the Germanic area of Switzerland, completely covered, scriptorium by scriptorium, in Alfons Bruckner's splendid *Scriptoria Medii Aevi Helvetica*.[8]

4. Gottlieb, *Über mittelalterliche Bibliotheken* (henceforward Gottlieb); Becker, *Catalogi Bibliothecarum Antiqui* (henceforward Becker); Gottlieb et al., *Mittelalterliche Bibliothekskataloge Österreichs* (henceforward Bibl. Öst.); Lehmann et al., *Mittelalterliche Bibliothekskataloge Deutschlands und der Schweiz* (henceforward Bibl.), so far covering the southern dioceses of Augsburg, Bamberg, Chur, Eichstätt, Erfurt, Freising, Konstanz, Mainz, Passau, Regensburg and Würzburg; and Derolez and Victor, *Corpus Catalogorum Belgii: The Medieval Booklists of the Southern Low Countries* (henceforward CCB).

5. Krämer, *Handschriftenerbe des deutschen Mittelalters*. See for instance the corrections signalled by Hotchin, 'Women's Reading and Monastic Reform in Twelfth-Century Germany', 152 n. 42 and 158 n. 61. Survival rates of twelfth-century books for some houses in medieval

Bavaria are given by Beach, *Women as Scribes*, 78.

6. Krämer, Vol. 1, ix-x.

7. Apart from those cited below: Bodarwé, *Sanctimoniales litteratae*, though mainly dealing with the tenth and eleventh centuries; Dengler-Schreiber, *Skriptorium und Bibliothek des Klosters Michelsberg in Bamberg*, unaccountably ending her account c. 1150; Glassner and Haidinger, *Die Anfänge der Melker Bibliothek*; Houben, *St Blasianer Handschriften des 11. und 12. Jahrhunderts*; Hoffmann, *Bücher und Urkunden aus Helmarshausen und Corvey*; Krämer, 'Die Bibliothek von Ranshofen im frühen und hohen Mittelalter', (a study is needed of the contents of the thirty-nine surviving twelfth-century books from this Augustinian house); Mazal, 'Die Salzburger Domkapitelbibliothek vom 10. bis zum 12. Jahrhundert'; Pfaff, *Scriptorium und Bibliothek des Klosters Mondsee im hohen Mittelalter*; Wirtgen, *Die Handschriften des Klosters St.*

At first sight, the huge gaps in the evidence would seem to preclude absolutely the construction of a 'panorama', that is, a reasonably complete survey of book-production in twelfth-century Germany. But this is not necessarily so. The key to understanding what the situation really was is the booklists. In a few cases many of the books in them still survive, but in most cases this is not so. This tells us that the fact that a large or medium-sized medieval religious community is represented today by only a handful of books, or none at all, is due to the accidents of post-Reformation history, war and secularization, not because the community had hardly any books in the first instance. This in turn means that we can view the communities with large collections (represented by contemporary booklists, substantial numbers of surviving books, or both), as the norm, and extrapolate from them to assume collections of comparable size in other communities with similar populations and longevity but with few surviving books and no medieval booklists. Thus, we can use a relatively small number of cases to stand as representative of the whole. In what follows I describe such a sample, moving geographically from north to south and east to west, and covering the types of community most involved: reformed Benedictine houses and regular canons, male, female and double, including the 'new orders', above all the Cistercians.

I begin in the north, with the double house of reformed Augustinian canons at Hamersleben in Lower Saxony, founded in 1108, transferred to its present site – for the church still stands – in 1112.[9] It was probably the earliest religious home of Hugh of St. Victor. Although only half-a-dozen twelfth-century books from Hamersleben survive, it must have quickly built up a great library, for ninety-three titles figure in its early thirteenth-century catalogue, and that is only of the schoolbooks.[10] It provides impressive evidence of the depth and breadth of the training of the house's novices. There was no eschewing of dialectic here: the list includes a copy of Abelard's *Logica 'Ingredientibus'* amid a number of dialectical texts. The only surviving book from the list contains the works of Virgil and a collection of 'rhetorica'.

Not far from Hamersleben was the Benedictine nunnery of Lippoldsberg, founded c. 1090, reformed c. 1100 by the archbishop of Mainz who introduced into it the customs of Hirsau.[11] But the communal life at Lippoldsberg was as much shaped by the man who became provost in late 1138, Gunther, a former Augustinian canon at Hamersleben. The surviving library-catalogue from 1151 lists fifty-five volumes,[12] including up-to-date non-German theology represented by works of Anselm, Hugh of St Victor, two 'libri sententiarum' and a good handful of liberal arts texts: Martianus Capella, a commentary on Porphyry's *Isagoge*, Cicero's *De inuentione* and Gerlandus's commentary on Priscian, *De constructionibus* (Fig. 25/Plate 25). Only four books from the catalogue survive, plus another two written locally during the twelfth century, suggesting that the catalogue is incomplete.

This was not the only example of the creative influence of Augustinians, specifically the canons of Hamersleben, on the intellectual life of women's houses in the area. Lamspringe, near Gandersheim, was founded in the ninth century as a collegiate community for women.[13] Between 1119 and 1130 it became a Benedictine nunnery with an Augustinian canon as provost. By the middle of the century in-house copying had begun, and although only the small number of twenty-two twelfth-century manuscripts survive, the Lamspringe scriptorium was sufficiently active and skilled to take in commissions from other houses. Two of its nun-scribes are names to us: Ermengarde and Odelgarde. Gerhard, its provost towards the end of the century, was the brother of Hermann, provost of

Peter und Paul zu Erfurt bis zum Ende des 13. Jahrhunderts; and Wolter-von dem Knesebeck, "'Die Weisheit hat sich ein Haus gebaut.'"

8. Bruckner, *Scriptoria Medii Aevi Helvetica* (henceforward Bruckner).

9. Cohen-Mushlin, *Scriptoria in Medieval Saxony*.

10. Milde, 'Mittelalterliche Bibliothekskataloge als Quellen der Bildungsgeschichte', and Cohen-Mushlin, *Scriptoria in Medieval Saxony*, 219-25.

11. Hotchin, 'Women's Reading and Monastic Reform in Twelfth-Century Germany', 139-89.

12. Becker, No. 88. See also the edition in Hotchin, 'Women's Reading and Monastic Reform', 178-89, with commentary, unfortunately containing many errors of identification.

13. What follows is based upon Wolter-von dem Knesebeck, 'Lamspringe, ein unbekanntes Scriptorium des Hamersleben-Halberstäter

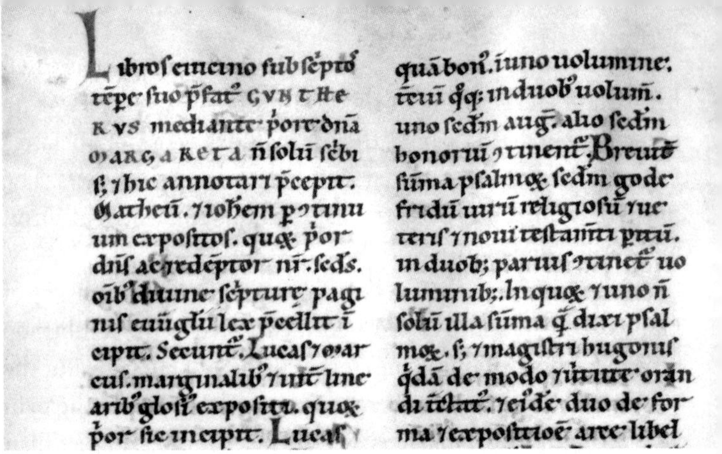

Fig. 25. Marburg, Hessisches Staatsarchiv, MS H77, fol. 12r (detail, enlarged). First leaf of the Lippoldsberg library catalogue.

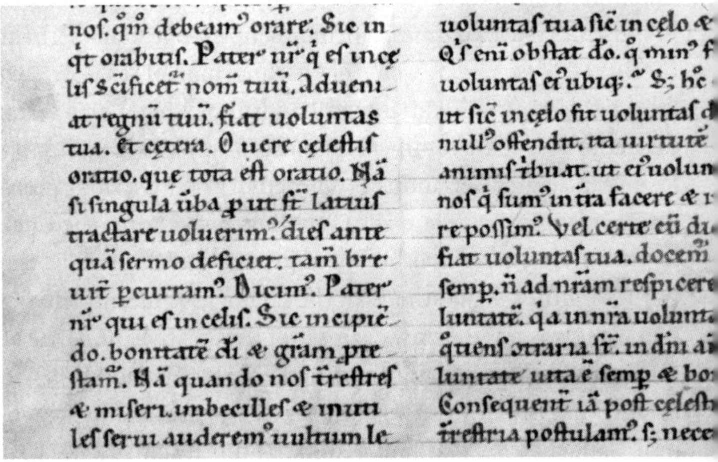

Fig. 26. Wolfenbüttel, Herzog August Bibliothek, Guelf. 204 Helmst., fol. 3v (detail, enlarged), of 1178-91: Lamspringe, script imitative of the Hamersleben style.

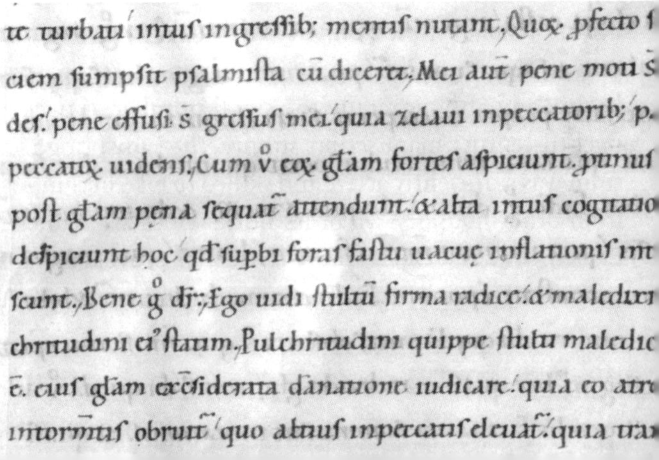

Fig. 27. Munich, Bayerische Staatsbibliothek, MS Clm 22009, fol. 4v (detail, enlarged). The hand of the Wessobrunn anchoress and scribe Diemut, c. 1100-50.

Hamersleben, and it is therefore no accident that the Hamersleben style of script recurs in books copied at Lamspringe in his time (Fig. 26/Plate 26).

Moving south, let us next consider the Augustinian house of Frankenthal near Worms, founded in 1119 by a local noble. Unfortunately, it has left no medieval booklists, and from the twelfth century only twenty-six manuscripts and four fragments.[14] From them, however, can be inferred the active building of a considerable library in which the whole community participated. By exemplary meticulous autopsy of the surviving books Aliza Cohen-Mushlin has identified more than sixty scribes, individually active for periods of between five and twenty-five years, during the second half of the century. Some of these books were written in as many as fourteen hands: this was doubtless for practice, but also because the scribes, being also canons, had to break off copying in order to perform their liturgical duties. By 1148 the scribes were being trained in the cloister, and thereafter a sequence of masters and pupils can be identified. One canon/scribe, John, went to Paris, perhaps to study Canon Law, and stayed there for at least ten years before returning, probably in 1204/5, bringing with him books copied or obtained by him in the interval.

The large Benedictine double house of Zwiefalten, southeast of Stuttgart, was founded from Hirsau in 1089: in 1138 it comprised seventy monks, 130 lay brothers and sixty-two nuns; at least a hundred of its twelfth-century books are known to survive.[15] A significant number of extant books have inscriptions by Ortlieb, local chronicler and librarian, who died 1140. The local necrology names two scribes who were members of the community, one a woman 'conversa' with the name of a noble house (Mahtilt de Nifen): 'Ista multos libros sancte Marie conscripsit'. Noteworthy is the presence among

Reformkreises zur Zeit Heinriches des Löwen'; Hotchin, 'Women's Reading and Monastic Reform', 167-71; Cohen-Mushlin, Scriptoria in Medieval Saxony, 155-70; Härtel, Geschrieben und Gemalt: Gelehrte Bücher aus Frauenhand.

14. What follows is based upon Cohen-Mushlin, A Medieval Scriptorium.

15. Löffler, Die Handschriften des Klosters Zwiefalten and Mews, 'Monastic Educational Culture Revisited'. Most of the manuscripts are in the Stuttgart Landesbibliothek; as publication of more volumes of its modern catalogue progresses more books of Zwiefalten provenance are likely to be identified.

16. Ruf, 'Die Handschriften des Klosters Schäftlarn' and Beach, Women as Scribes, Chapter 3.

17. Beach, Women as Scribes, 104-27.

18. What follows is based upon Beach, Women as Scribes, Chapter 4.

the surviving books of writings of Anselm of Canterbury, of a substantial number of glossed biblical books, and of texts associated with the school of Laon. Nonetheless, the contents and palaeography of the Zwiefalten books have yet to be studied in detail and Matilda's hand identified.

By contrast, Schäftlarn (south-west of Munich), was an ancient foundation, dating from 760, in ruins by 932, restored as a community of secular canons in the late tenth century.[16] Made Premonstratensian by Bishop Otto of Freising in 1140, it was colonised from the double monastery of Ursberg in Swabia. Its library at the beginning of this process was small: forty-seven volumes figure in the catalogue of c. 1150, 'duo uetera matutinalia' suggesting that they included items from a much earlier period. More were added as a gift by the priest Arbo von Hebertshausen c. 1160-62. Many more were added by internal copying, instigated by Prior Henry (1164-1200), as can be recognized from the colophons naming him or specifying a date of production in his time. The total number of surviving twelfth-century Schäftlarn books is a respectable sixty-six. Thirteen of the scribes named themselves, three of them female; Alison Beach has studied the production of these women, Adelheid, Sophia and Irmingart.[17] The sort of errors they made suggests that they were literate, not merely mechanical, copyists. Sophia worked closely with a male scribe, Adalbertus, who headed the scriptorium during the time of Prior Henry.

Not far away is Wessobrunn, another Benedictine foundation of the eighth century, refounded with secular canons until 1065-1110, when Prior Adalbero repopulated the house with monks from Regensburg and stayed on as abbot.[18] About 1138 it gained a women's community and became part of the Hirsau reform; in 1161 Liutold of Hirsau arrived as abbot, bringing with him six of his monks. The community included an *inclusa* named Diemut (d. 1130-50), who between c. 1100 and 1130 copied forty-seven volumes of which fourteen survive (Fig. 27/Plate 27). Some of these were produced in collaboration with two other nuns and the monk Lodevicus. Two lists of the books written by Diemut survive, one contemporary with her, the other from the late twelfth century: it seems that she concentrated on the patristic writings that were fundamental to the book collection in any religious community of the time. The later list occurs at the end of a twelfth-century copy of Sulpicius Severus (Munich, Bayerische Staatsbibliothek, MS Clm 22059); at the front, and in the same hand, occurs another booklist (see Fig. 28/Plate 28 and Fig. 29/Plate 29). It comprises 108 volumes including multiple copies: among them are liturgical books and 'libri scholastici': classical texts, grammar, rhetoric and dialectic. Headed 'Hi libri hic habentur', this list surely represents all of the Wessobrunn books *not* made by Diemut.[19] In other words, the two lists in combination constitute what the library of Wessobrunn held at that date, a total of some 155 volumes. To some extent this figure is corroborated by two later lists of books, one of those that survived a fire in 1221 and another of the whole library c. 1240. Thirty-two twelfth-century Wessobrunn books are still in existence. This is a comparatively respectable total, but comparison with the number of books in the twelfth-century lists makes the point that numbers of surviving books are usually much less than what the booklists show to have originally existed.

Some 275 km to the west, and slightly south, of Wessobrunn is Rheinau in modern-day Switzerland, a ninth-century Benedictine house reformed from Hirsau in the early twelfth. Nearly 200 of its books survive, most of them in the Zürich Zentralbibliothek. Some are older than the house itself, often made elsewhere until the twelfth century, when uniformity of script and decoration indicates the beginnings of a scriptorium.

19. A point missed by the editors of Bibl., 3, 60-2 and by Beach, *Women as Scribes*, 40-2.

Fig. 28. Munich, Bayerische Staatsbibliothek, MS Clm 22059, fol. 1r (detail, enlarged). Wessobrunn library catalogue, s. xii^ex.

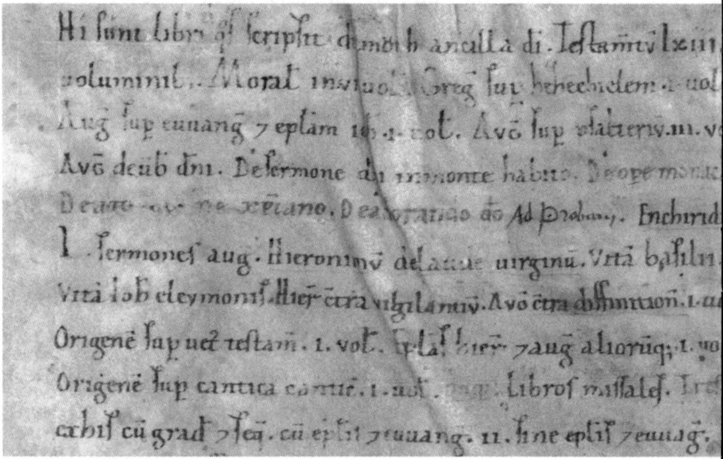

Fig. 29. Munich, Bayerische Staatsbibliothek, MS Clm 22059, fol. 72v (detail, enlarged). Wessobrunn library catalogue, s. xii^ex.

Fig. 30. Admont, Stiftsbibliothek, MS 672, fol. 1v (detail, enlarged). Hugh of St Victor.

A booklist from the late twelfth century lists the work of a single copyist, the monk Rudolf from Zürich: four books for study and meditation, three of them with glosses.[20] It is of interest that the style of the decorated initials in the Rheinau books can be paralleled at other monasteries reformed from Hirsau.[21]

Finally, moving east into central Austria, we encounter, for once in a way, a case of a medieval library that survives almost intact, though without any early catalogues. The great Benedictine house at Admont was founded in 1074 and reformed on the Hirsau pattern after 1115; between 1116 and 1120 a women's community was added.[22] Just over 200 of its twelfth-century manuscripts survive, apparently mostly products of the local scriptorium (Fig. 30/Plate 30 and Fig. 31/Plate 31), though the collection has never been studied intensively or as a whole. As at Schäftlarn and Wessobrunn, so at Admont there is abundant evidence for full participation in book-production by the women's community. The Admont nuns are known to have been for the most part aristocratic, literate and trained in the liberal arts,[23] normally speaking Latin in the cloister, holding their own chapter, occasionally even preaching. The community had its own school, open to external students, in which were taught the basics such as grammar, but also biblical interpretation. Not surprisingly, this activity gained the house a reputation and attracted commissions from elsewhere. In 1162 Archbishop Eberhard of Salzburg presented Abbot Godfrey with copies of correspondence sent or received by the archdiocese since 1119. The monks recopied the letters into a book, adding many of their own. From twelfth-century Admont we can name five female scribes and ten male.[24] By late in the century each community had its own library and librarian, and one female scribe, Adelheit, was remembered in the monastery's necrology. Beach has assigned forty-seven surviv-

20. Bibl., Vol. 1, No. 60.

21. Bruckner, Vol. 4, 45-50 and Heinzer, 'Rheinauer Handschriften und die Hirsauer Reform'. For the 'Hirsau' decorative style Bruckner refers to the plates in Löffler's Romanische Zierbuchstaben und ihre Vorläufer and Schwäbische Buchmalerei in romanischer Zeit.

22. Beach, Women as Scribes, 65-103 and Mews, 'Scholastic Theology'.

23. Beach, 'Voices from a Distant Land' and Lutter, Geschlecht und Wissen, Norm und Praxis, Lesen und Schreiben.

24. Stammberger, 'The Works of Hugh of St Victor at Admont', 235.

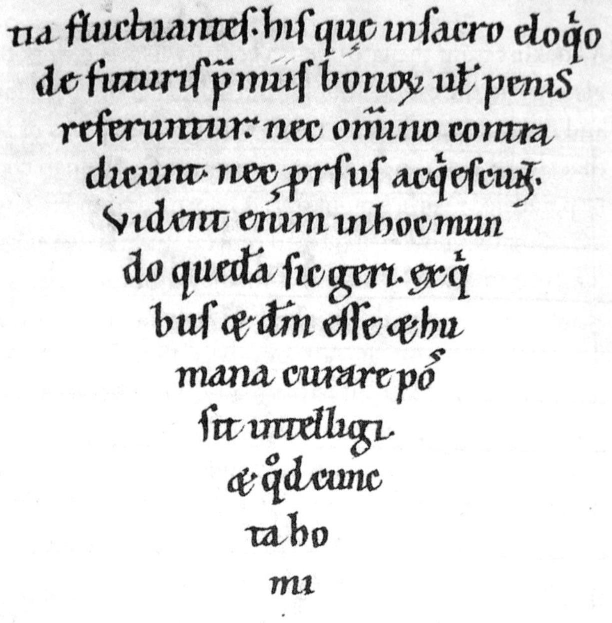

Fig. 31. Admont, Stifts-bibliothek, MS 672, fol. 41r (detail, enlarged). 'Bravura' formatting.

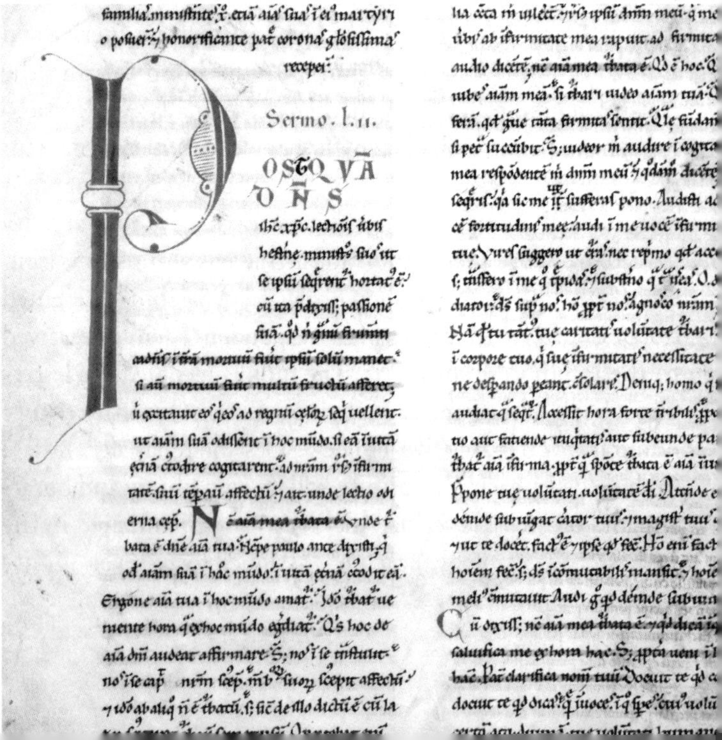

Fig. 32. Oxford, Bodleian Library, MS Laud. misc. 143, fol. 36v (detail, enlarged). A product of the Eberbach scriptorium, s. xii^{ex}.

ing books to the nuns' library. Monks and nuns collaborated in copying, including draft and finished versions of the sermons and biblical commentaries of Abbot Irimbert (1172-76). But the house was also keen to obtain copies of scholastic works written in France. Admont, SB, MS 593, contains Bernard of Clairvaux's *De Gratia et libero arbitrio*, preceded by Gilbert of Poitiers's commentary on Boethius's theological tractates and theological *sententiae* attributed to a Master Peter of Poitiers in a manuscript from (Cistercian) Zwettl. Two other manuscripts written at Admont contain copies of Abelard's *Theologia 'Summi boni'* and Thierry of Chartres's commentary on Boethius' *De trinitate*. The first shares an exemplar with a manuscript from another Cistercian house, Heilbronn, in which Abelard is described as 'master Peter, that most distinguished and learned man, with the nickname of "Adbaiolard".'[25] Another contains a sentence-collection associated with the school of Laon, and the *Sentences* ascribed to Abelard. Of two closely-related and near-contemporary copies of this last text, one was at the Benedictine house of Prüfening before passing to the monastery of St Emmeram at Regensburg, the other at the Augustinian house of St Nikolaus vor Passau. Here we have evidence of 'networking' that actually overrode the boundaries between different religious Orders.

Here, also, two important points converge: that German religious communities were eager to acquire scholastic works written further west, and that very often new or reformed Cistercian houses were prominent in this process. We may take as an example Heiligenkreuz just south of Vienna, founded by Otto of Freising in the 1130s. Heiligenkreuz, SB, MS 153, a locally-made book of the mid twelfth century, contains Abelard's *Theologia 'Scolarium'* and reports of the teaching of Abelard, Hugh of St. Victor and other Paris masters of the 1120s.[26]

25. Erlangen, Universitätsbibliothek, MS 182 and Mews, 'Scholastic Theology', 225 and n. 24.

26. Mews, 'Scholastic Theology', 221 and n. 14.

27. Palmer, *Zisterzienser und ihre Bücher*, Chapter 2 (1136-1221).

28. On the books of another Cistercian foundation, Maulbronn, 44 km north-west of Stuttgart, see Hein-zer, 'Maulbronn und die Buchkultur Südwestdeuts-chlands im 12. und 13. Jahrhundert'.

29. I wish to thank Erik Kwakkel for inviting me to give the first Lieftinck lec-ture, and Nigel Palmer for a critical reading of it.

Further north, not far from Frankfurt, lie the impressive phys-ical remains of Eberbach, founded as an Augustinian house probably soon after 1110/11, Cistercian from 1136 when its pop-ulation was 'seeded' with monks from Clairvaux.[27] About a quarter of its 195 surviving manuscripts were written between c. 1100 and the early thirteenth century, uniformity of script and decoration indicating that for a while there was an active local scriptorium (Fig. 32/Plate 32). But among the books dat-ing from the late twelfth century are, once again, imported items, for instance Bodl. MS Laud. lat. 105, given by a Master Hugo, containing sermons and biblical commentaries by Maurice de Sully, Andrew of St Victor, Peter Lombard, Robert of Melun and a copy of Priscian, written at Paris at various times from the early twelfth century on.[28]

The twelfth century was indeed a transformative period in the history of books and book-collections in Western Europe, no less in the German lands than elsewhere. Drawing together some of the threads of the foregoing discussion, it seems that 'reform' of an individual community was always closely followed by, indeed entailed, a sustained burst of activi-ty in copying books, above all the works of the Fathers but also texts for training in the Liberal Arts; about 100 new books seems to have been the norm, their copying carried out by members of the community who were usually highly trained by a master scribe. As the century wore on, consciousness grew of the works of biblical study and dialectical theology being produced in and around Paris, and these were acquired and copied locally. By c. 1200 there must have been tens of thou-sands of books, copied in religious communities, across the whole of Germany, many times more than there had been a century earlier, and many times more than exist now.[29]

Appendix

Twelfth-Century Booklists from German Religious Communities[29]

Augsburg Cathedral; Bishop Embrico's donation c. 1063-75 (Bibl. 3, No. 2).

Augsburg, St Ulrich and Afra (OSB); donation of Canon Werinher c. 1130 (Bibl. 3, No. 17). Over 600 MSS survive, mostly of s. xv; only half a dozen are from the twelfth century.

Bamberg, Michelsberg (OSB); cat. 1122-23 (Bibl. 3, No. 90); cat. 1172 x 1201 (Bibl. 3, No. 91).

Bamburg Cathedral; cat. 1127 (Bibl. 3, No. 83); cat. c. 1200 (Bibl. 3, No. 86).

Blaubeuren (OSB); cat. 1085-1101 (Becker, No. 74).

Ebersberg (OSB); cat. late s. xii (Bibl. 4, No. 74).

Engelberg (OSB); school-books of Abbot Frowin, 1142 x 1178 (Bibl. 1, No. 10). Bruckner, Vol. 8, 43.

Füssen (OSB); cat. late s. xi (Bibl. 3, No. 31).

Fulda (OSB); cat. s. xii (Becker, No. 128).

Göttweig (OSB); cat. c. 1114 (Bibl. Öst. 1, 8-9); donation of Brother Henry, s. xii (ibid., 9-12).

Hamersleben (OSA); cat. s. xiii[in], school library (ed. Cohen-Mushlin, *Hamersleben*, 219-25).

Heiligenkreuz (OCist.), cat. 1134-37 (Bibl. Öst. 1, 18-21).

Hildesheim, S. Godehard (OSB); gift of Abbot Friedrich 1136-51 (Becker, No. 85).

Hildesheim Cathedral; donation of Canon (later Bishop) Bruno c. 1150:
Urkundenbuch des Hochstifts Hildesheim und seiner Bischöfe, part 1, ed. K. Janicke and H. Hoogeweg (Hannover and Leipzig, 1896), 311-13, No. 324; K. Sudhoff, 'Die medizinischen Schriften, welche Bischof Bruno von Hildesheim 1161 in seiner Bibliothek besass, und die Bedeutung

29. Even the combined resources of Becker, Gottlieb and the more recent repertoria leave gaps, e.g. see below under Hamersleben and Hildesheim Cathedral. It is therefore possible that I have omitted some documents edited in other places, I hope not many.

des Konstantin von Afrika im 12. Jahrhundert', *Archiv für Geschichte der Medizin* 9 (1915-16): 348-56.

Hirsau (OSB); cat. later than 1165 (Becker, No. 100; Gottlieb, No. 84); Mews, 'Monastic educational culture', 185.

Klosterneuburg (OSA); cat. s. xii (*Bibl. Öst.* 1, 91-2); cat. early s. xiii (ibid., 92-5).

Lambach (OSB), two lists of c. 1210 (*Bibl. Öst.* 5. 53-8), the first mainly school-books, the second liturgica and patristica, obviously incomplete.

Liége, St-Laurent (OSB): cat. ascribed to s. xii[1]: J. Gessler, 'La bibliothèque de l'abbaye de Saint-Laurent à Liège au XIIe et XIIIe siècles', *Bulletin de la société des bibliophiles liégeois* 12 (1927): 91-135, at 105-11; CCB 2, 111-14. Cat. of the school library, s. xii: A.-C. Fraeys de Veubeke, 'Un catalogue de bibliothèque scolaire inédit du xiie siècle dans le ms. Bruxelles, B. R. 9384-89', *Scriptorium* 35 (1981): 23-38 and pl. 3; CCB 2. 114-18; cat. of s. xiii[1]: Gessler, 112-32; CCB 2, 118-24.

Lippoldsberg (OSB nuns); cat. 1151 (Becker, No. 88; ed. Hotchin, 178-89).

Lobbes, St Peter's (OSB): additions to the 1049 cat. of the conventual library, to c. 1158-60 (CCB 4., 269-75); catalogue of the school library, 1049, with additions to c. 1158-60 (ibid., 275-83). List of MSS rescued from a fire, s. xii[1] (ibid., 283-4).

Muri (OSB); cat. s. xii (*Bibl.* 1, Nos 40-44). Bruckner 7 (1955), 59-94.

Naumburg (OSB); cat. s. xii (Becker, No. 129).

Niederaltaich (OSB); cat. s. xii (Gottlieb, No. 134).

Oberaltaich (OSB); cat. s. xii[in] (*Bibl.* 4, No. 17).

Obermarchtal (OPrem.); cat. 1190-1224 (*Bibl.* 1, No. 45).

Petershausen (OSB); cat. 1086-1116 (*Bibl.* 1, No. 45).

Pfäfers (OSB); cat. 1155 (*Bibl.* 1, No. 96). Bruckner, Vol. 1, 50-8.

Prüfening (OSB); cat. c. 1150 (*Bibl.* 4, No. 40); Wolfger's books 1165 (*Bibl.* 4, No. 41). Forty-seven twelfth-century books survive.

Rastede (OSB); cat. c. 1150 (Becker, No. 87).

Regensburg, St Emmeram (OSB); donation-list 1162-63 (*Bibl.* 4, No. 28). Sixty-four twelfth-century books survive.

Rheinau (OSB); list of books written by the monk Rudolf, s. xii (Bibl. 1, No. 60).

Salzburg Cathedral; cat. late s. xii and cat. s. xiii (Bibl. Öst. 4, 19-20 and 20-2). The first lists only thirty MSS: 'Isti sunt libri Salzburgensis armarii'. All are patristic, with a preponderance of works of Augustine. The second is headed 'Hic annotauimus libros in camera sancti Roudberti quos Otto diaconus inuenit'. Twenty-nine books are listed, again mainly patristic. There is considerable overlap between the lists.

Salzburg, St Peter (OSB); cat. after 6 June 1164 (Bibl. Öst. 4, 66-72), including 'scolares libri' grouped at the end: there are about forty survivors of more than 200 titles (excluding the liturgica).

St. Lambrecht (OSB); cat. s. xii^2 and cat. c. 1200 (Bibl. Öst. 3, 81-2 and 83-4). The first includes liturgical, library and school-books, the latter two classes a little short of 100 volumes (including copies of Waltharius, Otto of Freising, Gesta anglorum and three glossed books). About ten books from this list survive. The second is library-books only: sixty-four volumes, but ending imperfectly, two leaves having been excised. Lanfranc is in both lists, Anselm in the later one, and three volumes of Rupert of Deutz. The later list includes at least six glossed books; four more survive.

Schäftlarn (OPrem.); cat. mid s. xii (Bibl. 4, No. 103); gift of the priest Arbo von Hebertshausen c. 1160-62 (Bibl. 4, No. 104).

Schaffhausen (OSB); cat. 1083-96 (Bibl. 1, No. 63). There are many surviving books, listed in Bruckner, Vol. 6, 81-119.

Schöntal (OCist.); late s. xii, books of the priest Henry (Bibl. 4, No. 123).

Steinfeld (OSB); cat. s. xii (Becker, No. 98; Gottlieb, No. 194).

Steterburg (OSA, nuns), cat. s. xiii (Becker, No. 124; Gottlieb, No. 195).

Trier Cathedral; cat. s. xi or xii (Becker, No. 76; Gottlieb, No. 206)

Vorau (OSA); list of school-books, mostly 'contulit' by the canon Goppold (but he could be from Seckau). Another list, c. 1200, comprises both liturgical and library-books: twenty-five of the latter, including five glossed books (Bibl. Öst. 3. 97 and 98-9). One book survives from each (in each case the book containing the list).

Weihenstephan (OSB); cat. late s. xi (Bibl. 4, No. 87).

Weingarten (OSB); books written under Abbot Berthold, 1200-1231 (Bibl. 1, No. 74).

Wessobrunn (OSB), late s. xi (Bibl. 3, No. 59); two lists of books written by Diemut, s. xii$^{2/4}$ and s. xii^{ex} (Bibl. 3, Nos 60-1; Beach, *Female Scribes*, 40-2); cat. c. 1180 (Bibl. 3, No. 62), books that survived the fire of 1221 (Bibl. 3, No. 63).

Würzburg Cathedral; bequest of the Scholasticus Iohannes c. 1176-9 (Bibl. 4, No. 130).

Zwettl (OCist.); cat. late s. xii (Bibl. Öst. 1, 510-11).

Bibliography

Ado of Vienne, *Chromicon* (reprint of Paris 1561 edition), Migne, Patrologia Latina, vol. 123, cols. 23-138

Alcuin, *De Orthographia*, ed. S. Bruni (Florence: SISMEL, 1997)

Arlt, W., and S. Rankin, eds., *Stiftsbibliothek Sankt Gallen Codices 484 & 381* (Winterthur: Amadeus, 1996)

Autenrieth, J., D. Geuenich and K. Schmid, eds., *Das Verbrüderungsbuch der Abtei Reichenau*, MGH Libri memoriales et necrologia nova series 1 (Hannover: Hahn'sche Buchhandlung, 1979)

Baesecke, G., *Der Vocabularius Sti Galli in der angelsächsischen Mission* (Halle: Verlag Max Niemeyer, 1933)

Barney, S.A. et al., *Etymologies of Isidore of Seville* (Cambridge: Cambridge University Press, 2006)

Bayless, M., 'Alcuin's Disputatio Pippini and the Early Medieval Riddle Tradition', in G. Halsall, ed., *Humour, History and Politics in Late Antiquity and the Early Middle Ages* (Cambridge: Cambridge University Press, 2002), 157-78

Beach, A., 'Voices from a Distant Land: Fragments of a Twelfth-Century Nuns' Letter Collection', *Speculum* 77 (2002): 34-54

—, *Women as Scribes: Book Production and Monastic Reform in Twelfth-Century Bavaria*, Cambridge Studies in Palaeography and Codicology 10 (Cambridge: Cambridge University Press, 2004)

Becker, G.H., *Catalogi Bibliothecarum Antiqui* (Bonn: Max Cohen, 1885; repr. Hildesheim: Georg Olms Verlag, 1973)

Bede, *De temporum ratione*, ed. C. Jones, *Bedae opera didascalica*, Corpus Christianorum, Series Latina 123B (Turnhout: Brepols, 1977)

Béjoint, H., *The Lexicography of English from Origins to Present* (Oxford: Oxford University Press, 2010)

Benediktson, D.T., 'Voces animantium', *Mnemosyne* 53 (2000): 71-9

Benson, R.L., and G. Constable, eds., *Renaissance and Renewal in the Twelfth Century*, Medieval Academy Reprints for Teaching (Toronto: Toronto University Press, 1991)

Bischoff, B., *Aratea: Kommentar zum Aratus des Germanicus MS. Voss lat Q. 79* (Luzern: Faksimile Verlag, 1989)

—, *Latin Palaeography: Antiquity and the Middle ages*, trans. D. Ganz and D. Ó Cróinín (Cambridge; New York: Cambridge University Press, 1990)

—, *Paläographie des römischen Altertums und des abendländischen Mittelalters*, 2nd edn., Grundlagen der Germanistik 24 (Berlin: Erich Schmidt Verlag, 1986)

— et al., *The Épinal, Erfurt, Werden and Corpus Glossaries (Épinal Bibliothèque Municipale 72(2), Erfurt, Wissenschaftliche Bibliothek Amplonianus 2°42, Düsseldorf, Universitätsbibliothek Fragm. K 119:Z 9/1; Munich, Bayerische Staatsbibliothek cgm 187. III (e.4), Cambridge, Corpus Christi College 144*, Early English Manuscripts in Facsimile 22 (Copenhagen: Rosenkilde and Bagger, 1988)

Bishop, T.A.M., 'The Prototype of Liber glossarum', in M.B. Parkes and A.G. Watson, eds., *Medieval Scribes, Manuscripts and Libraries* (London: Scolar Press, 1978), 69-86

Bodarwé, K., *Sanctimoniales litteratae: Schriftlichkeit und Bildung in den ottonischen Frauenkommunitäten Gandersheim, Essen und Quedlinburg* (Münster: Aschendorff, 2004)

Bremmer Jr, R.H., 'Leiden, Universiteitsbibliotheek, Vossianus Latinus Q. 69 (Part 2): Schoolbook or Proto-Encyclopaedic Miscellany?' in R.H. Bremmer Jr and K. Dekker, eds., *Practice in Learning: The Transfer of Encyclopaedic Knowledge in the Early Middle Ages*, Mediaevalia Groningana New Series 16 (Paris, Leuven and Walpole MA: Peeters, 2010), 19-54

—, and K. Dekker, eds., *Foundations of Learning: The Transfer of Encyclopaedic Knowledge in the Early Middle Ages*, Mediaevalia Groningana New Series 9 (Paris, Leuven and Dudley MA: Peeters, 2007)

—, *Anglo-Saxon Manuscripts in Microfiche Facsimile: Vol. 13, Manuscripts in the Low Countries*, Medieval and Renaissance Texts and Studies 321 (Tempe, AZ: Arizona Center for Medieval and Renaissance Studies, 2006)

—, *Practice in Learning: The Transfer of Encyclopaedic Knowledge in the Early Middle Ages*, Mediaevalia Groningana New Series 16 (Paris, Leuven and Walpole MA: Peeters, 2010)

Brett, M., 'Theodore and Latin Canon Law', in M. Lapidge, ed., *Archbishop Theodore: Commemorative Studies on his Life and Influence*, Cambridge Studies in Anglo-Saxon England 11 (Cambridge: Cambridge University Press, 1995): 120-40

Bruckner, A., *Scriptoria Medii Aevi Helvetica*, 14 vols. (Geneva: Roto-Sadag, 1935-78)

Brown, M., *A Guide to Western Historical Scripts from Antiquity to 1600* (London: British Library, 2002)

Burgers, J.J.W., *De paleografie van documentaire bronnen in Holland en Zeeland in de dertiende eeuw*, 3 vols. (Leuven: Peeters, 1995)

Burgess, R.W., 'Jerome Explained: An Introduction to his Chronicle and a Guide to its Use', *Ancient History Bulletin* 16 (2002): 1-32

—, *Studies in Eusebian and Post-Eusebian Chronography*, Historia Einzelschriften 135 (Stuttgart: Franz Steiner, 1999): 90-8

Butzer, P.L., and D. Lohrmann, eds., *Science in Western and Eastern Civilization in Carolingian Times* (Basle: Birkhäuser Verlag, 1993)

Butzman, H., *Corpus Agrimensorum Romanorum, Codex Arcerianus A der Herzog August Bibliothek zu Wolfenbüttel (Cod. Guelf. 36.23.A)* (Leiden: Sijthoff, 1970)

Caillet, J.P., 'Caractères et statut du livre d'apparat carolingien: origines et affirmation', in J.P. Caillet and M.P. Laffitte, eds., *Les manuscrits carolingiens: Actes du colloque de Paris. BnF, le 4 mai 2007*, Bibliologia 27 (Turnhout: Brepols, 2009), 1-43

Cassiodorus, *De Orthographia*, ed. P. Stoppacci, *De orthographia: tradizione, manoscritta, fortuna, edizione critica* (Florence: SISMEL, 2010)

Cohen-Mushlin, A., *A Medieval Scriptorium: Sancta Maria Magdalena de Frankendal* (Wiesbaden: Harrassowitz, 1990)

—, *Scriptoria in Medieval Saxony: St Pancras in Hamersleben* (Wiesbaden: Harrassowitz, 2004)

Daly, L.W., *Contributions to a History of Alphabetization in Antiquity and the Middle Ages*, Collection Latomus 90 (Brussels: Latomus, 1967)

Damian-Grint, P., *The New Historians of the Twelfth-Century Renaissance: Inventing Vernacular Authority* (Woodbridge: Boydell and Brewer, 1999)

Declercq, G., ed., *Early Medieval Palimpsests*, Bibliologia 26 (Turnhout: Brepols, 2007)

Demollière, C.J., ed., *L'art du chantre carolingien* (Metz: Editions Serpenoise, 2004)

Dengler-Schreiber, K., *Skriptorium und Bibliothek des Klosters Michelsberg in Bamberg*, 2nd edn. (Graz: Akademische Druck-u. Verlagsanstalt, 1979)

Derolez, A., and B. Victor, *Corpus Catalogorum Belgii: The Medieval Booklists of the Southern Low Countries*, 7 vols. (Brussels, 1966-1997; new edn. of vol. 1, 1997)

Derolez, A., 'Observations on the Aesthetics of the Gothic Manuscript', *Scriptorium: International Review of Manuscript Studies* 50 (1996): 3-12

—, *The Palaeography of Gothic Manuscript Books from the Twelfth to the Early Sixteenth Century*, Cambridge Studies in Palaeography and Codicology 9 (Cambridge: Cambridge University Press, 2003)

—, 'Anglo-Saxon Glossography', in R. Derolez, ed., *Anglo-Saxon Glossography* (Brussels: Koninklijke Academie voor Wetenschappen, Letteren en Schone Kunsten, 1992), 9-42

Dickey, E., *Ancient Greek Scholarship: A Guide to Finding, Reading and Understanding Scholia, Commentaries, Lexica, and Grammatical Treatises, from their Beginnings to the Byzantine Period* (Oxford: Oxford University Press, 2007)

Dilke, O.A.W., *The Roman Land Surveyors: An Introduction to the Agrimensores* (Newton Abbot: David and Charles, 1971)

Dionisotti, A.C., 'Greek Grammars and Dictionaries in Carolingian

Europe', in M.W. Herren, ed., *The Sacred Nectar of the Greeks: The Study of Greek in the West in the Early Middle Ages* (London: King's College London, 1988), 1-56

—, 'On the Nature and Transmission of Latin glossaries', in J. Hamesse, ed., *Les manuscrits des lexiques et glossaires de l'antiquité tardive à la fin du moyen âge*, Textes et études du moyen âge 4 (Louvain-la-Neuve, 1996), 205-52

Disputatio regalis et nobilissimi iuvenis Pippini cum Albino scholastico, ed. L.W. Daly and W. Suchier, *Altercatio Hadriani Augusti et Epicteti philosophi* (Urbana: University of Illinois Press, 1939)

Doody, A., *Pliny's Encyclopaedia: The Reception of the Natural History* (Cambridge: Cambridge University Press, 2010)

Duchesne, L., *Le Liber pontificalis*, 2 vols. (Paris: Ernest Thorin, 1886-92)

Dutton, P., *Carolingian Civilization*, 2nd edn. (Peterborough, Ont.: Broadview Press, 2004), 139-46

Eastwood, B., and G. Grasshoff, *Planetary Diagrams for Roman Astronomy in Medieval Europe, ca. 800-1500*, Transactions of the American Philosophical Society Vol. 94, Part 3 (Philadelphia: American Philosophical Society, 2004)

—, *Ordering the Heavens: Roman Astronomy and Cosmology in the Carolingian Renaissance* (Leiden: Brill, 2007)

—, *The Revival of Planetary Astronomy in Carolingian and Post Carolingian Europe* (Aldershot: Ashgate, 2002)

Elm, K., ed., *Literarische Formen des Mittelalters: Florilegia, Kompilationen, Kollektionen*, Wolfenbütteler Mittelalter-Studien 15 (Wiesbaden: Harrassowitz in Kommission der Herzog August Bibliothek, 2000)

Erhart, P., and J.K. Kuratli-Hüeblin, eds., *Bücher des Lebens – Lebendige Bücher* (St Gallen: Stiftsarchiv St Gallen, 2010)

Eucherius, ed. K. Wotke, 'Glossae spiritales secundum Eucherium episcopum', *Sitzungsberichte der phil.-hist. Klasse der kaiserlichen Akademie der Wissenschaften* (Wien) 115 (1888): 425-39

Eusebius-Jerome, *Chronicon*, ed. R. Helm, *Eusebius-Werke*, Vol. 7: *Die griechis-*

chen-christlichen Schriftsteller der ersten Jahrhunderten 70, 2nd edn. (Berlin: Kommission für Spätantike Religionsgeschichte der Deutschen Akademie der Wissenschaften zu Berlin, 1956)

Euw, A. von, ed., *Liber viventium Fabariensis: Das karolingische Memorialbuch von Pfäfers in seiner liturgie- und kunstgeschichtlichen Bedeutung*, Studia Fabariensia 1 (Bern and Stuttgart: Franke Verlag, 1989)

Finch, C.E., 'Suetonius's Catalogue of Animal Sounds in Vat. lat. 6018', *The American Journal of Philology* 90 (1969): 459-63

Fotheringham, J.K., ed., *The Bodleian Manuscript of Jerome's Version of the Chronicle of Eusebius, Reproduced in Collotype* (Oxford: Oxford University Press, 1905)

Freculph, *Chronicon*, ed. M. Allen, *Frecvlfi Lexoviensis episcopi opera omnia*, Corpus Christianorum, Continuatio Medievalis 169 (Turnhout: Brepols, 2003)

Ganz, D., 'Book Production in the Carolingian Empire and the Spread of Carolingian Minuscule', in McKitterick, ed., *The New Cambridge Medieval History Vol. 2: c. 700-c. 900* (Cambridge: Cambridge University Press, 1995), 786-808

—, 'The "Liber Glossarum": A Carolingian Encyclopaedia', in P.L. Butzer and D. Lohrmann, eds., *Science in Western and Eastern Civilization in Carolingian Times* (Basle: Birkhäuser Verlag, 1993), 127-38

—, 'The Preconditions for Caroline Minuscule', *Viator* 18 (1987): 23-44

Gatti, P., *Synonima Ciceronis*, Lexicographica 2 (Genoa: Università di Genova, 1993)

—, *Un glossario bernense* (Bern, Burgerbibliothek, A. 91 [18]), Labarinti 55 (Trento: Università degli Studi di Trento, 2001)

Geertman, H., 'La genesi del *Liber Pontificalis romano*: un processo de organizzazione della memoria', in F. Bougard and M. Sot, eds., *Liber, gesta, histoire: Écrire l'histoire des évêques et des papes de l'Antiquité au XXI siècle*, (Turnhout: Brepols 2009), 37-108

Gerritsen, W., *Het alphabet als zoekinstrument: Een beschouwing over de* geschiedenis van de alfabetische index, Scaliger-Lezingen 2 (Leiden: Primavera Pers, 2006)

Geuenich, D., 'A Survey of the Early Medieval Confraternity Books from the Continent', in D. Rollason et al., eds., The Durham Liber Vitae and its Context (Woodbridge: Boydell & Brewer, 2004), 151-8

Glassner, C., and A. Haidinger, Die Anfänge der Melker Bibliothek (Melk, Austria: Stift Melk, 1996)

Goetz, G., ed., Corpus glossariorum latinorum, 7 vols. (Leipzig: Teubner, 1888-1923)

Gottlieb, T., Über mittelalterliche Bibliotheken (Leipzig: Harrassowitz, 1890; repr. Graz: Akademische Druck-u. Verlagsanstalt, 1955)

— et al., Mittelalterliche Bibliothekskataloge Österreichs, 6 vols. (Cologne, Vienna and Graz: Böhlau, 1915-70)

Grafton, A., Joseph Scaliger: A Study in the History of Classical Scholarship. 2. Historical Chronology (Oxford: Oxford University Press, 1993)

—, and M. Williams, Christianity and the Transformation of the Book: Origen, Eusebius, and the Library of Caesarea (Cambridge, MA: Harvard University Press, 2006)

Grand, G., ed., Les manuscrits datés: Premier bilan et perspectives. Die datierten Handschriften: Erster Bilanz und Perspectiven. Neuchâtel/Neuenburg 1983, Rubricae 2 (Paris: CEMI, 1985)

Griffiths, A., 'The Leiden Glosses on the Regula S. Benedicti in Leiden, Vossianus Lat. Q. 69: A Systematic Sifting, Old and New', in R.H. Bremmer Jr and K. Dekker, eds., Practice in Learning: The Transfer of Encyclopaedic Knowledge in the Early Middle Ages, Mediaevalia Groningana New Series 16 (Paris, Leuven and Walpole MA: Peeters, 2010), 55-83

Gumbert, J.P., and M.J.M. de Haan, eds., Essays Presented to G.I. Lieftinck, Litterae textuales, 4 vols. (Amsterdam: A.L. van Gendt, 1972-76)

Härtel, H., Geschrieben und Gemalt: Gelehrte Bücher aus Frauenhand: Eine Klosterbibliothek sächsischer Benediktinerinnen des 12. Jahrhunderts, Ausstellungskataloge der Herzog August Bibliothek 86 (Wiesbaden: Harrassowitz, 2006)

Haskins, C.H., *The Renaissance of the Twelfth Century* (Cambridge, MA: Harvard University Press, 1927)

Heinzer, F., *Klosterreform und mittelalterliche Buchkultur in deutschen Südwesten* (Leiden: Brill, 2008)

—, 'Maulbronn und die Buchkultur Südwestdeutschlands im 12. und 13. Jahrhundert', in Heinzer, *Klosterreform und mittelalterliche Buchkultur in deutschen Südwesten* (Leiden and Boston: Brill, 2008), 409-36

—, 'Rheinauer Handschriften und die Hirsauer Reform', in Heinzer, *Klosterreform und mittelalterliche Buchkultur in deutschen Südwesten* (Leiden and Boston: Brill, 2008), 386-405

Henderson, J., *The Medieval World of Isidore of Seville: Truth from Words* (Cambridge: Cambridge University Press, 2007)

Hessels, J.M., *An Eighth-Century Latin-Anglo-Saxon Glossary Preserved in the Library of Corpus Christi College, Cambridge* (Cambridge: Cambridge University Press, 1890)

—, ed., *An Eighth-Century Latin-Anglo Saxon Glossary Preserved in the Library of Corpus Christi College Cambridge* (Cambridge: Cambridge University Press, 1890)

Heyse, E., *Hrabanus Maurus Enzyklopädie De rerum naturis: Untersuchungen zu den Quellen und zur Methode der Kompilation* (Munich: Arbeo Gesellschaft, 1969)

Hoffmann, H., *Bücher und Urkunden aus Helmarshausen und Corvey* (Hannover: Hahn, 1992)

Holtz, L., *Donat et la tradition de l'enseignement grammatical: Etude sur l'Ars Donati et sa diffusion (IVe-IXe siècle) et édition critique* (Paris: CNRS Institut de Recherche et d'Histoire des Textes, 1981)

Hotchin, J., 'Women's Reading and Monastic Reform in Twelfth-Century Germany: The Library of the Nuns of Lippoldsberg', in A. Beach, ed., *Manuscripts and Monastic Culture: Reform and Renewal in Twelfth-Century Germany* (Turnhout: Brepols, 2007), 139-90

Houben, H., *St Blasianer Handschriften des 11. und 12. Jahrhunderts: unter beson-*

derer Berücksichtigung der Ochsenhausener Klosterbibliothek (Munich:
Arbeo-Gesellschaft, 1979)

Hüllen, W., English Dictionaries 900-1700: The Topical Tradition (Oxford:
Oxford University Press, 1999)

Inglebert, H., Les romains chrétiens face à l'histoire de Rome: histoire, christian-
isme et romanités en occident dans l'antiquité tardive (IIIe-Ve siècles) (Paris:
Institut d'études augustiniennes, 1996)

Isidore, Etymologiae, ed. W.M. Lindsay, Isidori Hispalensis episcopi
Etymologiarum sive originum libri XX (Oxford: Oxford University Press,
1911); English translation Stephen A. Barney et al, Etymologies of
Isidore of Seville (Cambridge: Cambridge University Press, 2006)

Jaeger, C.S., 'Pessimism in the Twelfth-Century "Renaissance"', Speculum:
78 (2003): 1151-83

Kamesar, A., Jerome, Greek Scholarship and the Hebrew Bible (Oxford: Oxford
University Press, 1993)

Ker, N.R., Catalogue of Manuscripts Containing Anglo-Saxon (Oxford:
Clarendon Press, 1957; repr. 1990)

—, English Manuscripts in the Century After the Norman Conquest (Oxford:
Oxford University Press, 1960)

Kelly, C., 'Past Imperfect: The Formation of Christian Identity in Late
Antiquity', in T. Minamikawa, ed., Material Culture, Mentality and
Historical Identity in the Ancient World: Understanding the Celts, Greeks,
Romans and the Modern Europeans (Kyoto: Kyoto University, 2004), 55-64

—, 'The Shape of the Past: Eusebius of Caesarea and Old Testament history', in C. Kelly, R. Flower and M. Williams, eds., Unclassical Traditions:
1. Alternatives to the Classical Past in Late Antiquity, Cambridge Classical
Journal: Proceedings of the Cambridge Philological Society,
Supplementary 34 (Cambridge: the Cambridge Philological Society,
2010), 13-27

Koningsveld, P.S. van, 'The Latin-Arabic Glossary of the Leiden University Library: A Contribution to the Study of Mozarabic Manuscripts and Literature', unpublished Ph.D. dissertation, University of Leiden (1976)

Kramer, J., *Glossaria bilingua in papyrus et membranis reperta* (Bonn: Habelt, 1983)

Krämer, S., 'Die Bibliothek von Ranshofen im frühen und hohen Mittelalter', in P.F. Ganz, ed., *The Role of the Book in Medieval Culture*, 2 vols. (Turnhout: Brepols, 1986), 41-72

—, *Handschriftenerbe des deutschen Mittelalters*, 3 vols. (Beck'sche Verlag: Munich, 1989-90)

Lagarde, P. de, C. Morin and M. Adriaen, eds., *S. Hieronymi presbyteri opera, Pars 1: Opera exegetica 1, Hebraicae quaestiones in libro Geneseos; Liber interpretationis hebraicorum nominum, Commentarioli in Psalmos; Commentarius in Ecclesiasten*, Corpus Christianorum, Series Latina 72 (Turnhout: Brepols, 1959)

Lagorio, V., 'Three More Vatican Manuscripts of Suetonius's Catalogue of Animal Sounds', *Scriptorium* 35 (1981): 59-62

Lapidge, M., 'Old English Glossography: The Latin Context', in M. Lapidge, ed., *Anglo-Latin Literature, 600-899* (London: Hambledon, 1996), 169-81

—, 'The School of Theodore and Hadrian', *Anglo-Saxon England* 15 (1986): 45-72

Law, V., *Grammar and Grammarians in the Early Middle Ages* (London: Longman, 1997)

Lehmann, P. et al., *Mittelalterliche Bibliothekskataloge Deutschlands und der Schweiz*, 4 vols. (Munich: Beck'sche Verlag, 1918-1977)

Lemerle, P., *Byzantine Humanism: The First Phase. Notes and Remarks on Education and Culture in Byzantium from its Origins to the 10th century*, trans. H. Lindsay and A. Moffatt (Canberra: Australian Association for Byzantine Studies, 1986)

Lieftinck, G.I., *De Middelnederlandsche Tauler-handschriften* (Groningen: Wolters, 1936)

—, 'Het oudste schrift uit de abdij van Egmond', in A. Beekman, ed., *Tien eeuwen Egmond: Ontstaan, bloei en ondergang van de voormalige regale abdij van Egmond* (Heemstede, 1950), 110-17

—, *Bisschop Bernold (1027-1054) en zijn geschenken aan de Utrechtse kerken* (Groningen: J.B. Wolters, 1948)

—, *Codicum in finibus Belgarum ante annum 1550 conscriptorum qui in Bibliotheca Universitatis asservantur Pars I: Codices 168-360 Societatis cui nomen Maatschappij der Nederlandsche letterkunde, Bibliotheca Universitatis Leidensis, Codices manuscripti 5* (Leiden: Brill, 1948)

—, 'Het evangeliarium van Egmond', in *Huldeboek Pater Dr. Bonaventura Kruitwagen O.F.M.* [...] (The Hague: Martinus Nijhoff, 1949), 261-75

—, 'Het oudste schrift uit de abdij van Egmond', in A. Beekman, ed., *Tien eeuwen Egmond: Ontstaan, bloei en ondergang van de voormalige regale abdij van Egmond* (Heemstede, 1950), 110-7

—, 'Drie handschriften uit de librije van de abdij van Sint Bernards opt Schelt (Brussel K.B. 19545, 19546 en Kon. Ned. Akad. v. Wetensch. XXIV)', *Tijdschrift voor Nederlandse Taal- en Letterkunde* 69 (1952): 1-30

—, *De librijen en scriptoria der Westvlaamse Cisterciënser-abdijen Ter Duinen en Ter Doest in de 12ᵉ en 13ᵉ eeuw en de betrekkingen tot het atelier van de kapittelschool van Sint Donatiaan te Brugge, Mededelingen van de Koninklijke Vlaamse Academie voor Wetenschappen, Letteren en Schone Kunsten van België, Klasse der letteren 15, No. 2* (Brussels: Paleis der Academiën, 1953)

—, '"Methodologische" en paleographische opmerkingen naar aanleiding van een hert met een wit voetje', *Tijdschrift voor Nederlandse Taal- en Letterkunde* 72 (1954): 1-17

—, 'Middelnederlandse handschriften uit beide Limburgen: Vondsten en ontdekkingen – Het Lutgart-handschrift', *Tijdschrift voor Nederlandse Taal- en Letterkunde* 72 (1954): 184-200

—, 'Pour une nomenclature de l'écriture livresque de la période dite goth-ique: Essai s'appliquant spécialement aux manuscrits originaires des Pays-Bas médiévaux', in B. Bischoff, G.I. Lieftinck and G. Battelli, eds., *Nomenclature des écritures livresques du XIe au XVIe siècle* (Paris: Centre National de la Recherche Scientifique, 1954), 15-34

—, 'Le ms. d'Aulu-Gelle à Leeuwarden executé à Fulda en 836 (Leeuwarden, Bibl. Prov. de Frise, ms. B.A.Fr. 55)', *Bullettino dell' 'Archivio Paleografico Italiano'* N.S. 1 (1955): 11-17

—, 'The "Psalterium Hebraycum" from St Augustine's Canterbury Rediscovered in the Scaliger bequest at Leyden', *Transactions of the Cambridge Bibliographical Society* 2 (1955): 97-104

—, *Problemen met betrekking tot het Zutphens-Groningse Maerlant-handschrift*, Mededelingen der Koninklijke Nederlandse Akademie van Wetenschappen, Afd. Letterkunde, N.R. 22 (1959), No. 2

—, *Servii Grammatici in Vergilii carmina commentarii: Codex Leidensis B.P.L. 52*, Umbrae codicum occidentalium 1 (Amsterdam: North-Holland Publishing Company, 1960)

—, 'Medieval Manuscripts with "Imposed' Sheets"', *Het Boek* 34 (1961): 210-20

—, *Manuscrits datés conservés dans les Pays-Bas [...] Tome premier: Les manuscrits d'origine étrangère (816-c. 1550)*, 2 vols. (Amsterdam: North-Holland Publishing Company, 1964)

—, 'Pleidooi voor de philologie in de oude en eerbiedwaardige ruime betekenis van het woord', *Tijdschrift voor Nederlandse Taal- en Letterkunde* 81 (1965): 58-84

—, *Boekverluchters uit de omgeving van Maria van Bourgondië, c. 1475 – c. 1485*, Verhandelingen van de Koninklijke Vlaamse Academie voor Wetenschappen, Letteren en Schone Kunsten van België, Klasse der letteren 31, No. 66 (Brussels: Paleis der Academiën, 1969)

Lindsay, W.M., *Sexti Pompeii Festi De verborum significatu quae supersunt cum Pauli Epitome* (Leipzig: Teubner, 1913)

—, *The Corpus, Épinal, Erfurt and Leiden Glossaries* (London and New York: Oxford University Press for the Philological Society, 1921)

—, ed., *Glossaria latina*, 5 vols. (Paris: Les Belles Lettres, 1926-31)

—, 'Note on the Use of Glossaries for the Dictionary of Medieval Latin', in

W.M. Lindsay, *Studies in Early Medieval Latin Glossaries*, ed. M. Lapidge
(Aldershot: Ashgate, 1996)

—, *Studies in Early Medieval Latin Glossaries*, ed. M. Lapidge (Aldershot:
Ashgate, 1996)

Löffler, K., *Die Handschriften des Klosters Zwiefalten*, Archiv für Bibliographie,
Buch- und Bibliothekswesen 6 (Linz: Winkler, 1931)

—, *Romanische Zierbuchstaben und ihre Vorläufer* (Stuttgart: Matthaes, 1927)

—, *Schwäbische Buchmalerei in romanischer Zeit* (Augsburg: B. Filser, 1928)

Lowe, E.A., 'Some Facts About Our Oldest Latin Manuscripts', *Classical
Quarterly* 19 (1925): 197-208

—, 'More Facts About Our Oldest Latin Manuscripts', *Classical Quarterly* 22
(1928): 43-62

—, *Codices Latini Antiquiores*, 12 vols. (Oxford: Oxford University Press, 1935-1972)

—, *Palaeographical Papers*, ed. L. Bieler, 2 vols. (Oxford: Oxford University
Press, 1972)

Luscombe, D., 'Thought and Learning', in D. Luscombe and J. Riley-Smith,
eds., *The New Cambridge Medieval History Volume iv: c. 1024-c. 1198 Part
1* (Cambridge: Cambridge University Press, 2004), 461-98

Lutter, M.C., *Geschlecht und Wissen, Norm und Praxis, Lesen und Schreiben:
Monastische Reformgemeinschaften im 12. Jahrhundert* (Vienna:
Oldenbourg, 2005)

Mandolfo, C., ed., *Eucherii Lugdunensis, Formulae Spiritalis intelligentiae,
Instructionum libri duo*, Corpus Christianorum, Series Latina 66
(Turnhout: Brepols, 2004)

Marcovich, M., 'Voces animantium and Suetonius', *Ziva Antika: Antiquité
vivante* 21 (1971): 399-416

Martin, H.J., and J. Vezin, eds., *Mise en page et mise en texte du livre manuscrit*
(Paris: Éditions du Cercle de la librairie – Promodis, 1990)

Mazal, O., 'Die Salzburger Domkapitelbibliothek vom 10. bis zum 12.
Jahrhundert', in G. Silagi, ed., *Paläographie 1981* (Munich: Arbeo-
Gesellschaft, 1982), 71-91

McGurk, P., *Latin Gospel Books from A.D. 400 to A.D. 800*, Les Publications de
  Scriptorium 5 (Anvers and Amsterdam: Editions 'Erasme'; Paris and
  Bruxelles: Standaard-Boekhandel, 1961)

McKitterick, R., 'Knowledge of Canon Law in the Frankish Kingdoms
  before 789', *Journal of Theological Studies*, N.S. 36/1 (1985): 97-117

—, *The Carolingians and the Written Word* (Cambridge: Cambridge University
  Press, 1989)

—, ed., *The Uses of Literacy in Early Mediaeval Europe* (Cambridge: Cambridge
  University Press, 1990)

—, 'Carolingian Book Production: Some Problems', *The Library*, Sixth Series
  12 (1990): 1-33

—, 'Nuns, Scriptoria in England and Francia in the Eighth Century', *Francia*
  19/1 (1992): 1-35

—, *Books, Scribes and learning in the Frankish Kingdoms, 6th – 9th Centuries*
  (Aldershot: Ashgate, 1994)

—, ed., *Carolingian Culture: Emulation and Innovation* (Cambridge: Cambridge
  University Press, 1994)

—, *History and Memory in the Carolingian World* (Cambridge: Cambridge
  University Press, 2004)

—, *Perceptions of the Past in the Early Middle Ages* (Notre Dame IND: University
  of Notre-Dame Press, 2006)

—, *Charlemagne: The Formation of a European Identity* (Cambridge: Cambridge
  University Press, 2008)

—, 'Roman Texts and Roman History in the Early Middle Ages', in C. Bolgia,
  R. McKitterick and J. Osborne, eds., *Rome Across Time and Space:
  Cultural Transmission and the Exchange of Ideas, c. 500-1400* (Cambridge:
  Cambridge University Press, 2011), 19-34

Mercati, G., 'Codici del convento di S. Francesco in Assisi nella Biblioteca
  Vaticana', *Miscellanea Francesco Ehrle: Scritti di storia e paleografia pubblicati
  sotto gli auspici di S. S. Pio XI in occasione dell'ottantesimo natalizio dell' e. mo.
  Cardinale Francesco Ehrle: Vol. 5 Biblioteca ed Archivio Vaticano, biblioteche
  diverse*, Studi e testi 41 (Rome: Biblioteca Apostolica Vaticana, 1924), 83-127

Mews, C., 'Monastic Educational Culture Revisited: The Witness of
Zwiefalten and the Hirsau Reform', in G. Ferzoco and C. Muessig,
eds., *Medieval Monastic Education* (Leicester, London, New York:
Leicester University Press), 182-97

—, 'Scholastic Theology in a Monastic Milieu in the Twelfth Century: The
Case of Admont', in A. Beach, ed., *Manuscripts and Monastic Culture:
Reform and Renewal in Twelfth-Century Germany* (Turnhout: Brepols,
2007), 217-39

Meyïer, K. de, *Codices Vossiani Latini*, 4 vols. (Leiden: Brill, 1973-84)

Migne, J.P., ed., *Patrologia Latina*, 221 vols. (Paris: Garnier et Migne, 1844-64)

Milde, W., 'Mittelalterliche Bibliothekskataloge als Quellen der
Bildungsgeschichte: das Beispiel Hamersleben im 12./13.
Jahrhundert', in J. Luckhardt and F. Niehoff, eds., *Heinrich der Löwe
und sein Zeit*, 3 vols. (Munich: Brunswick, 1995), Vol. 2, 478-83

Murphy, T.M., *Pliny the Elder's Natural History: The Empire in the
Encyclopaedia* (Oxford: Oxford University Press, 2004)

Nonius Marcellus De compendiosa doctrina, ed. W.M. Lindsay, *Nonius
Marcellus' Dictionary of Republican Latin* (Oxford: Oxford University
Press, 1901)

O'Sullivan, S., *Early Medieval Glosses on Prudentius' Psychomachia: The Weitz
Tradition* (Leiden: Brill, 2004)

Palmer, N.F., 'Simul cantemus, simul pausemus: Zur mittelalterlichen
Zisterzienserinterpunktion', in E. Conrad Lutz, M. Backes and S.
Matter, eds., *Lesevorgänge: Prozesse des Erkennens in mittelalterlichen
Texten, Bildern und Handschriften* (Zürich: Chronos, 2010), 483-569 and
715-28

—, *Zisterzienser und ihre Bücher: die mittelalterliche Bibliotheksgeschichte von
Kloster Eberbach im Rheingau [...]* (Regensburg: Schnell & Steiner,
1998)

Parkes, M.B., *Pause and Effect: An Introduction to the History of Punctuation in the West* (Aldershot: Scolar Press, 1992)

—, *Their Hands Before Our Eyes: A Closer Look at Scribes: The Lyell Lectures Delivered in the University of Oxford 1999* (Aldershot and Burlington, VT: Ashgate, 2008)

Pfaff, C., *Scriptorium und Bibliothek des Klosters Mondsee im hohen Mittelalter* (Vienna: Böhlau (in Kommission), 1967)

Pheifer, J.D., *Old English Glosses in the Épinal and Erfurt Glossaries* (Oxford: Oxford University Press, 1974)

Placidus, *Liber glossarum*, ed. G. Goetz, *Corpus Glossariorum Latinorum* 5 (Leipzig: Teubner, 1894)

Porter, D.W., 'On the Antwerp-London Glossaries', *Journal of English and Germanic Philology* 98 (1999): 170-92

—, ed., *The Antwerp-London Glossaries: The Latin and Latin-Old English Vocabularies from Antwerp, Museum Plantin-Moretus 16.2-London, British Library Add. 32246*, Texts and Indexes 1, Publications of the Dictionary of Old English (Toronto: Toronto University Press, 2011)

Powell, J., 'Pastor Bonus: Some Evidence of Honorius III's Use of the Sermons of Pope Innocent III', *Speculum* 52 (1977): 522-37

Rankin, S., 'Carolingian Music', in R. McKitterick, ed., *Carolingian Culture: Emulation and Innovation* (Cambridge: Cambridge University Press, 1994), 274-316

—, 'On the Treatment of Pitch in Early Music Writing', *Early Music History* 30 (2011): 105-75

Reynolds, L.D., ed., *Texts and Transmission: A Survey of the Latin Classics* (Oxford: Oxford University Press, 1983)

Ribémont, B., *Les origines des encyclopédies médiévales d'Isidore de Séville aux Carolingiens*, Nouvelle Bibliothèque du Moyen Âge 61 (Paris: Honoré Champion, 2001)

Roberts, C.H., and T.C. Skeat, *The Birth of the Codex* (Oxford: Oxford University Press for the British Academy, 1983)

Rouse, R.H., and M.A. Rouse, 'Statim invenire: Schools, Preachers and New Attitudes to the Page', in R.L. Benson and G. Constable, eds., *Renaissance and Renewal in the Twelfth Century* (Toronto: Toronto University Press, 1991), 201-25

Ruf, P., 'Die Handschriften des Klosters Schäftlarn', in S. Mitterer, ed., *1200 Jahre Kloster Schäftlarn, 762-1962* (Schäftlarn, 1962), 22-122

Sauer, H., 'Glosses, Glossaries and Dictionaries in the Medieval Period', in A.F. Cowie, ed., *The Oxford History of English Lexicography 1 General-Purpose Dictionaries* (Oxford: Oxford University Press, 2009), 17-40

Schiaparelli, L., *Il codice 490 della Biblioteca capitolare di Lucca e la scuola lucchese (sec. VIII-IX): contributi allo studio della minuscola precarolina in Italia*, Studi e testi 36 (Rome: Biblioteca Apostolica Vaticana, 1924)

—, *Il codice 490 della Biblioteca capitolare di Lucca: ottantatre pagine per servire a studi paleografici* (Rome: Biblioteca Apostolica Vaticana, 1924)

Schneider, K., *Paläographie und Handschriftenkunde für Germanisten: Eine Einführung*, Sammlung kurzer Grammatiken germanischer Dialekten 8 (Tübingen: Max Niemeyer, 1999)

Somfai, A., 'The Transmission and Reception of Plato's *Timaeus* and Calcidius's Commentary During the Carolingian Renaissance', unpublished PhD dissertation, University of Cambridge (1998)

Stammberger, R., 'The Works of Hugh of St Victor at Admont', in R. Berndt, ed., *Schrift, Schreiber, Schenker: Studien zur Abtei Sankt Viktor in Paris und den Viktorinern*, Corpus Victorinum 1 (Berlin: Akademie Verlag, 2005)

Swanson, R.N., *The Twelfth-Century Renaissance* (Manchester: Manchester University Press, 1999)

Sweet, H., *The Épinal Glossary, Latin and Old English of the Eighth Century* (London: Trübner, 1883)

Teresi, L., 'Anglo-Saxon and Early Anglo-Norman *Mappaemundi*', in R.H. Bremmer Jr and K. Dekker, eds., *Foundations of Learning: The Transfer*

of *Encyclopaedic Knowledge in the Early Middle Ages*, Mediaevalia
Groningana New Series 9 (Paris, Leuven and Dudley MA: Peeters,
2007), 341-78

Thomson, R.M., 'Richard Southern on the Twelfth-Century Intellectual
World', *Journal of Religious History* 26 (2002): 264-73

—, 'The Place of Germany in the Twelfth-Century Renaissance', in A.
Beach, ed., *Manuscripts and Monastic Culture: Reform and Renewal in
Twelfth-Century Germany*, Medieval Church Studies 13 (Brepols:
Turnhout, 2007): 19-42

Tremp, E., K. Schmuki and T. Flury, *Karl der Grosse und seine Gelehrten: Zum
1200 Todesjahr Alkuins (†804)* (St Gallen: Stiftsbibliothek, 2004)

Uhlfelder, M.L., *De proprietate sermonum vel rerum: A Study and Critical Edition
of a Set of Verbal Distinctions*, American Academy Papers and
Monographs 15 (Rome: American Academy in Rome, 1954)

Vaciago, P., ed., *Glossae Biblicae*, Pars I, Corpus Christianorum, Continuatio
Medievalis 189A (Turnhout: Brepols, 2004)

—, *Glossae Biblicae Pars II*, Corpus Christianorum, Continuatio Medievalis
189B (Turnhout: Brepols, 2004)

Vezin, J., 'L'emploi des notes tironiennes dans les manuscrits de la region
parisienne', in P. Ganz, ed., *Tironischen Noten*, Wolfenbütteler
Mittelalter-Studien 1 (Wiesbaden: Harrassowitz in Kommission der
Herzog August Bibliothek, 1990), 60-74

Wallis, F., 'Bede and Science', in S. De Gregorio, ed., *The Cambridge
Companion to Bede* (Cambridge: Cambridge University Press, 2010),
114-26

Webber, T., 'Script and Manuscript Production at Christ Church,
Canterbury, After the Norman Conquest', in R. Eales and R. Sharpe,
eds., *Canterbury and the Norman Conquest: Churches, Saints and Scholars,
1066-1109* (London: Hambledon Continuum, 1995), 145-58

Werner, H., *English Dictionaries 800-1700: The Topical Tradition* (Oxford: Oxford University Press, 1999)

Wirtgen, B., *Die Handschriften des Klosters St. Peter und Paul zu Erfurt bis zum Ende des 13. Jahrhunderts* (Gräfenhainichen: A. Heine, 1936)

Wolter-von dem Knesebeck, H., '"Die Weisheit hat sich ein Haus gebaut": Bilder, Buchkunst und Buchkultur in Hildesheim während des 12. Jahrhunderts', in M. Brandt, ed., *Abglanz des Himmels: Romanik in Hildesheim: Katalog zur Ausstellung des Dom-Museums Hildesheim* (Hildesheim: Schnell & Steiner, 2001), 97-113

—, 'Lamspringe, ein unbekanntes Scriptorium des Hamersleben-Halberstäter Reformkreises zur Zeit Heinriches des Löwen', in J. Luckhardt and F. Niehoff, eds., *Heinrich der Löwe und sein Zeit: Herrscheft und Repräsentation der Welfen 1125-1235*, 3 vols. (Munich: Hirmer, 1995), Vol. 2, 468-77

Wright, D., 'Latin Gospel Books from A.D. 400 to A.D. 800 by Patrick McGurk', *Speculum* 37 (1961), 637-43

Zechiel-Eckes, K., *Katalog der frühmittelalterlichen Fragmente der Universitäts- und Landesbibliothek Düsseldorf vom beginnenden achten bis zum ausgehenden neunten Jahrhundert* (Wiesbaden: Dr Ludwig Reichert Verlag, 2003)

—, 'VII.42 Corpus glossarum', in C. Stiegemann and M. Wemhoff, eds., *Kunst und Kultur der Karolingerzeit*, 3 vols. (Mainz: Philipp von Zabern, 1999), Vol. 2, 490-1.

Ziolkowski, J., *Talking Animals: Medieval Latin Beast Poetry, 750-1150* (Philadelphia: University of Pennsylvania Press, 1993)

Notes on the Authors

Rosamond McKitterick is Professor of Medieval History in the University of Cambridge and Fellow of Sidney Sussex College. She is a Fellow of the Royal Historical Society and of the Royal Society of Arts, Manufacturing and Commerce, a *Korrespondierendes Mitglied* of the Monumenta Germaniae Historica and of the Austrian Academy of Sciences, and Corresponding Fellow of the Medieval Academy of America. She was awarded the Dr A.H. Heineken Prize for History by the Royal Dutch Academy in 2010. Rosamond McKitterick has published on literacy, manuscript transmission, perceptions of the past and political culture in the early Middle Ages. Her most recent monographs are *Ego Trouble: Authors and Their Identities in the Early Middle Ages* (with R. Corradini, I. van Renswoude and M. Gillis, 2010) and *Rome Across Time and Space: Cultural Transmission and the Exchange of Ideas, c. 500-1400* (with C. Bolgia and J. Osborne, 2011). Her current interests are the migration of ideas in the early Middle Ages and the implications and impact of the historical and legal texts produced during the sixth and seventh centuries in Rome.

Erik Kwakkel is *Universitair Docent* (University Lecturer) in palaeography at Leiden University Institute for Cultural Disciplines and Principle Investigator of the NWO-funded research project 'Turning Over a New Leaf: Manuscript Innovation in the Twelfth-Century Renaissance' ('Vidi' innovation scheme). In March 2012 he was appointed to De Jonge Akademie (The Young Academy) of The Royal Netherlands Academy of Arts and Sciences (KNAW). His research interests are related to the changing physical features of manuscripts, in particular those from the eleventh and twelfth centuries, and how these changes relate to the objects' use and readers. His publications include a monograph on Carthusian book production (2002), a co-edited volume on Middle Dutch Bible translations (2007) and a variety of articles and book chapters devoted to Middle Dutch and Latin manuscripts, including in such journals as *The Library, The Transactions of the Bibliographical Society, Viator, Medieval and Renaissance Studies* and the *Gazette du Livre Médiévale*. Among his forthcoming publications is a co-edited volume on medieval authorship (University of Toronto Press, 2012).

Rodney Thomson is Emeritus Professor of Medieval History at the University of Tasmania and Honorary Research Fellow in its School of History and Classics. He is a historian and palaeographer, whose research has focussed on intellectual and cultural life in twelfth-century England, with special attention to Benedictine monasteries and men of learning, their books and libraries. Since the early 1980s he has produced a series of descriptive catalogues of the medieval manuscripts at Lincoln, Hereford and Worcester Cathedrals, Merton and Corpus Christi Colleges Oxford. He has also edited and translated medieval Latin texts, above all (with Michael Winterbottom) the historical works of the monk William of Malmesbury (d. c. 1142), and contributed to the history of the Latin classical tradition in Western Europe before c. 1500.

Colour Plates

2. Leiden, Universiteits-
bibliotheek, MS VLQ 9, fols
24v-25r (reduced)

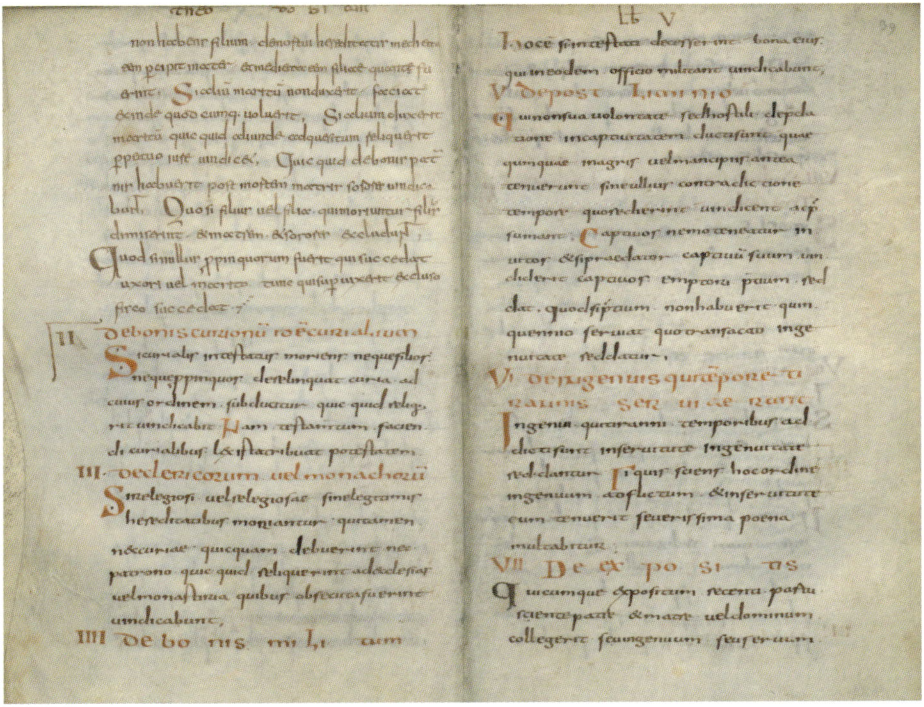

3. Leiden, Universiteitsbibliotheek, MS BPL 114, fols 38v-39r (reduced)

4. Leiden, Universiteits-
bibliotheek, MS BPL 48, fols
8v-9r (reduced)

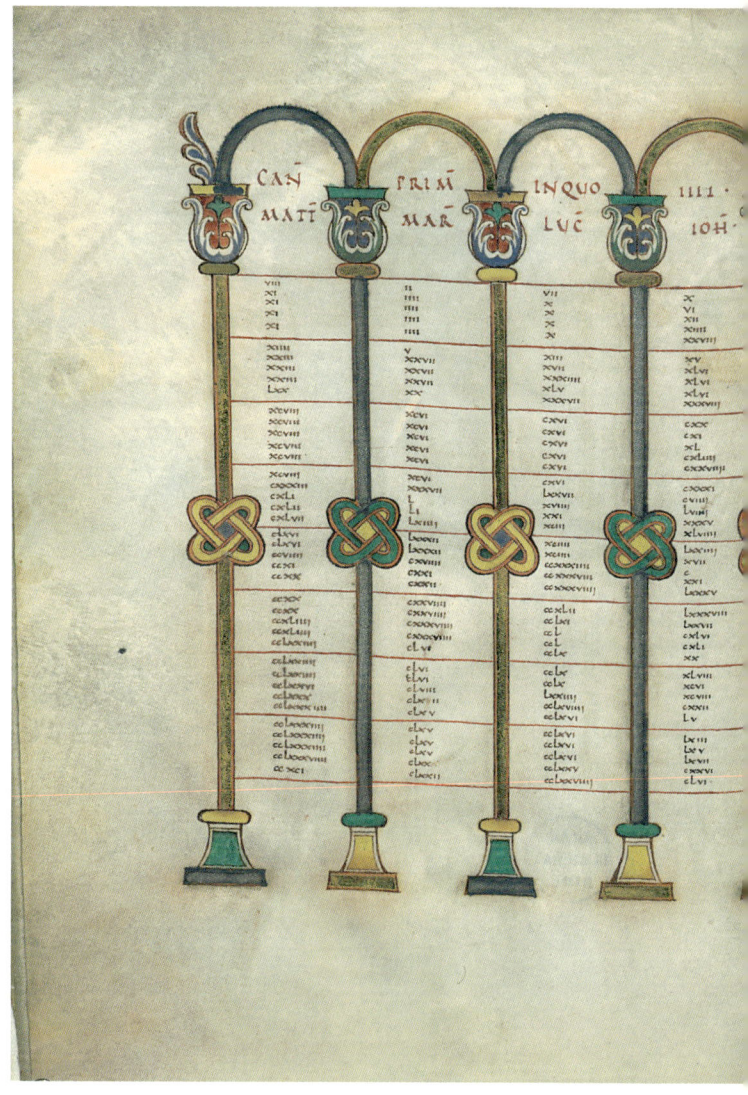

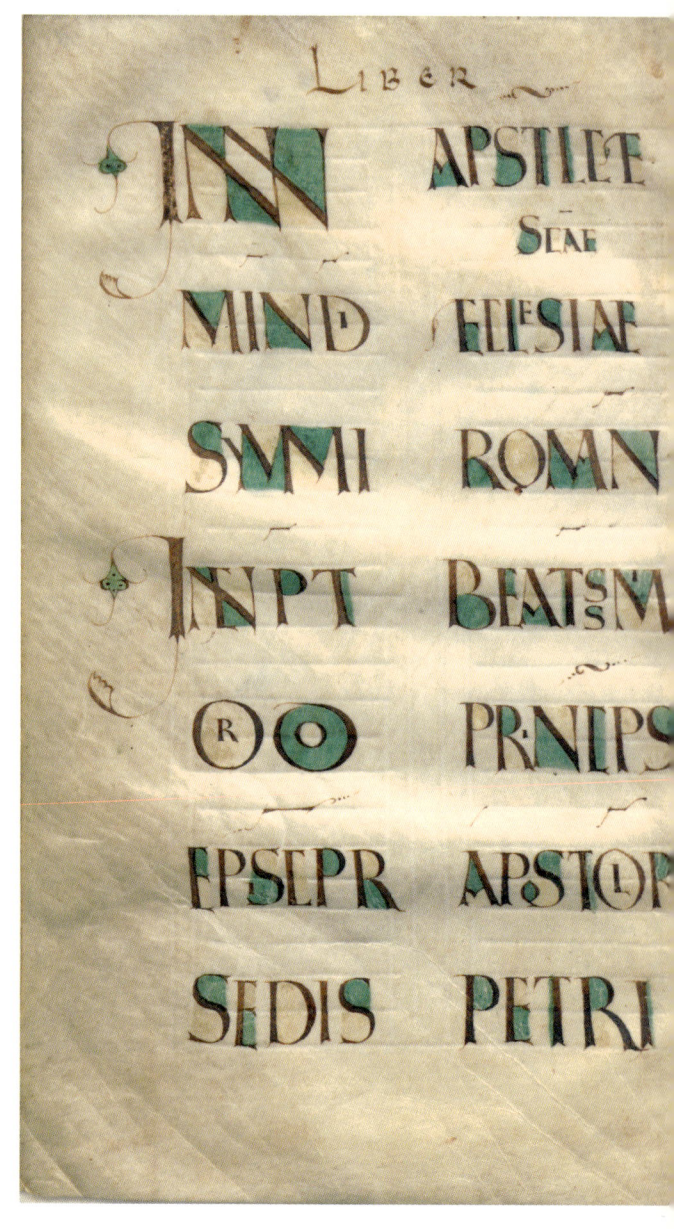

IN NOMINE SEAE ECCLESIAE ROMANAE INCIPIT BEATISSIMO PRINCIPIS EPISCOPORUM APOSTOLORUM SEDIS PETRI

LIBER

IN NOMINE

SEAE

APOSTLEE

ECCLESIAE

SVMI

ROMN

INCIPIT

BEATISSIMO

R O O

PRINCIPS

EPSEPR

APOSTO L

SEDIS

PETRI

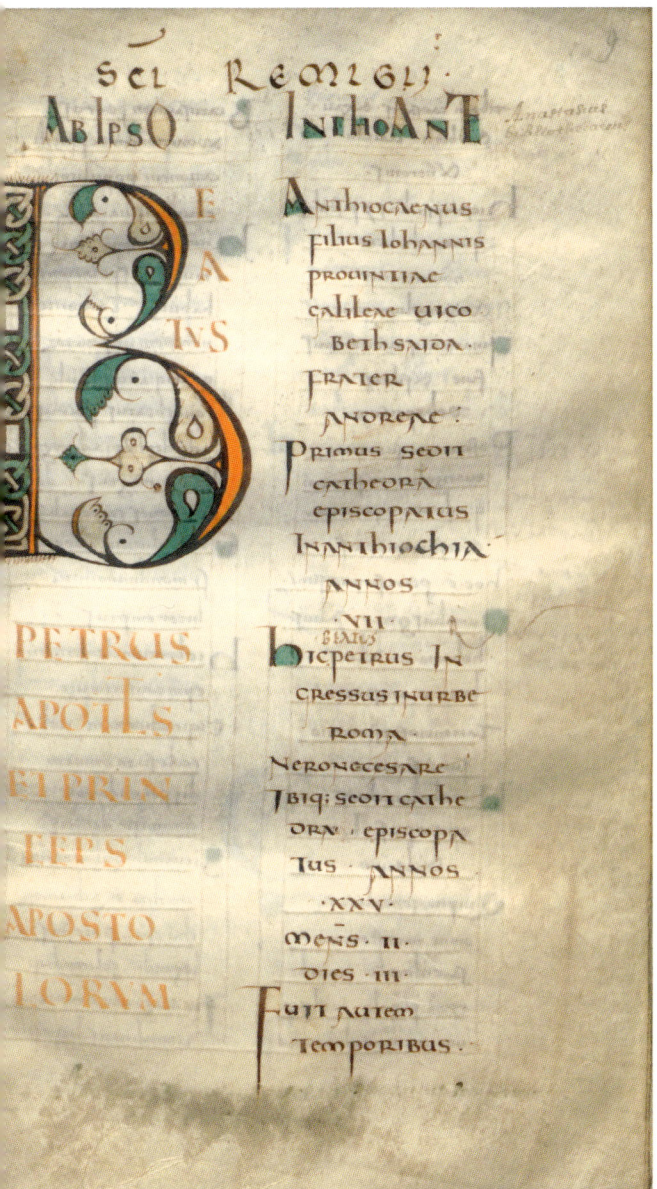

5. Leiden, Universiteits-
bibliotheek, MS VLQ 60, fols
8v-9r (reduced)

ocorbe — DE ORBE

Orbis a rotunditate circuli dictus quia sicut rota est, unde breuis etiam rotella orbiculus appellatur. undique enim oceanus circumfluens eius in circulo ambit fines. diuisus est autem trifarie, ex quibus una pars Asia altera Europa tertia Africa nuncupatur. quas tres partes orbis ueteres non aequaliter diuiserunt. Nam Asia a meridie per orientem usque ad septentrionem peruenit. Europa uero a septentrione usque ad occidentem. Atque inde Africa ab occidente usque ad meridiem. unde euidenter orbem diuiduntasia sola tenet dimidium, duae partes reliquae faciunt alterum dimidium...

DE ASIA

Asia ex nomine cuiusdam mulieris est appellata quae apud antiquos imperium tenuit orientis. haec in tertia orbis parte disposita ab oriente habet ortum solis a meridie oceano a occiduo nostro mari finitur. A septentrione meotidis lacu et Tanai flumine terminatur. habet autem prouincias multas et regiones quarum breuiter nomina et situs expediam sumpto initio a paradiso. Paradisus est locus in orientis partibus constitutus cuius uocabulum ex greco in latinum uertitur hortus, porro hebraice eden dicitur quod in nostra lingua delicie interpretatur. quod utrumque iunctum facit hortum deliciarum. est enim omni genere ligni et pomiferarum arborum consitus habens etiam lignum uitae. non ibi frigus non aestus sed perpetua aeris temperies. e cuius medio fons prorumpens totum nemus inrigat diuiditurque in quatuor nascentia flumina...

Indua ab Indo flumine...
occidens mari clauditur... haec Aemerluuiano mari...
porrecta usque ad Ortis solis et a septentrione nostri
admonse mons clauditur qui... habens gentes multas et oppida, insulam quoque Taprobanen et gemmis et elephantis referta. etiam Chrisen et Argirem in auro et argento fecundas. et regionem Tylen arboribus folia numquam carentem. habet et flumen Ganges et Indus et Hypanis inlustrantes Indos...

Parthia ab Indo usque ad Mesopotamiam regionem...

Assyria uocata ab Assur filio Sem qui eam regionem post diluuium primus incoluit. haec ab Ortu...

J gnibus & ignis umorem umoribusesse
C etera consimili fingit ratione putatque
H ec tamen esseulla idenparte inrebusmane
C oncedit neque corporibus finemesseseaundis
q uaremutraque mihi pariter rationeuidetur
e rrare atq; illis utraquoddyximus ante
A dde quod inbecilli animis primordia fingit
f ipr mordia funtsimili quaepraedita constant
η atura atqueipseressunt aequeq; laborant
& pereunt neque abgenio refullarefrenat
H am quid inoppressu ualido durabiteorum
u t mortem efficiat letisubdentibus ipsis
J gnis an umor anaura quidhotx sanguisanos
H ihilutopinor ubi &aequore fundituromnis
T am mortaliserit quamq; manifestaui demus
& oculis nostris aliquamineta perire
a tneq; recedere adnibilum respossenteq; autem
C rescere denibilo restorres anteprobatas
p raeterea qm cibus auget & corpus alitque
f circelice & nobis uenas &sanguine &ossa

6. Opposite, Leiden, Universiteitsbibliotheek, MS VLF 82, fol. 120v (reduced)

7. Leiden, Universiteitsbibliotheek, MS VLF 30, fol. 22v (reduced)

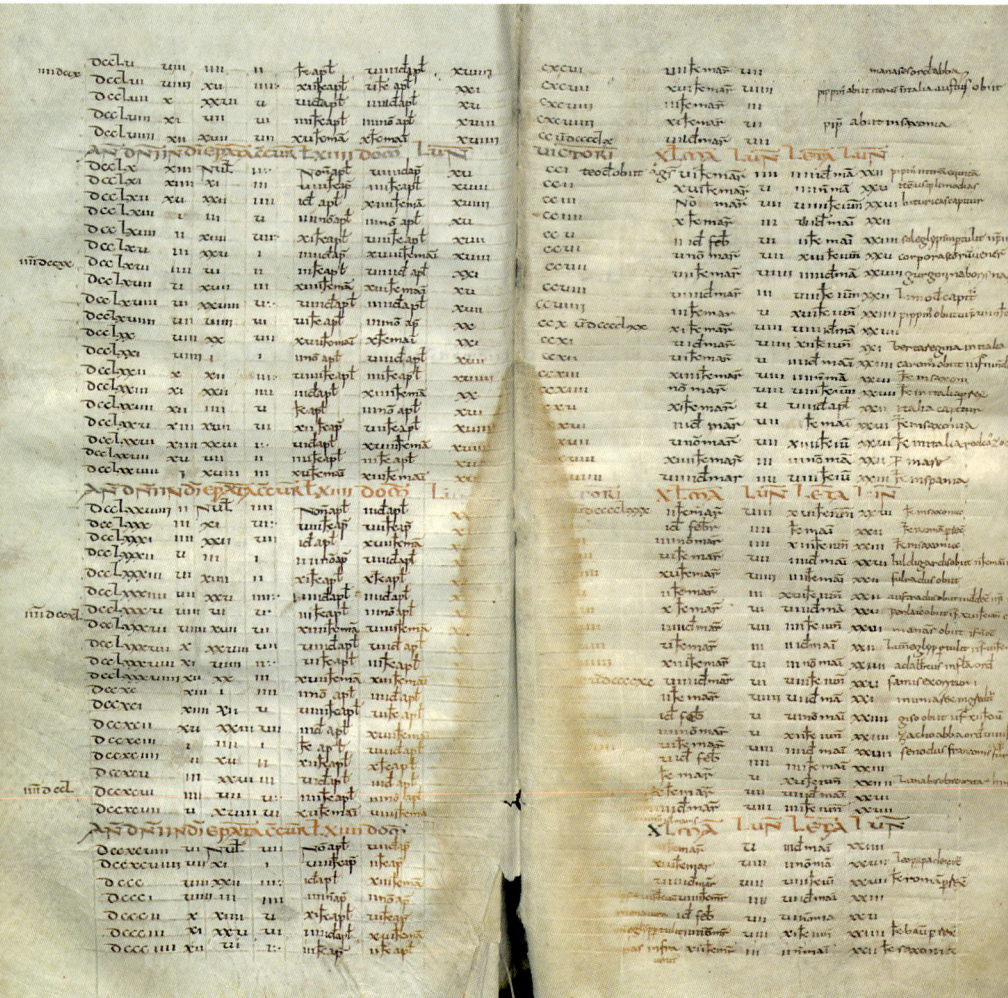

8. Leiden, Universiteits-

bibliotheek, MS Scaliger 28,

fols 17v-18r (reduced)

9. Leiden, Universiteits-
bibliotheek, MS VLQ 110 A,
fols 1v-2r (reduced)

10. Leiden, Universiteitsbibliotheek, MS VLQ 110,
fols 48v-49r (reduced)

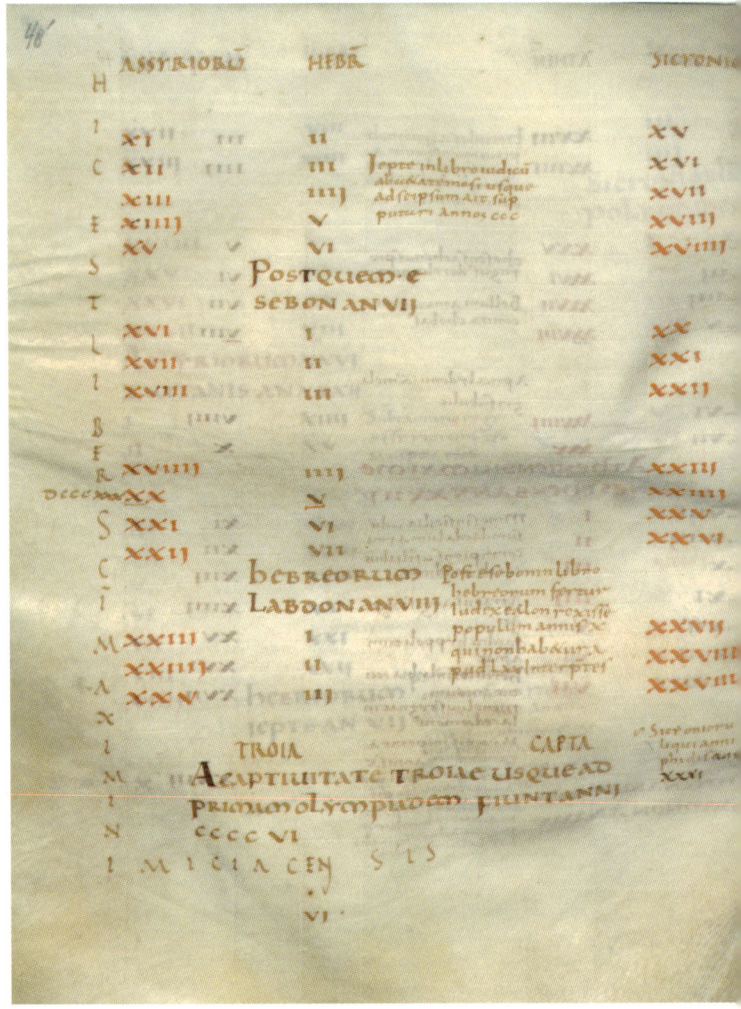

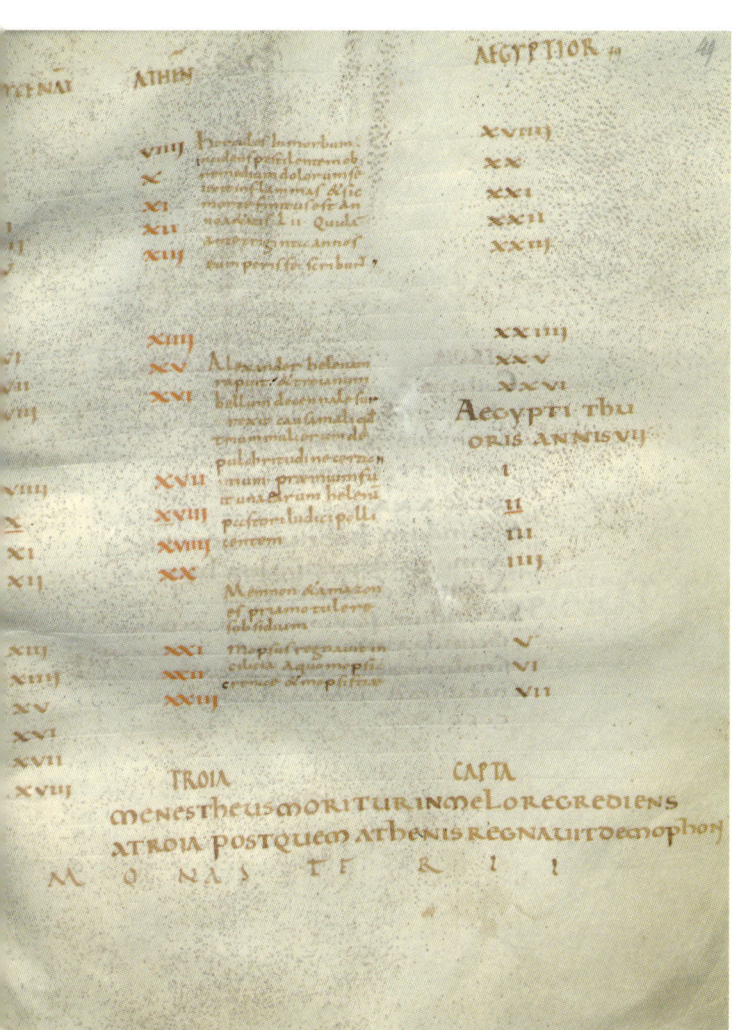

...ENAI	ATHIN		AEGYPTIOR...
	VIIII	Herodes humorbum...	XVIIII
	X	...deis pestilontem ob...	XX
	XI	...rentiam dolorum si...	XXI
	XII	...ram inflammat & sic	XXII
	XIII	...um perisse scribunt	XXIII
	XIIII		XXIIII
...I	XV	Alexander helenam	XXV
...II	XVI	rapuit: & erecunum	XXVI
...III		bellum decennale sur...	**Aecypti Thu**
		rexit cau samali est	**ORIS ANNIS VII**
		troam maior orndo	I
VIIII	XVII	pulchritudine corum...	
X	XVIII	mam prain num fu...	II
XI	XVIIII	truna clarum helen...	III
XII	XX	pisson ludici polli...	IIII
		tencem	
		Memnon & amazon...	
XIII	XXI	... priamo tulere	V
XIIII	XXII	...sub sidum	VI
XV	XXIII	Mopsus regnavit in...	VII
		cilia Aquo mopsu...	
XVI		cronus & mopsistia	
XVII			
XVIII			

TROIA   **CAPTA**

MENESTHEUS MORITUR IN MELO REGREDIENS
A TROIA POSTQUEM ATHENIS REGNAVIT DEMOPHON

M O N A S T E R I I

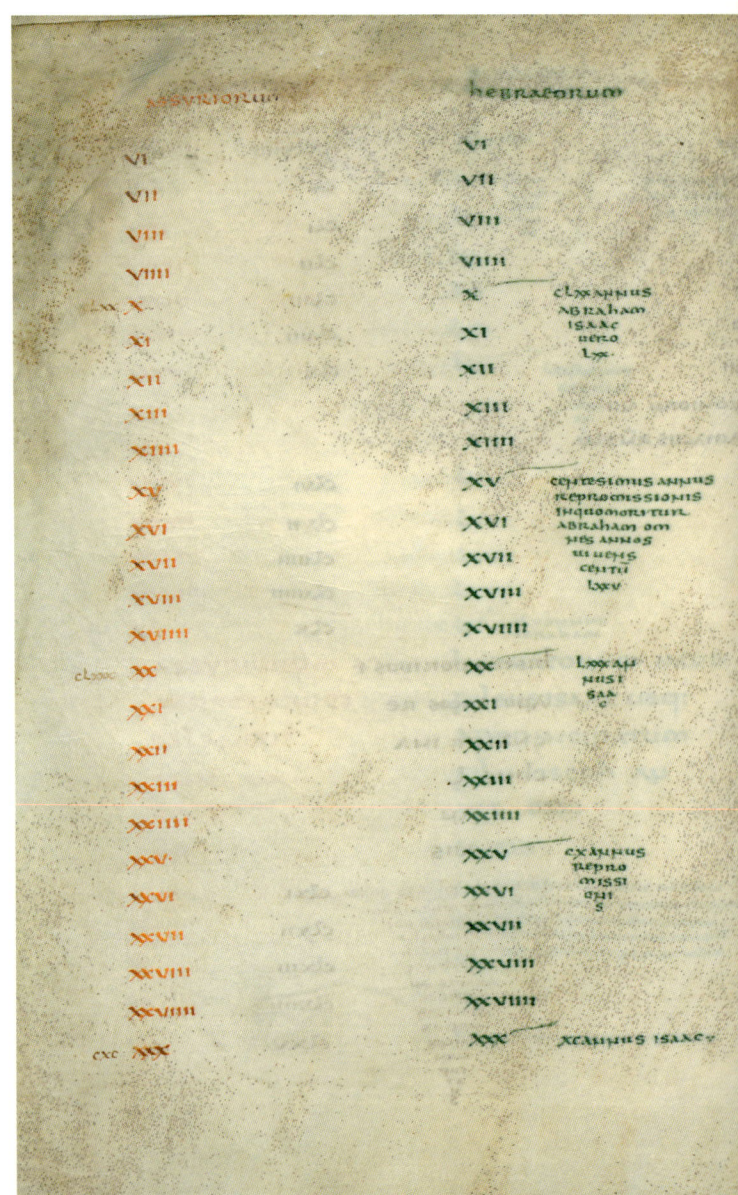

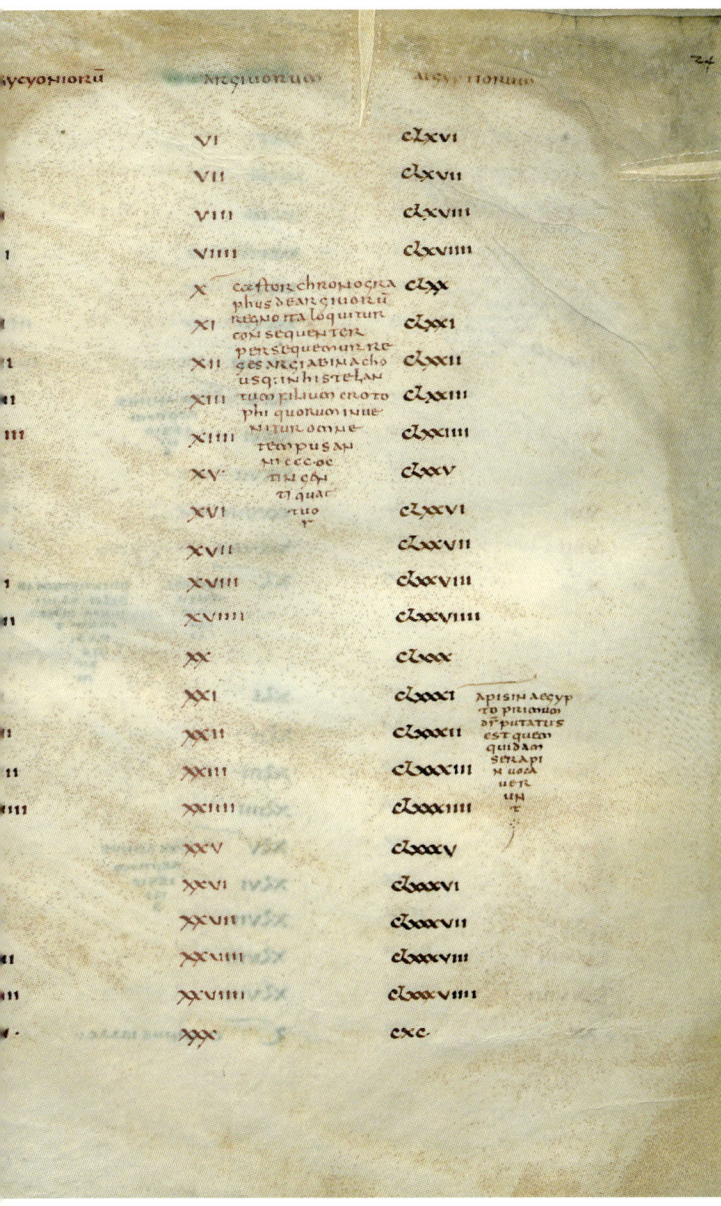

12. Leiden, Universiteitsbibliotheek, MS BPL 30, fols
14v-15r (reduced)

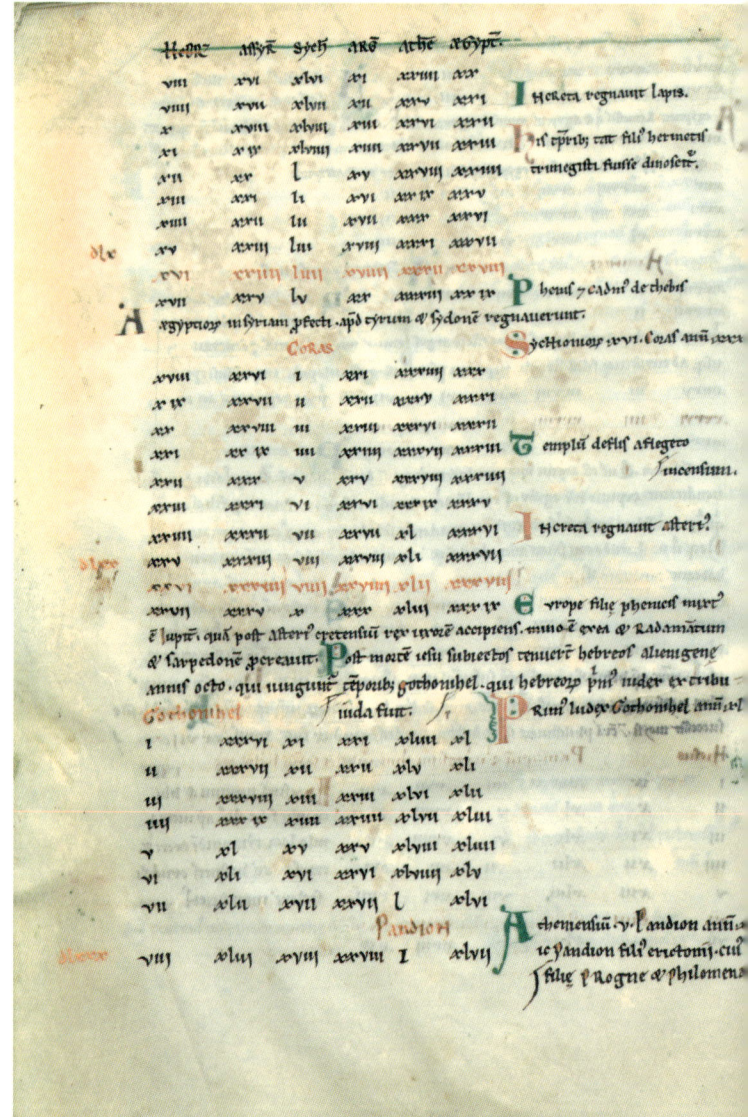

Apud hebreos pontificatum suscepit phinees.

viiii	xliiii	xviii		ii	urben	
x	xlv	xx	xl	iii	xl	vi

Apd argos scedorio tunctu ent hypmestra danai filia.

Assyriorum nono decimo bolochus ann. xxv. huic filia costa q̄ semiramis regnauit t̄ pat ann̄

bolochus

| xi | i | xvi | xli | iiii | l | |
| xii | ii | xvii | xli | v | li | |

Radamanctꝰ et sarpedon reges iouior fuerunt.

xiii	iii	xviii	xlii	vi	lii	
xiiii	iiii	xviiii	xliiii	vii	liii	
xv	v	xxv	xlv	viii	liiii	

Hoc tp̄re rapta europa.

Cadmꝰ regnauit thebis. ex cuiꝰ filia semele nat̄ e dionisi? id̄ lib̄ pat̄ sub q̄ lin̄

| xvi | vi | xxvi | xlvi | | lv | |
| xvii | vii | xxvii | xlvii | x | lvi | |

thebeus musicus fuit.

| xviii | viii | xxviii | xlviii | xi | lvii | |
| xviiii | viiii | xxviiii | xlviiii | xii | lviii | |

Oelus et paphꝰ et thiasus qui alesta urbes condidt.

| xx | | xxx | l | xiii | lx | |

Cropeus linceus

Schonieus xxvii. cropeꝰ annꝰ xxv.

| xxi | vi | i | i | xiiii | lx | |

Arguiorum xvi linceꝰ ann̄ xli.

| xxii | vii | ii | ii | xv | lxi | |

Prima edita a phenicib q pruium Artadena uocabat.

xxiii	viii	iii	iii	xvi	lxii	
xxiiii	viiii	iiii	iiii	xvii	lxiii	
xxv	xv	v	v	xviii	lxiiii	

Linꝰ thebeus et zetus et amphi on in musica arte claruerunt.

| xxvi | xvi | vi | vi | xviii | lxv | |
| xxvii | xvii | vii | vii | xx | lxvi | |

Idei t̄ dactili his tp̄ribus erant ḡ ferrum repperierunt.

| xxviii | xviii | viii | viii | xxi | lxvii | |

Aegyphon t̄ rex thebis regnabant.

| xxx | x | x | x | xxii | lxviii | |

menops

Principũ q̄ argisimi sedi iubeleꝰ

| xxx | xx | xx | xx | xxiii | |

egyptios asenopes ann̄ xl.

| xxxi | xxi | xxi | xxi | xxiiii | ii |

In dardania regnauit erie tonius filius dardani.

| xxxii | xxii | xii | xii | xxv | iii |
| xxxiii | xxiii | xiii | xii | xxvi | iiii |

Eaq̄ de demetria q̄ isd̄e ē auint. et dane euꝫ ipseuis nascent̄ dict̄. his fuere gẽta tp̄rib.

| xxxiiii | xxiiii | xiiii | xiii | xxvii | v |
| xxxv | xxv | xv | v | xxviii | vi |

bellesparis

Assyriorum xxviii bellesparis ann̄ xxx.

| xxxvi | i | xvi | xvi | xxv iv | vii |

Ephira q̄ nc chorinū uocat a sisipho condita.

| xxxvii | ii | xvii | xvii | xxx | viii |

13. Leiden, Universiteits-

bibliotheek, MS BPL 30, fols

66v-67r (reduced)

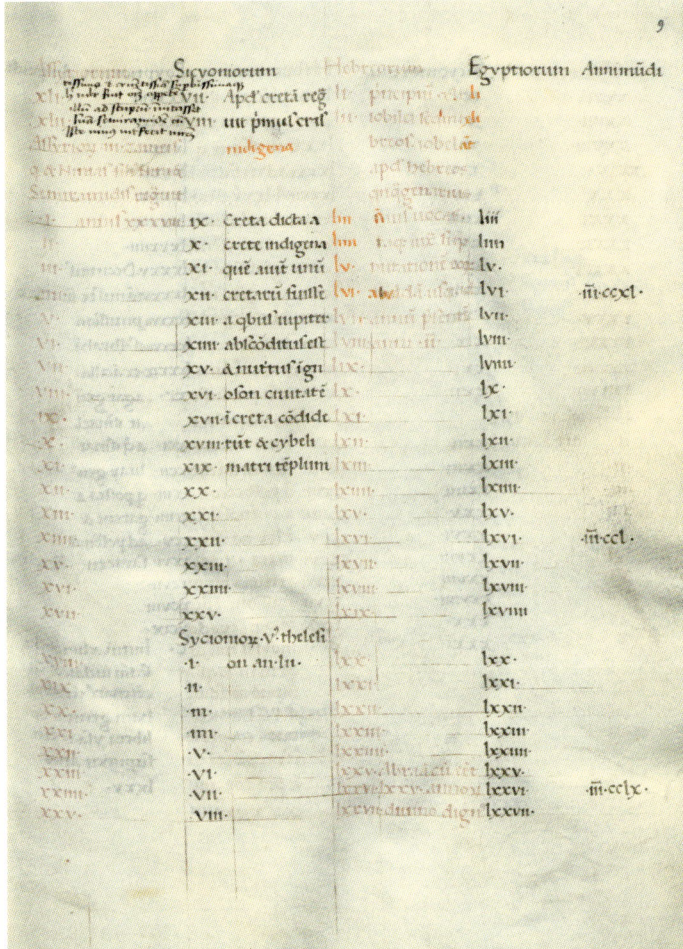

14. Leiden, Universiteitsbibliotheek, MS BPL 97 B,
fol. 9r (reduced)

187

15. Leiden, Universiteitsbibliotheek, MS VLF 26, fol.
1r (reduced)

16. Opposite, Leiden,
Universiteitsbibliotheek,
MS VLF 73, fol. 133v
(reduced)

acsumar et uelius lib xx yr rem cognoscas et
dicas annuu astendas postulo pompomus par
sapapipolom agis turaba abi cognorint omnet
una assentiam tenentur mandri xeopa c̄o
cognauura me consilium meu cognoseieri eg
georg libr urefugis tenuta q pigēt cognos
cerecurat Cognoscere. noscitul pr̄spicere
uerg lib unis uenant assiduo et cecui cognio
uamus amne idē georg libr tuneq quam
quemodapossis cognoscere dicxm cullius in
hostense Unde aut facilius quia exaliu
monumentis aut bellicgres Autoris r eipubl
disciplinē cognoscam ·idē ecelesenecatur
neq uerueroipse cognos utfecis illos ecuā dequa
b eraudius leg t eius conscripsi Cognoscere
agnoscerequerg imbucolias inti pepar uepue
rit sucognoscere mae benit ullius der epubl
lib r Cognoscere mehercule iniquid consuetudi
nest̄a et taud iusermone qua equa rros esqui
exquire corneme quoq; cum domu Abilio
cossum reuerter orprae cor canē cognoscas
nemo Cōpecer et significat quodlē honoro
uel omni gratia.

velquandut aliquad aduersuralia pecere
unde cōspecer et uel scope Cōpecer ero pater
so 'uel similis ende ca nac estimatione rerū hoc
illi cōpecit dicamus Cōpecer e reticaus
qi meminisse. Aut confiant uale resalius
tur historiarul lib r sicuero quasi formi
dine astrontur neq; animo neq; auribus
aut lingua cōpetere

Damnare ē damno adficere· un
de et condempnare dici uit eo cōra
rio nulla damno adfectu indempnem pba
mus Damnare est excheredare et ualius
satirarul lib xv cartius gaius hic opera
rius quam cesalonem dicamus sectorem
furium q; hanc ullius· quam index here
dem facet et clamnat alii omnes Dam
na necet sirare constringtere et uius in
formione uuise damnatur natus eon
tis Damnare ē· et mor adare uerg aeris
eidos lib iiii; nondū illi slauis pserpria uer
nec

17. Leiden, Universiteitsbibliotheek, MS BPL 67 D,
fol. 1r (reduced)

18. Opposite, Leiden,
Universiteitsbibliotheek,
MS VLF 24, fol. 108v
(reduced)

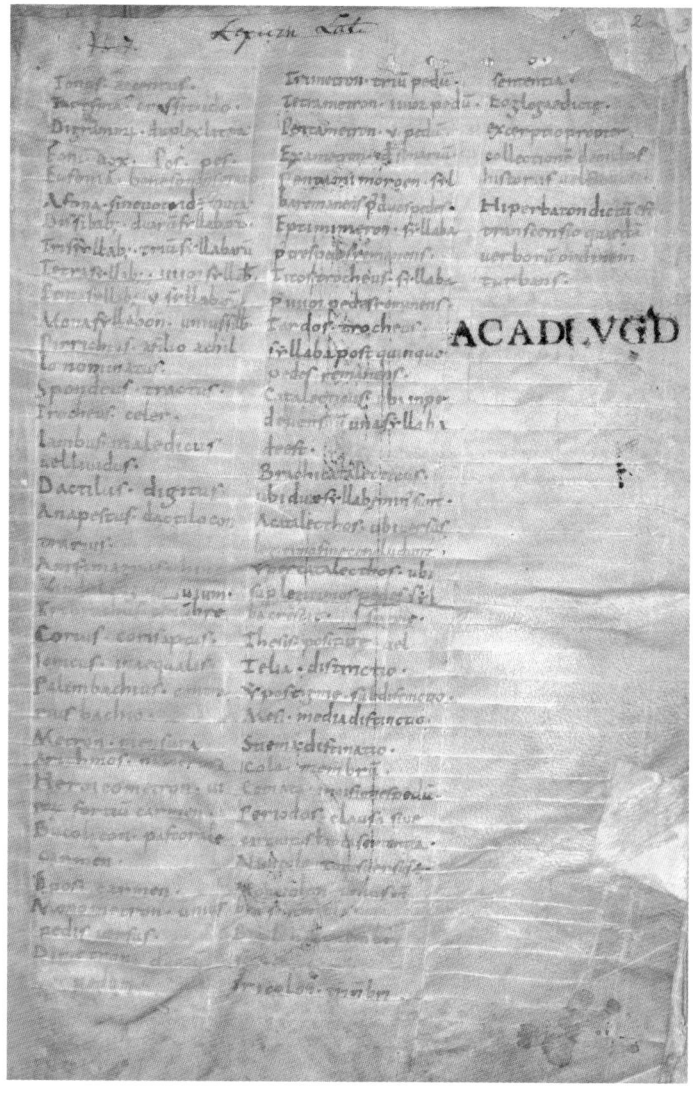

19. Leiden, Universiteits-

bibliotheek, MS VLQ 69, fol.

20r (reduced)

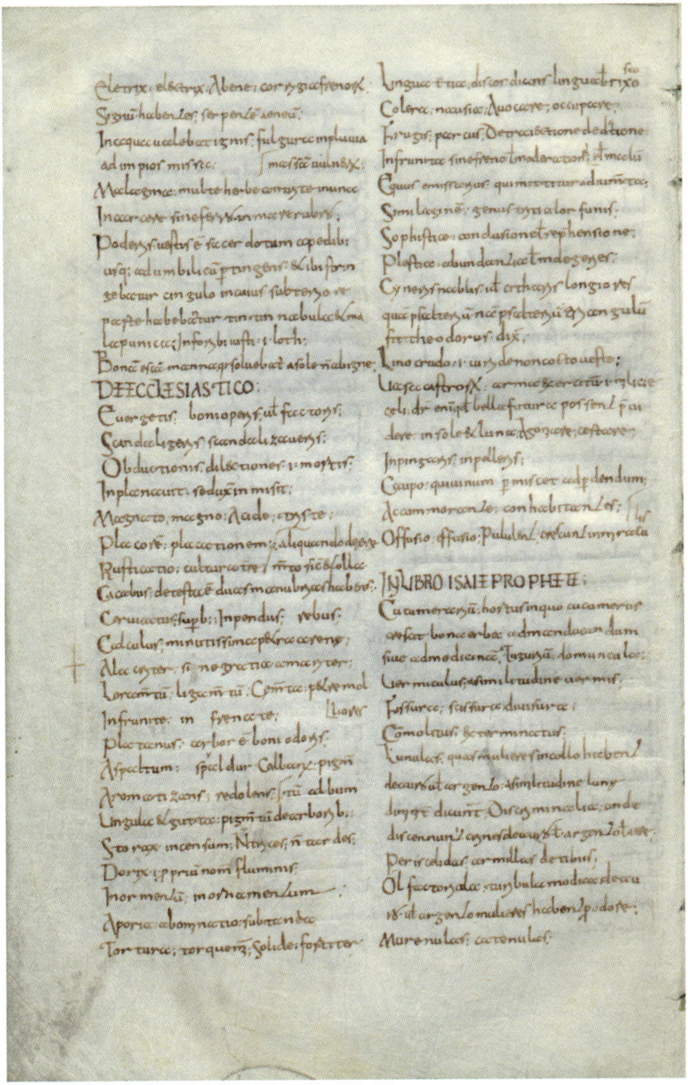

20. Leiden, Universiteitsbibliotheek, MS VLQ 69, fol. 24v (reduced)

21. Leiden, Universiteits-bibliotheek, MS Vulcanius 46, fol. 130v (reduced)

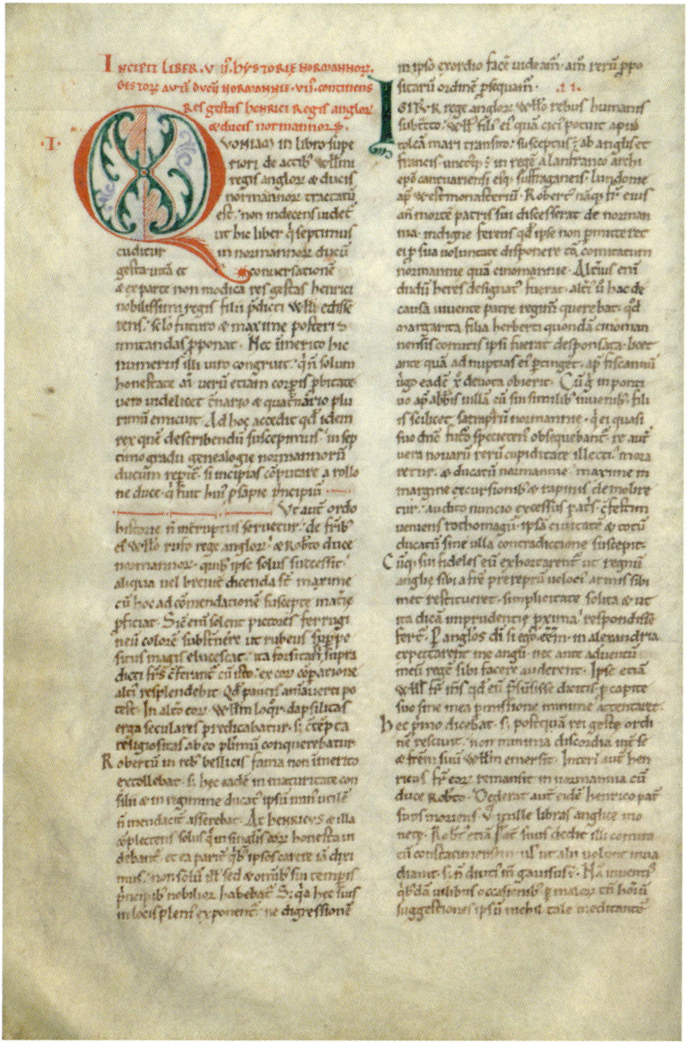

22. Leiden, Universiteitsbibliotheek, MS BPL 20, fol. 22v (reduced)

23. Leiden, Universiteitsbibliotheek, MS BPL 196, fol.
129v (reduced)

24. Opposite, Leiden,
Universiteitsbibliotheek,
MS VLF 8, fol. 17v (reduced)

urbs exultat cleri letat senat gaudet popls. Tercio die
escensionis ei augusti uelcens cu dono papa epulat e
in xpo eo finito conuiuio cesare speciale filiu deoscu
lat e unimo amore. His gestis impr urbe discesse
sede. in loco q agno dr collocauit. Et psul baudiens
adecclonis ei copuls plentudine. cu acerrito ae optima
tib romanis ad eund locu ppaurt. August eu uidens
obuia ei occurrit strenuiq; pontifices cesar marul
sius apphendens pedestri more quanta sagitte icul
extendit uxro. Cu ingssi centorum impiale. i salu
bri adnuuce fruebunt eloqis misicq; epuls pomatas
speciale alacrentie parte cibu super. Sacati misicq;
remotis plum cesar bo psula dona consulto. Quib sus
cepet equi conscendens conaluit reita. Cui amore
sres August impiale sup scandens equi medebar cu
animu uoluntate. Cuq; puemisset ad quenda graciosis
simu truneru locu umpr eq descende equiq; pontifices
terru ut susmemunt uxro dulcissimis; osout adu
uico pomantes se luesse pgratulatis? Cesar u ren
toru iraxerat arripuit ib. Preslai aut nobilissi
mox cetb; contabat roma ingssi magnifica conuta
 one almifica. To n cetb indutc uiii. fluui tybis alueu
siu egssi e ae sous urbe omia ae infra multa deser
tauit. fecit multa onamta in ecclosi fee ona u p
m ml. Eptos xo diae ui. epos p duila loca ae. Sepule
e in basilica bi leeri et cest epite d. xxvi.

Adrianus papa cu iu nat rom patre uullo sedit
ann. v. hic ecclui omantia multa paeola supd
ministrauit. Hic antephonario gregoriani tio anteo
adriani duisa p loca corroborauit ae sedin plogu usib;
exameris admissa maiore in die pmo aduent dni nri
ihu xpi decantaudu instruxit. Qui similit incipto sic
anteoua adriani pemuit qd ille ad omi missas in eade
diuca pma aduent decantandu strictissimi sfecerot
s; plurib; iste cantat usib; hic statut p monasd ad
missa maiore in sollepnizatib; seapuis n soli in hymno
anglico gla in excelsis do canere ymnol iufunectos as
laudes appellant uersicul in psalmis dauiticis as in
tronis dicunt moserta cantet decantate q romani
festuas laudes finnt tropos appellant qa inepreat
figura omantis in laudib; dii. Aelodias seq; ante euan
glui conmendas tradidit as dicet conseqntias ep sequt
cui euanglui. Ceq; adono papa gregorio pmo iu smodo
abadriano una cu alceuno abbe delectos magni imprs
karole bee cantalene festualee statue ac coposite fue
tunt mutet in hic delecceto psuleto cesure karolo s;
negligentia cantorer u imtatu uidebant ab ipso al
misico psilute de q loquim tu corrobeate st ad laude
ae glam dni nri ihu xpi. ut diligenta studiosop

cu antiphonario simul deinceps ae trophari insol
lepnub; dieb; ad missa maiore cantilenis frequenten
honestis hic statuit ut clerici romani instruerent
puipes dni nri ihu xpi siis nros ut ante dricu sa
cratissimi die pasche erib dieb; hoc e dni cena puri
socue ae sca sepultura dni ii alic pecerere elemosinu
hane romana n excelsa uoce cantilena dicendo p pla
teas ae ante monasteria ae ecclias ui m. Hyrleyson.
xpeeleyson. dne miserere nob xpis dris siet e obedienti
usq; ad monte fecit ord p m dech e mr. Eptos u. diae
v. epos. lx.   I

Marinus ex sed ann. i. m. iiii.   Terci
Adrianus exs sed ann. i. m. uiii.   Stephanus
ceu sed ann. un. ox. un. d xu.

vi. Bonefacui sed e. xcu.   xuui. Iohs sed an. ui.
vi. Stephan sed annu. i. oa.   xuui. Ohs ann. v.
dxuu.   xuu. Sergi sed an. ii. ox un. d. xii.
Foamos ann. ii. ii. ox n. dxuu. xu. Benedict sed an. vi. ox n d. yu.
Roman sed ox. un. d. xx.   xx. Iohs sed an. ou. ox. uu.
Theodou sed ox. xxui.   xx. Benedict sed an. ou. und. xx.
vui. Iohs sed an. ii.   xuu. Siluest sed diet sed. lvi.
iii. Benedict sed ann. iii. ox.
v. Leo sed ox. ui.   vi. Gregori sed an. v. ox. vi.
xposu sed ox. vi.   vi. Clemens sed ox. u. dxxu.
iii. Sergi sed an. u. ox n. d. xii. u. d amaseo sed an. u. cessau equi ox n.
u. Anastasi sed an. u. oa. d. xiu. u. eo sed an. u. ox. d. xi.
Landosed ox. u. d. xu.   u. Iohs sed an. u. ox. n. ox. d. xui.
x. Iohs sed an. xiu. ox n. d. iii. u. eph an sed ox. u. d. xxviu.
vi. Leo sed an. u. d. xu.   xx. Benedict sed ox. ou. d. xxu.
vi. Stephan sed an. u. d. xv.   iii. Nicolaus sed an. ou. ox n. iii. cessau
vu. Iohs sed an. uu. ox. x.   equus ox. n. d. vu.
vu. Leo sed an. iii. ox. vi.   iii. Alexander sed an. x. ox n. d. vu.
vui. Stephan sed an. un. ox.   vu. Gregori sed an. von. ox. i. d. vu.
vu. ou arni sed an. un. ox.   u. Urbeo sed an. uu. xou. cessau equ
Acapit sed an. uun. ox n. d.   ox. n. ox. vu.
xx. viii.   u. Urban sed an. xu. ox n. diex. xou.
xu. Iohs sed an. uun. ox. iii.   cessau equi. d. xu.
v. Benedict sed an. ii. d. v.   u. Paschal sed an. uiii. ox d. xu.
vu. Leo sed ann. iii. ox.   u. Gelasii sed an. i. d. v.
xu. Iohs sed an. ox i. d. ii.   u. Caluri sed an. v. ox i. d. xiu.
xu. Benedict sed an. ou. d. xu. ii. honorius sed an. u.   + 1130
Bonus sed an. i. ox.   ii. Innocenti
v. Bonefaci sed an. ou. d. xu.   ii. Celestinus
vu. Benedict sed ann. von.   Lucuis
xu. Iohs sed ox. ui.   iii. Eugeni
xxu. Iohs sed an. x. ox i. d. x. iii. Anastasius
v. Gregori sed an. ii. ox. ui.   com Adrian
xuu. Iohs sed ox. x.   Alexander iii.
ii. Siluest sed an. iii. ox n. ox. d. xui. Lucuis. iii.
                                 Vrbanus iii.

25. Marburg, Hessisches Staatsarchiv, MS H77, fol. 12r (reduced)

Augustin' de dominica
oratione.

constitui, et
ppe est dies quo ad
celestis regis uelun consisto
riu uenuatis. moneo uos kmi.
ut prece legitima patri & do
offerenda ante discatis. Ha qa
stupida mens hominu & igna
ra celestiu. nec scire nec inueni
re potuit queadmodu dm di
gne pcaret. ipse uerus dns et
magister ostendit & docuit p
se quide seos aplos. p illos aute
nos. qm debeam orare. Sic in
qt orabitis. Pater nr q es ince
lis scilicet nom tuu. Adueni
at regnu tuu. fiat uoluntas
tua. & cetera. O uere celestis
oratio. que tota est oratio. Ha
si singula uba p ut sc latius
tractare uoluerim. dies ante
qua sermo deficiet. tam bre
uit pcurram. Dicim. Pater
nr qui es incelis. Sic incipie
do. bonitate di & gram pre
stam. Ha quando nos trestres
& miseri. umbecilles & inuti
les serui auderem uultum le

uantes ad celu dicere. pat nr.
n ipse psuu unigenitu hanc
fiducia prestitit. Sic septu
e. Qtqt eu recepit. dedit illis
potestate filios di fieri. his q
credit innoie ei. Accepta q po
testate. patri uocat dm. qa
p fide spm adoptionis accepi
m. ut nos factos di filios gra
tulem. Bein dicim. Scificet
nom tuu. Hoc actio graru est.
uelut si dicat. scim sit & bn
dictu nom tuu. Decet eni gras
agere. q gram meruit. A due
niat regnu tuu. Non utiq: in
cipiat ille regnare. cui regnu
regnu est omniu seloz. s. hoc
optam. ut sine nris faciat ma
lis. & ueniens de celo nos assu
mat in regnu. Hoc eni dicto
ammonemur. u urta nram &
substantia. & regnu spare de
beam. Similit dicim. Fiat
uoluntas tua sic in celo & in tra.
Qs eni obstat do. q min fiat
uoluntas ei ubiq. S; hc oram.
ut sic in celo sit uoluntas di. ubi
null offendit. ita uirtute nris
animis tbuat. ut ei uoluntate
nos q sum in tra facere & imple
re possim. Vel certe eu dicim
fiat uoluntas tua. docem ad di
semp. ii ad nram respicere uo
luntate. qa in nra uoluntate ali
quens otraria st. in dni au uo
luntate urta e semp & bonitas.
Consequent ia post celestia. eni
trestria postulam. s; necessario.

non mansa bibim̄.'quia n̄ fracta sorbemus̄. Hęc subintelle
ctu mystico breui locutione transcurrim̄.'neqd forsitan
pretcrisse uideretr.,S; quia beati iob amei ē n̄ possent.m
si inquibṛdā quoqꝫ magna morū honestate fulgerent.'restat.
ut meoꝗ uerbis uirtute sensuum moralī inquiram.'quatinuſ
dū locutionis eoꝗ pondus discutī.' cuiuſ doctrine fuerint often
datur.Ego uidi stultū firma radice.'c̄ maledixi pulchritudim
eiuſ statim.Quasi firma radice stultuſ interra figit.'quia tot̄ū
desideriuſ interreno amore solidat̄.Vnde c̄ primū eam ciuitatē min
c̄struxisse describit.'ut apte monstraretur.'quia ipse interra
fundam̄tum posuit.qui asoliditate celestiſ patriꝗ alienſ sunt.,
Quasi firma radice stultuſ attollit.'quando hic temporali p
speritate fulcit̄.'ut omne qd'appetit assequat̄.'aduerſa nul
la sustineat.'contra infirmoſ sine repugnatione pualeat.'
bene agentibꝫ ex.inuentute ceradicat.'ad maiora c̄moda ex
peiore semp actione puenat.'ut unde uiam uite deserit.in
de adtempuſ felicior uiuat.,S; cū maloſ florere infirmi con
spiciunt. trepidant.'c̄ apud semetipsoſ peccantiū psperita
te turbati intuſ ingressibꝫ mentiſ nutant.Quoꝗ psecto spe
ciem sumpsit psalmista cū diceret.Mei aut pene moti ſ pe
des.'pene effusi ſ gressuſ mei.quia zelaui inpeccatoribꝫ pace
peccatoꝗ uidens.Cum v eoꝗ glam forteſ aspiciunt. punisūq;
post glam pena sequat̄ attendunt.'c̄ alia intuſ cogitatione
despiciunt hoc qd'superiuſ foraſ fastu uacue inflationiſ intumē
scunt.,Bene g̃ dr̄.Ego uidi stultū firma radice.'c̄ maledixi pul
chritudini cā statim.Pulchritudini quippe stulti maledicere
ē. cuiuſ glam excōsiderata dānatione iudicare.'quia eo atrociuſ
intormiuſ obruet̄ 'quo altiuſ inpeccatiſ eleuat̄.'quia transit

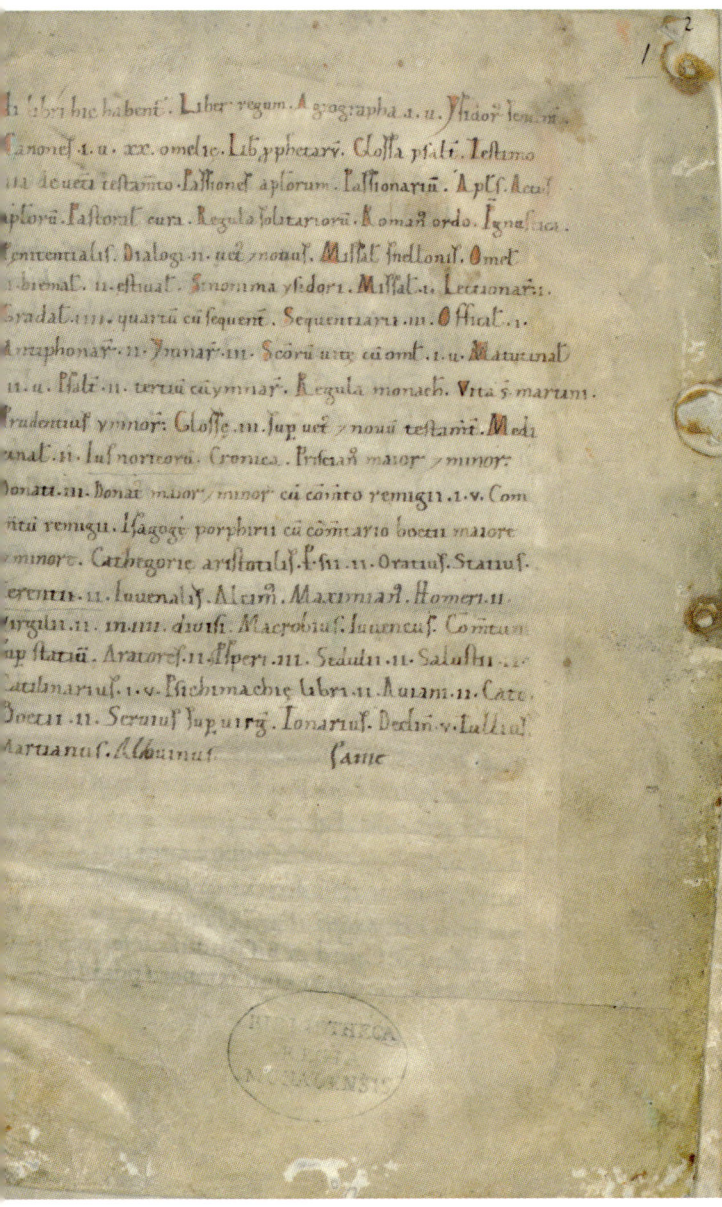

h libri hic habent. Liber regum. Agiographa .i. u. Ysidor lento mi.
Canones .i. u. xx. omelie. Lib. yphetaru. Glossa psalt. Testimo
ni̅ de uet̅i testamto. Passiones aplorum. Passionariu. Apl̅s Act̅
aplorum. Pastoral cura. Regula solitariorum. Roman ordo. Ignasti ca.
Penitentialis. Dialogi .ii. uet noui̅. Missal snellonis. Omel
i hiemal. .ii. estiual. Sinonima ysidori. Missal .ii. Lectionari.
Gradal .iiii. quartu cu sequent. Sequentiaru .iii. Offical .i.
Antiphonar .ii. Ionnar .iii. Scoru antē cu omt .i. u. Matutinal
.ii. u. Psalt .ii. tertiu cu ymnar. Regula monach. Vita s̅ martini
Prudentiuf ymnor. Glosse .iii. sup uet̅ 7 noui̅ testamt̅. Medi
cinal. .ii. Iusnorteoru. Cronica. Priscian maior 7 minor.
Donati .iii. Donat maior 7 minor cu comito remigii .i. u. Com
mitu remigii. Isagoge porphirii cu commtario boetii maiore
7 minore. Cathegorie aristotilis. f. sii. .ii. Oratiuf. Statiuf.
Terenti .ii. Iuuenalif. Alcim. Maximiani. Homeri .ii.
Virgili .ii. in .iiii. diuisi. Macrobiuf. Iuuencuf. Comtum
sup statiu. Aratoref .ii. Psperi .iii. Seduli .ii. Salusti
Catilinariuf .i. u. Psichimachie libri .ii. Auiani .ii. Cato
Boeti .ii. .ii. Seruiuf sup uirg. Ionariuf. Declin .v. Tulliuf
Martianuf. Albuinuf.   Same

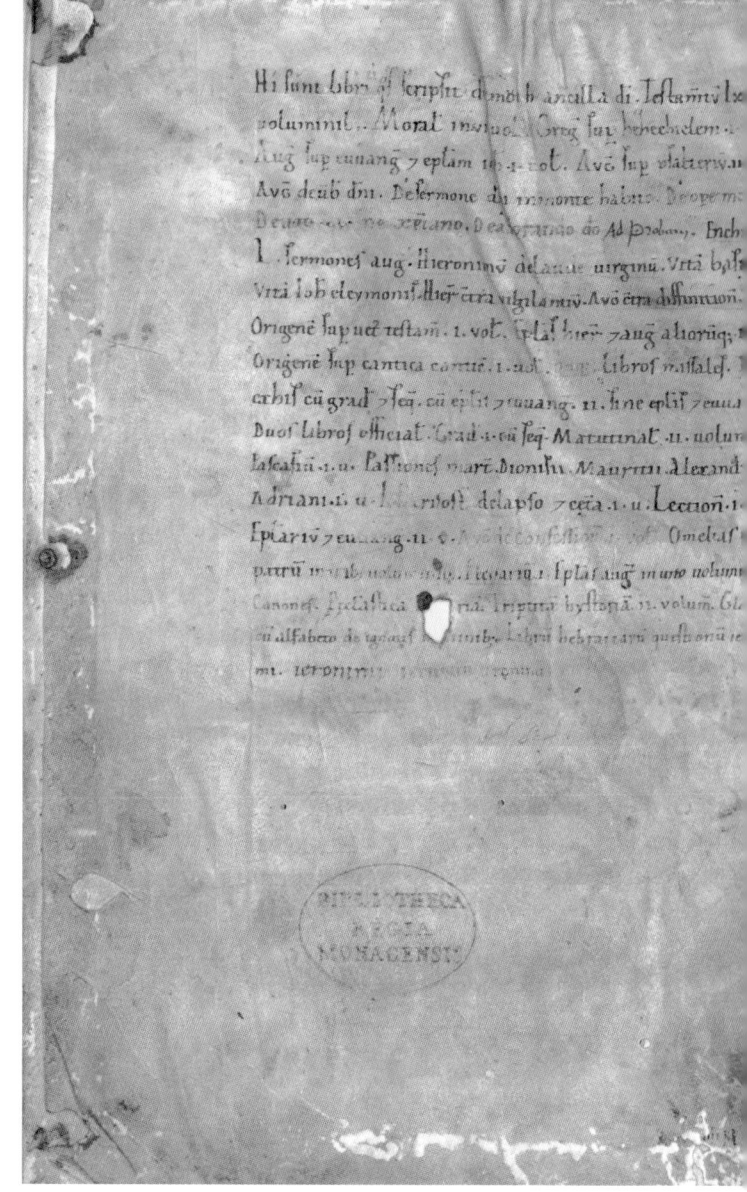

Incipit liber primus Hvbonis magistri de archa noe p archa sapientie cum archa ecclesie . & archa matris GRE;

CVM SEDE REM

aliqvando in conventv

30. Admont, Stifts-
bibliothek, MS 672, fol. 1v
(reduced)

tia fluctuantes. his que in sacro eloquio
de futuris primus bonorum ut penis
referuntur: nec omnino contra
dicunt nec prius acquiescunt.
Vident enim in hoc mun
do queda sic geri. ex q
bus ea dm esse ea hu
mana curare po
sit intelligi.
ea qd cunc
ta ho
mi

num
facta seu
bona seu ma
la reseruentur
adiudicium. Hoc
ergo considerantes ti
mere incipiunt qd mi
natur deus atq; hoc timo
re copulsi quod iubet face
re ea phibet uitare pponunt ea sit

Sermo . L . ii .

Graphs

see p. 90

Graph 1: Style of feet at minims (as encountered in m and n)

——— Caroline
——— Gothic
——— Mix
——— No Turns

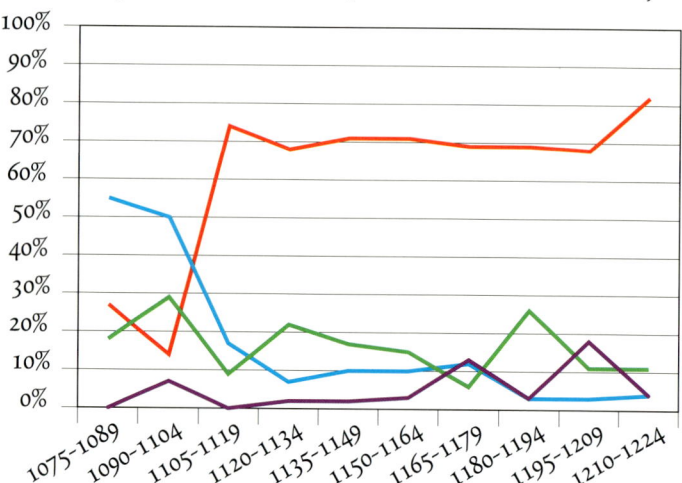

see p. 91

——— France
——— England
——— Austria,
Germany and
Switzerland

Graph 2: Minims in Gothic Style by Country

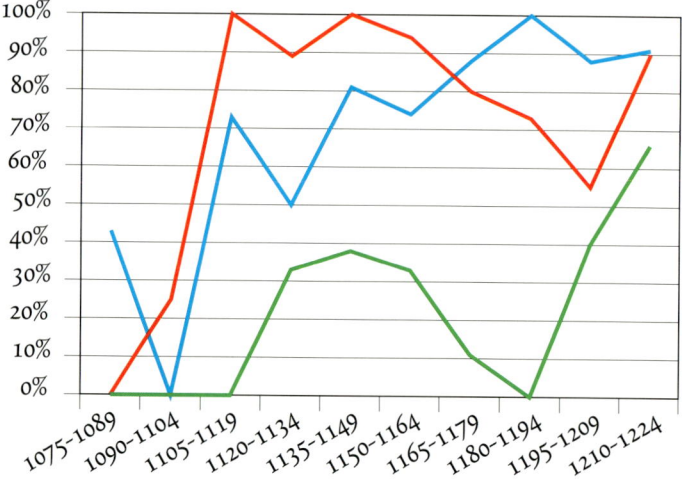

Graph 3: Angularity (as encountered in **c**, **e**, **h**, **o** and **r**) see p. 94

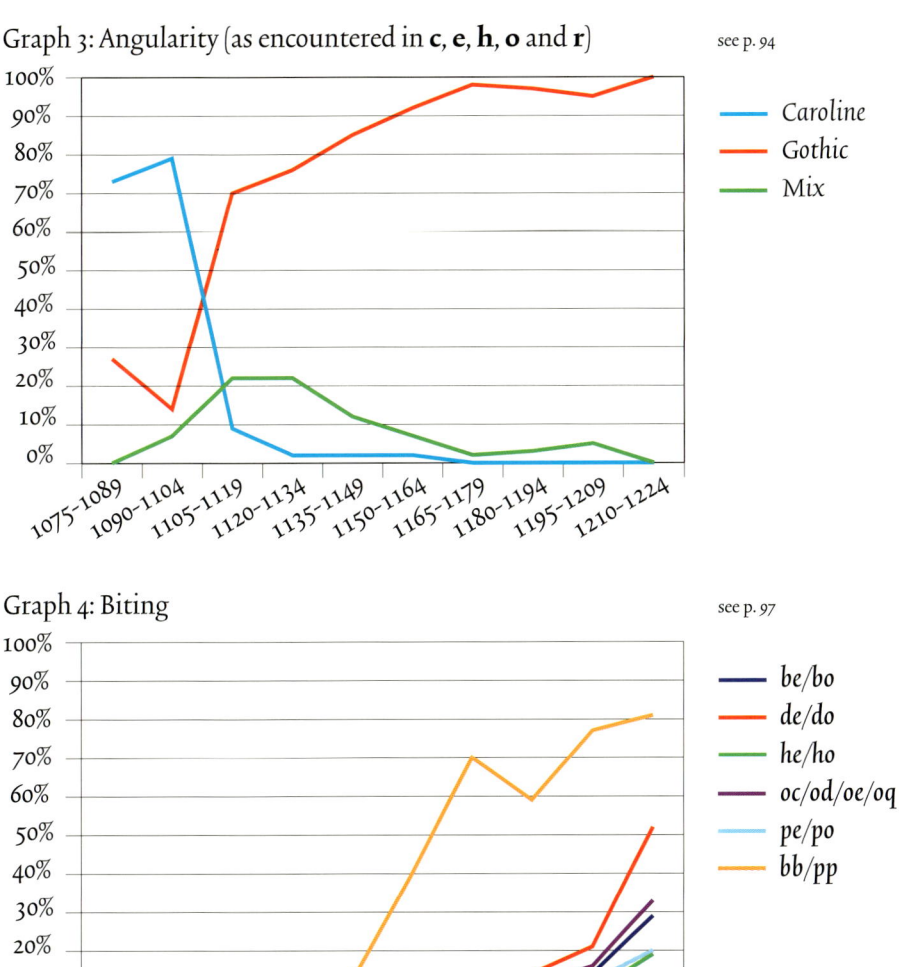

Graph 4: Biting see p. 97

see p. 100

Graph 5: Biting Following Round **d**

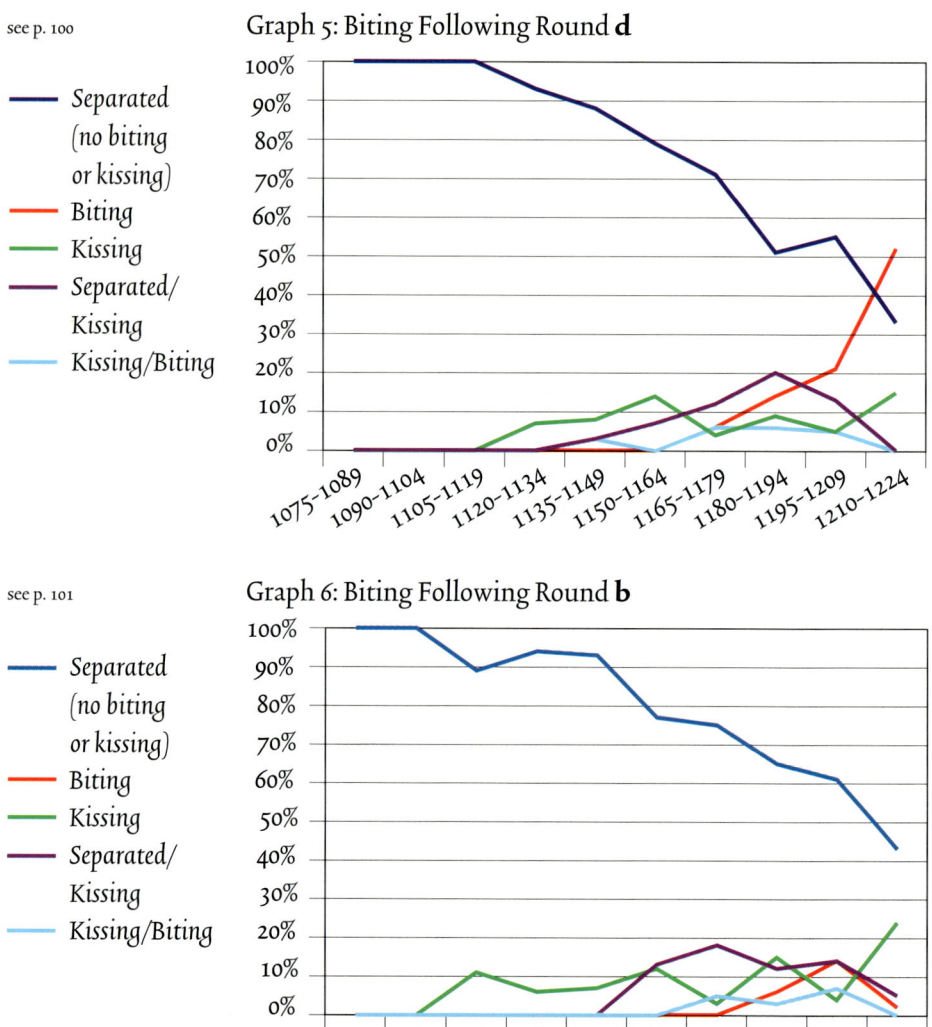

- **Separated** (no biting or kissing)
- **Biting**
- **Kissing**
- **Separated/ Kissing**
- **Kissing/Biting**

see p. 101

Graph 6: Biting Following Round **b**

- **Separated** (no biting or kissing)
- **Biting**
- **Kissing**
- **Separated/ Kissing**
- **Kissing/Biting**

Index of Manuscripts

General Index

Servius 19, 25, 28, 47-8
Sigibert of Gembloux 38-9
Sinonima 47, 49, 71-2
Soissons 44
Solomon 35
Sophia, canoness of Schäftlarn 134
Spain 41, 51, 56, 79, 82
Steinfeld 143
Steterburg 143
Stuttgart 133, 140
Suda 50
Suetonius 45
Sulpicius Severus 60, 65, 135
Swabia 132
Switzerland 63, 89, 91-2, 102-3, 127, 133

Tauler, Johannes 16
Ter Doest 17
Ter Duinen 17
Thierry of Chartres 139
Theodore of Tarsus 56, 60-1
tironian notes 70, 74
Titus 35
Tours 27, 46, 58, 69, 72
Trier 143
Troy 35

Ursberg 134
Utrecht 17

van Wijn, H. 15
Verona 65
Verrius Flaccus 47

Vienna 139
Virgil 57, 131
Vita Sanctae Eugeniae 63, 66
Vorau 143-4
    see Goppold
Vossius, Isaac 42

Waltharius 143
Weihenstephan 143
Weingarten 144
    see Berthold
Werden 54
Werinher, canon of Augsburg 141
Wessobrunn 132, 134-7, 144
    see Adalbero, Diemut, Liutold, Lodevicus
Werdo 67
Willibrord 53
Winithar 44, 53, 67
Wolfger of Prüfening 142
Worms 133
Würzburg 129, 144
    see Iohannes

Zürich 135
Zwettl 139, 144
Zwiefalten 131-2
    see Mahtilt, Ortlieb